*Professional
Service
Management*

Professional Service Management

William Joseph

McGraw-Hill Book Company

New York   St. Louis   San Francisco   Auckland
Bogotá   Singapore   Johannesburg   London   Madrid
Mexico   Montreal   New Delhi   Panama   São Paulo
Hamburg   Sydney   Tokyo   Paris   Toronto

Library of Congress Cataloging in Publication Data

Joseph, William.
  Professional service management.

  Includes index.
  1. Service industries—Management. I. Title.
HD9980.5.J67   658   82-6563
ISBN 0-07-039267-6   AACR2

Copyright © 1983 by William J. Lynott. All rights reserved.
Printed in the United States of America. Except as permitted
under the United States Copyright Act of 1976, no part of this
publication may be reproduced or distributed in any form or by
any means, or stored in a data base or retrieval system, without
the prior written permission of the publisher.

1234567890   DOCDOC   898765432)

ISBN 0-07-039267-6

*The editors for this book were William Newton and
Carolyn Nagy, the designer was Richard A. Roth, and the
production supervisor was Paul A. Malchow. It was composed
by Lorraine Spence in the McGraw-Hill Book Company
Publishing Technology Department and typeset in Caledonia by
Benjamin H. Tyrrel, Inc.*

Printed and bound by R. R. Donnelley & Sons Company.

To Betty Lou

My use of generic words such as "repairman" and "handyman" is simply a convenience. It certainly isn't intended to discriminate against women. I am personally acquainted with a number of successful female service managers, and I hope that this book will be helpful to readers of either sex. To highlight that point, I have made use of both male and female pronouns because I feel that the use of the artificial "him/her" constructions would be awkward and distracting.

Contents

Preface xi
Acknowledgment xiii

1. ***How It All Began* 1**
   Early Growth in the Service Industry 2
   The Service Business Today 3
   Today's Consumer 4
   The Effects of Changing Technology 4
   Service Comes into Its Own 5
   The Business Community Responds 7
   The Customer Speaks Out 9
   Life as a Service Manager 10
   What Your Customers Expect 11

2. ***Service—A People Business* 13**
   The Importance of "People Skills" 14
   The Laws of Human Relations 17
   The Fundamental Physical Needs 25

3. ***The Magic of Communicating* 29**
   It Starts with Good Listening 30
   A Good Vocabulary Helps 30
   Where Do You Fit In? 32
   But Don't Overdo It 35
   Skill with the Spoken Word 37
   Making a Speech? 38
   The Written Word 39
   Why Bother to Write? 40
   Meeting Manners 41

4. Productivity—The Big Challenge 43

The Service Factory	44
Better Productivity Means Better Profit	45
Motivation	46
Measuring Productivity	49
What You Can Do	53
Road Technicians	57
All Technicians	59
Housekeeping	61
Financial Incentives	61

5. Routing and Dispatching 63

Road Calls	63
Suggested Changes	65
Alternative Systems	67
The Daily Gathering	75
Shop Technicians	77

6. Shop Layout and Work Flow 79

Remember the Factory Concept	79
Accessibility to Repair Parts	82
Storage Areas	84
Shop Records	85
Carry-in Service	86
Houskeeping	87

7. Repair Parts Inventories 89

The Orphans of the Service Business	89
Level of Service	90
The 80/20 Rule	92
How Much Inventory?	93
How to Keep Records	95
Inventory Deletions	97
Out of Stocks	98
Stocking the Truck	100
Profits from the Parts Department	102

8. Setting Service Rates 105

It Must Be Done with Care	105
No Easy Formula	107

CONTENTS ix

    The Hourly Rate System 108
    Productive-Time Ratio 112
    Flat-Rate Systems 114
    Other Systems 118
    Charging for Estimates 118
    Inflation 119
    Moderate or Premium Rates 119

9. *Selling Service Contracts* 121

    Genesis 121
    Should You Be Selling Service Contracts? 122
    Fulfillment Costs 123
    How to Sell Them 125
    Selling Renewals 128
    Wording the Contract 131

10. *Selling Your Service* 135

    The First Step 136
    Bringing in New Customers 137
    Other Forms of Advertising 140
    New Business from Old Customers 142
    Your Image 143

11. *Controlling Expenses* 146

    Technical Payroll 146
    Other Payroll 147
    Supplies 148
    The Telephone 151
    Energy 154

12. *You and Your Customer* 155

    What is a Service Manager? What
       Does He Do? 155
    It's the Customer Who Counts 156
    Who's Listening 158
    Broken Promises 160
    Telephone Complaints 161
    How to Say "No" 163
    The Customer Satisfaction Audit 166
    Your Personal Development 168

13. Managing a Healthy Business 169

The Discipline of the P&L 170
Accounting 170
The Balance Sheet 173
The Basic Ratios 176
Managing for Profit 178
The Technician's Role 181
What About Expenses? 184

14. Legal Considerations 188

Warranties and Guarantees 189
The Magnuson-Moss Warranty Act 191
Implied Warranties 193
Product Liability 194
Insurance 196
Equal Opportunity 200
Consumer Reports 201
Service Legislation 202

15. Letters to Help You Manage 205

Good Advice from Malcolm Forbes 206
Writing to Your Boss 209
Letters to Customers 212
Letters that Say "No" 213
Letters from Satisfied Customers 215
Consumer Agencies 216
Sales Promotion Letters 217

Preface

My first exposure to the service business came in the early days of television. I was working for a small appliance dealer as a repairman (we weren't called technicians in those days).

Since there were several of us working in the shop, someone had to be designated as the "boss." I remember him now only as Mr. Messenger. He was the eldest of us—more important, he knew how to fix those new television sets.

Mr. Messenger knew little and probably cared less about the professional management techniques discussed in this book. In looking back, though, I am reminded that I was not at all offended by his lack of credentials, since I knew nothing about such things either. What I do remember, despite the passage of all those years, is that I did not like having Mr. Messenger for a boss.

None of this is intended to fault my erstwhile colleague. Back in those days, the concept of service management had hardly progressed beyond its embryonic stage. Indeed, business management itself, in the professional sense that we think of it today, was still in its formative stages. As far as I know, Peter Drucker had yet to publish his first words on the subject.

A great deal has happened to me and to the service industry in the intervening years. Both, I like to feel, have matured considerably.

While there is still a tendency in some quarters to promote service managers on the basis of their technical skill rather than on their business and management potential, the practice is at last losing ground. We can expect this trend to accelerate as more and more industry leaders come to realize that service management is an exacting discipline, at least as demanding as other forms of general business management.

Working one's way up through the ranks has been, and I hope will always be, a perfectly acceptable path to service-management responsibility. However, as the industry grows even more sophisticated, the choice of candidates must inevitably reflect the fact that management potential, not technical skill, provides the surest foundation for success. Whether you are a practicing service manager, an owner/manager of some form of service business, or a technician trying to gain the management skills that will enable you to improve your lot, I believe that this book can help you.

Professional Service Management is a book neither on the abstract concepts of product service nor on the relationships among the manufacturing, marketing, and servicing arms of our distribution systems. These themes have been adequately explored in any number of scholarly works—and this certainly isn't a book on how to repair things. Instead, this book has been written specifically for the manager who must deal with the immediate and practical problems inherent in every type of service operation—how to run the business; how to satisfy the customer; how to make a profit.

Whether your business is involved in repairing airplanes, typewriters, or anything in between, the techniques discussed in these pages will help you do your job more effectively. If I have done my job well, you will find the book you are holding to be a permanent reference of the sort that will stimulate new thoughts and ideas each time you review it.

If you happen to be the type of person who insists on getting to the bottom line with dispatch, you may find yourself skimming through the first three chapters. Whether you choose to read them first, or come back to them later, I urge you to give them a fair share of your time. They provide what I feel is the kind of bedrock foundation that will add meaning and substance not only to the rest of the book but to the balance of your career as well.

The title of this book is no accident. By any set of parameters that one may choose, service management has earned the right to be regarded as a true profession. It is my hope that *Professional Service Management* will make some positive contribution toward the furthering of that premise.

William Joseph

Acknowledgment

When the final words of a manuscript have been set to paper, it's time to recall the names of those who have in some way made a contribution to the work.

What an impossible task. . . .

In my own effort to do so, I quickly became aware that such a list for this book would be unacceptably long. Yet to mention one or a few names would be to run the risk of slighting others.

Instead, allow me to make a general but sincere acknowledgment.

In a career in the service business that began in 1948, I have met and worked with many hundreds of service managers, service technicians and mechanics, executives, educators, and consultants. It has been the collective teaching of all these people that has given me the courage to embark on this project. To each and every one of them, my sincere gratitude for an education that could not have been gained in any other way.

W. J.

*Professional
Service
Management*

About the Author

William Joseph is a veteran of more than 30 years in the service industry. During his career, he has operated his own small television repair business, has been employed as a service manager, and, for the past 20 years, has been a service executive in one of the country's largest corporations.

Since the appearance of his first published article in 1958, he has become one of the most widely published authors on service-management subjects. More than 200 of his articles have appeared in leading magazines and trade journals.

He is the author of two monthly columns on business management: "It's YOUR Business," appearing in *Appliance Service News*, and "The Business Side of Things," in *Alarm/Installer Dealer*. He is also an active speaker and lecturer on service-management subjects and has appeared as a featured speaker at service-management seminars.

Chapter 1
How It All Began

The electric light bulb, the printing press, and Burt Reynolds all share one important thing in common: the precise times and places of their births have been clearly established.

Not so with the service industry.

In the earliest days of our civilization, the producer and the consumer were one and the same. If one of our forefathers was in need of a plow, he was expected to make it himself. Having done so, he most probably would not have been inclined to look to someone else for help when the plow fell into a state of disrepair.

At some point, of course, the first chap with more natural talent for fixing things than for making them came on the scene. Although history does not afford us a view of the event, we can assume that a market for his services slowly, and perhaps grudgingly, took shape.

It remained, however, for the industrial revolution to generate a clear distinction between those who produced goods and those for whom the goods were produced. When the American worker moved off the farm and into the factory, the groundwork for today's service industry was laid.

Of course, old habits are not readily dismissed. In recognition of this, much of the early output of our factories was designed to accommodate the American penchant for doing it yourself. Early farm machinery, for example, often came complete with tool kit, maintenance instructions, and the implicit understanding that malfunctions would require a considerable amount of tender loving care on the part of the owner. There were few, if any, service facilities in the bigger cities, much less in the rural areas.

However, advancing technology and an increasingly sophisticated system for bringing manufactured goods to the ultimate consumer served to strengthen the need for an industry designed to keep our assembly line society in good working order.

In 1887, when Richard W. Sears placed the classified ad that resulted in the hiring of Alvah C. Roebuck, he was looking for someone capable of repairing the malfunctioning pocket watches being returned by some customers. In doing so, Sears was responding to his perception that, to be successful, a merchant selling mechanical goods would need the support of a behind-the-scenes service organization.

In 1908, when William Crapo Durant merged the Buick and Oldsmobile motor car companies to form the colossus General Motors Corporation, the automobile industry had already begun to piece together the highly specialized service network without which our so-called mobile society would not have been possible.

Although the precise moment of its birth was not recorded in any ledger, the service industry had indeed been born.

EARLY GROWTH IN THE SERVICE INDUSTRY

By 1950, the annual cost of services in the United States was $88.2 billion, or about $583 per person. By 1970, the cost of the same services had grown to more than $424.6 billion, slightly more than $2090 for every man, woman, and child in the country. Inflation notwithstanding, the providing of services in America had become a gigantic industry.

In recent years, the market for services has been expanding even more rapidly. In 1975, a much-predicted milestone was reached. In that year, services became the largest item in the gross national product (GNP). For the first time in our history, more money was spent for services than for the purchase of tangible goods. By 1978, services accounted for nearly 46% of the entire gross national product.

To be sure, the government's description of services is broad, including not only the kinds of repair services that involve the professional service manager but also such diverse activities as dry cleaning, medical and dental services, house painting, etc. You get the idea: any business transaction that results in the exchange of a service instead of tangible goods is included in the government's statistical analysis of "services." Despite the breadth of the category, however, the repair segment alone constitutes a multibillion dollar industry, one of the largest in American business. It is the world of today's professional service manager.

The Department of Transportation estimates that automotive repairs and maintenance alone amounted to $50 billion in 1978. This is a tidy sum when you consider that it is nearly one-half the amount spent for the purchase of new cars a year earlier.

THE SERVICE BUSINESS TODAY

The American economy, then, can be seen as having experienced three different phases. In the beginning, we were an almost totally agrarian society, with the bulk of our population living or working on farms. When the so-called industrial revolution came along, tangible goods were manufactured at a furious pace with an abundance of cheap labor and many of the workers were happy to leave the farm behind. Recent statistics indicate clearly that we are being ushered into the third phase of our economy—a service-oriented society. A summary of these statistics is presented in Table 1.1.

TABLE 1.1 *Services as a Percentage of Gross National Product*

	Total GNP, billions of dollars	Services, billions of dollars	Services, % of total GNP
1950	282.6	88.2	30.8
1955	399.3	135.3	33.9
1960	506.0	193.2	38.2
1965	688.1	272.7	39.6
1970	982.4	424.6	43.2
1975	1528.8	699.2	45.7
1976	1706.5	782.0	45.8
1979	2368.8	1085.1	45.8

Source: *Statistical Abstract of the United States*, 1980.

The principal force behind the current evolutionary process is a relatively simple one: appliances; automobiles; scientific, medical, and office equipment; and other durable goods being sold today are expensive and complicated. When these goods break down, the user expects them to be repaired promptly and properly. Providing that service is a big and a costly business.

More important to today's businessperson than the cost of service, though, is the cost of no service—or poor service.

TODAY'S CONSUMER

Along with more sophisticated technology and manufacturing techniques, we have also been quite successful in developing an infinitely more perceptive and demanding consumer. And woe to the producers or sellers of consumer or industrial goods who are insensitive to the demands of their customers or to the role played by service in the modern merchandising equation.

THE EFFECTS OF CHANGING TECHNOLOGY

With few exceptions, the merchandise sold during the early years of our industrial development was a tinkerer's dream. Even the early automobiles were designed with consideration for the do-it-yourself owner. In fact, the buyers of that ubiquitous Model T Ford had to be well-prepared to tinker, or else their travels were likely to be limited and distressingly intermittent. The first mechanical household appliances, such as washing machines, were also constructed in a basic and simple manner conducive to easy repairs.

Then a funny thing happened on the way to the market place. American ingenuity combined with the pressures of free competition resulted in increasingly fancy gadgets designed to catch the imagination of the emerging consumer.

Basic wringer washers became semiautomatic and then fully automatic washing machines. Auto gear boxes became transmissions and then automatic transmissions. Mechanical phonographs became electronic radios. Ice boxes became refrigerators, and coal furnaces in the cellar became thermostatically controlled heating/cooling systems in the basement.

The handymen-tinkerers viewed this transition first with apprehension and then with outright panic. They had become an endangered species, destined to be replaced by an army of trained mechanics and service technicians. Even within the industry itself, the subtle implications involved could be felt. Those who had started their careers as "repairmen" or "servicemen" found they had become "service technicians."

Finally, with the close of World War II, a furious burst of technological creativity dealt the remaining die-hard handymen a mortal blow. Color television, electronic garage-door openers, microwave ovens, central air conditioners, ad infinitum—all conspired to ensure that the service technician and the service manager would become almost as familiar as members of the family in most American homes.

While all this was going on, such fields as business and medicine were being advanced through the development of complex scientific equipment. In 1950, a few years after the close of World War II, tangible goods were being produced at such a prodigious rate that services accounted for only about 31% of the gross national product, a modern low. From that point on, the need for services has resulted in a steadily increasing percentage.

Much of the postwar appliance boom was aimed directly at improving the lot of the beleaguered homemaker. Chores that had previously been hard manual labor—such as the family wash—were reduced to not much more than an annoyance. Dishwashers proved to be the first guaranteed cure for dishpan hands; ovens became self-cleaning; refrigerators became self-defrosting.

Of course, Dad wasn't overlooked by the purveyors of the new leisure lifestyle. He saw himself demeaned on the situation comedies that were beginning to appear with frightening regularity on the new TV screen in the den, but he was able to benefit from a stream of gadgets that were being developed especially to make his life easier. There were dehumidifiers to keep the workshop dry during the damp summer months, humidifiers to put the dampness back in during the dry winter months, and a garage door that could be opened by a push button from inside the car. To make driving an even more pleasurable experience, such amenities as power steering, power brakes, thermostatically controlled heating/cooling systems, and electrically operated windows and doors were developed.

SERVICE COMES INTO ITS OWN

Unfortunately, some early fulfillments of the American dream were destined to end on a sour note. Too often, the sellers of some of these first-generation modern miracles were ill-prepared to answer the call when their products failed to perform satisfactorily. Probably the most dramatic illustration of this problem occurred during the early years of the television industry.

In the late 1940s, domestic television receivers were being snapped up by an eager public almost as quickly as they could be produced. The pace was frantic as manufacturers geared up to meet what seemed to be a limitless demand. In all this scurry of commercial bliss, it appeared that no one had given enough thought to a very fundamental problem: who was going to repair these devices (which were infinitely more subject to malfunction than are the advanced solid-state receivers being manufactured today)?

In 1948, when the first practical TV sets appeared on the domestic market, there were large numbers of radio repairmen who had been doing a creditable job of maintaining the 37 million radio sets then in use. In addition to the many full-time professionals in the field, there was an army of moonlighters, many of whom were learning their trade through the correspondence schools recently qualified to give training to World War II veterans under the new GI bill.

However, even though both were electronic in nature, radio was one thing, television quite another. The proper repair and maintenance of television sets required special advanced training, and the equipment needed was highly specialized and very expensive.

TELEVISION AND ITS INFLUENCE

Between 1948 and 1952, TV ownership grew from a few thousand to 15 million. During this period the industry was hard-pressed to produce qualified technicians in sufficient numbers. The industry's reputation was damaged as a result of the large number of fly-by-night repair companies that were formed to take advantage of the demand for television repair work.

Fortunately, the problem was relatively short-lived. American enterprise would not permit a market potential as powerful as that of television to suffer just because of a mere oversight. Manufacturers, industry groups, and commercial schools combined their resources to turn the tide. Since then, for the most part, the industry has been able to meet the demand.

This was no mean task, considering the immensity of the television industry which, for all practical purposes, did not even exist prior to 1948. According to Arbitron, an independent research firm, 97.5% of all American households had at least one television receiver by 1978. The U.S. government places this figure at 99.5% of all households wired for electricity. At best, statistics of this kind are necessarily only estimates, but it is interesting to note that *TV Digest Magazine* calculated the total number of television receivers in use in the United States during 1978 at 128 million—not bad for an industry only 30 years old.

The television experience provided what was probably the most visible evidence that an uninvited guest had sneaked into the marketing scene. From that time on, service was a factor to be reckoned with in merchandising strategies, not only for television but for home appliances, automobiles, industrial and scientific equipment, and most other forms of durable goods as well. Service, as a profession, had been born.

Much as the technological revolution was responsible for the demise of the do-it-yourself home handyman, it also made short work of the jack-of-all-trades within the repair profession. Radio repairmen who were unwilling or unable to absorb the advanced training required for television work continued on as radio and phonograph specialists. At the same time, appliance mechanics who had been expected to repair almost anything in the customer's home began to specialize in such specific fields as refrigeration, heating, or laundry equipment. More and more automobile mechanics began to drift toward such specialties as transmissions, front ends, and tune-ups.

All of this new professionalism seemed to add a cachet of sorts to the business. However, as you might suspect, not everyone was happy with the uninvited appearance of service in the world of merchandising.

THE BUSINESS COMMUNITY RESPONDS

To the retail merchant whose business instincts had been sharpened on the excitement and satisfaction inherent in the buying and selling of merchandise, the problems and demands of service were often looked on as an unwelcome intrusion. Along with such operating considerations as credit, warehousing, and delivery, service in many retail organizations became the unwanted but difficult-to-get-rid-of boarder.

Nevertheless, the increasing importance of customer service was becoming evident to some of the more perceptive retailers even in the 1940s. Those who foresaw the greatly expanded role of the customer service activity began to build their organizations and facilities to accommodate the need. Professional service managers were trained and given the necessary authority to enable them to resolve customer complaints. Corporate policies guaranteeing customer satisfaction were originated or given renewed emphasis. Such efforts were evident not only in the big national chains and manufacturing companies but in many of the smaller local businesses as well.

Those who resisted the encroachment of service, though, often did so with a vengeance. Some businesspersons who regarded service as too much of a bother "solved" the problem by ignoring it or by farming out their service responsibilities to other concerns. While the latter solution sometimes appeared to solve the problem for a while, more often it turned out to be a serious threat to the precious goodwill of the companies involved. With increasing competition for the consumer's dollar, many businesspersons came away from the experience convinced that relying on some other firm to resolve customer dissatisfaction was hardly the way to build customer confidence.

Despite these early lessons, the response of the business community to the challenge of satisfying today's knowledgeable and demanding consumer is far from uniform. Even the persistent efforts of consumer organizations and the results of sophisticated marketing surveys have not been enough to persuade some business people of the clear need for an enlightened and aggressive customer satisfaction policy. It no doubt is this void that has allowed self-proclaimed consumer advocates, such as Ralph Nader, to develop huge and influential followings.

A recent national survey conducted by an independent research organization turned up the fact that an average retail store loses 15 out of every 100 of its regular customers every year. Of that loss, 18% leave because of unavoidable circumstances such as moving away or death. However, a whopping 68% go elsewhere because of bad treatment or poor service, and another 14% leave because of unadjusted or poorly adjusted complaints: *a total of 82% due to poor customer relations.*

For most businesses, the never-ending challenge of developing new customers is a very expensive and difficult process. Recently, a nationwide survey of 100 major U.S. companies revealed that the average cost of acquiring a new customer was $118.16. The cost of maintaining existing customers in the same companies came to only $19.76.

Given these facts, it should be evident that doing everything reasonable to keep old customers happy is simply good business. For any business selling serviceable merchandise, an effective and a professional service department is one of the more obvious ways to keep customers happy.

THE CUSTOMER SPEAKS OUT

If you are not especially impressed by statistics, then consider the more direct evidence. In an internal survey, one national chain asked its own customers, who were shopping in the appliance departments of its stores, why they had chosen that company for their shopping. By far, the most frequent single response was "because of service." You may want to reflect on the significance of that reply. . . . Not price. Not features. Not quality. *Service!*

In recent years, similar marketing studies have shown with equal clarity that the American consumer is being influenced more and more by service considerations when the time comes to select a supplier of durable goods. Considering the ready availability of these facts and the incontrovertible nature of the evidence, we can assume that the great majority of businesses are closely tuned in to the need for good customer relations. Right?

Wrong!

Unfortunately, one does not have to look very carefully to uncover endless stories of lost sales and profits due to indifferent and even hostile treatment of customers.

In 1977, two college professors set out to gather their own data on this subject. Arthur Best of Western New England College, School of Law, and Alan Andreason of the University of Illinois conducted a survey of 2400 households throughout the United States. Their findings were published in the *Harvard Business Review* in an article entitled "Consumers Complain—Does Business Respond?"

Hardly. According to the professors, nearly every consumer had an unpleasant experience to tell. Some customers, they learned, are so used to being treated poorly that they don't even bother to complain; they simply take their business elsewhere. Some customers, of course, do lodge formal complaints. When they do, the study revealed, one out of every three complaints goes unresolved.

On the brighter side of all this is the fact that an increased awareness of this situation is finally developing in most areas of the business community. As the more progressive businesspersons come to realize that good customer relations is essential to business success, the job of the customer service manager is assuming increased significance and satisfaction.

And Business Listens

Recently, some of the country's largest corporations have created entire departments charged with the sole responsibility of customer satisfaction and goodwill. Often, these departments are headed by newly designated corporate officers. The title "vice president, customer relations" is now seen frequently on corporate organization charts. In most cases, these executives have real muscle in the boardroom where corporate policies are formulated.

This, then, is the background against which the modern customer service manager must function.

Consumers have clearly shown that they will return to do business with firms that have treated them fairly and made reasonable efforts to resolve their complaints. If mistreated, however, they will simply take their business to a more accommodating competitor. As service manager, it is your job, and that of the people working with you, to see to it that your firm's most valuable assets (its customers) are treated in such a manner as to cause them to want to do business with you again.

LIFE AS A SERVICE MANAGER

If you are an experienced service manager, you already know that developing and implementing an effective program of customer relations is not as easy as it sounds. If you are not yet experienced, you will quickly learn that your skills will be constantly put to the test.

As a service manager, you should understand from the very beginning that service is truly a people business and that the human element is by far the most important consideration in your development as a professional. Dealing effectively with difficult customers (yes, some customers can be *very* difficult) on the one hand, and sometimes recalcitrant employees on the other, is a challenge that some service managers must deal with almost every day.

Well, whoever said it was easy?

Depending on the nature of your firm and the scope of your duties, there can be many important but separate responsibilities for you to deal with. Technical training, productivity, expenses and profits, and equipment maintenance are just a few of the responsibilities you may be required to manage. With few exceptions, however, each of these areas of the business will eventually relate back to people and to your ability to deal with them skillfully. This important subject is discussed more fully in the next chapter.

Customers are people too, and leaving them satisfied is the reason for the existence of every service department and the manager who supervises it. The job is sometimes much more demanding than one might suppose, however.

Competent technicians or mechanics who do their jobs quickly and skillfully are obviously of fundamental importance. But hold on, there's a lot of evidence that it's not quite that simple.

WHAT YOUR CUSTOMERS EXPECT

For example, a study done by the Energy Products and Services Association (E.P.S.A.) of San Diego, California, reveals that many consumers also expect a little sociological and psychological pampering to help ease the blow when they find their favorite appliance in need of doctoring.

Working from the results of this study, E.P.S.A. drew up a list of five points that will help any service organization to develop a high degree of customer satisfaction. Listed in the order of their importance as determined by the study, these points are:

1. A pleasant attitude on the part of the service technician is necessary. Most customers said they were tired of dealing with servicers who were sullen and uncommunicative. A smile and a courteous attitude were rated as top requirements. *Many people, were more concerned about technicians' attitudes than the size of the repair bill* [italics added].

2. Consumers are more informed than they used to be, and they expect responsive and correct answers to their questions about their appliances. They also appreciate advice on how to get the best service from their appliances and how to avoid future service problems.

3. Consumers expect technicians to be well equipped and to perform their work in an efficient and a businesslike manner.

4. Consumers are concerned about the skill and training of the technicians to whom they entrust their appliances. They feel the technician should inspire confidence and display a genuine concern for the customer's appliance-related problems.

5. Consumers insist on punctuality. Some customers must take time off from work or interrupt otherwise busy schedules in order to be home for the service technician. While the study noted that most consumers understand that it is difficult to set an exact time for the technician's arrival, they are highly pleased when the technician shows up within the time frame allocated.

I hope that you took particular notice of the first of the five points listed above. Remember, they are listed in the order of their importance as defined by the customer. Any service manager would do well to memorize these points and the order of their importance. While they are all essential to customer satisfaction, the first and most important is often the most frequently ignored.

While a properly done repair job is obviously the primary target for any service organization, it must be accompanied by good customer relations if the job is to be considered complete. Any time a customer remains less than satisfied, the cost to the business in lost future sales can be substantial. Repeated often enough, customer dissatisfaction will be disastrous.

It is your job as service manager to see to it that the highest possible number of your customers is entirely satisfied, that they are happy to have done business with you and your firm, and that they will want to do business with you again. All this would be reasonably simple to accomplish provided you were given a bottomless purse from which to draw. Unfortunately, the lot of the service manager is not that uncomplicated. All your objectives must be accomplished within the limits dictated by conditions in the real world. Costs must be strictly controlled, and in those service departments doing out-of-warranty work, service sales and profits must be developed.

Have heart. Experience clearly shows that good service to the customer and good service profits are not conflicting objectives as you might be inclined to think. In fact, the two go together quite nicely. The chapters that follow will show you how.

Chapter 2

Service—a People Business

Do you like people? I hope so; if you do not, you are almost surely in the wrong business. To be sure, almost every form of modern business activity involves some degree of interpersonal relationships, but there are probably not many quite so dependent on the human element as is the profession of service management.

If this news comes as a mild surprise to you, you have lots of company. It's only natural to associate service with mechanical things. It might seem to follow logically that a manager in a business that deals with mechanical things would be mainly concerned with mechanical things.

Not so.

While a technical knowledge of what her mechanics and technicians are doing can sometimes be an advantage to a service manager, such knowledge is by no means a primary requirement. Experience has clearly shown us that skill in managing people is far more important to a service manager than is skill in repairing things. In fact, I have known executives in the service business who state flatly that technical expertise is actually a disadvantage to the modern service manager. While I'm not certain that I can subscribe to such an unequivocal position on the matter, there is absolutely no doubt in my mind about the paramount importance of people skills in our business.

THE IMPORTANCE OF "PEOPLE SKILLS"

In the early days of the service profession—and even today in some locations—mechanics and technicians were promoted to management status solely on the basis of their technical skills. That program was a mistake then, and it is a mistake now. Certainly, when we find a high degree of technical skills plus lots of know-how in dealing with people all wrapped up in the same person, we have a great candidate for service management (or any number of other good jobs, for that matter).

Alas, such a combination is relatively rare. If you feel that you are blessed with both talents, you are fortunate indeed. If, on the other hand, your technical skills are limited, have heart. There are lots of ways for a service manager to work around a lack of technical skills; there is no way that I know of for her to be successful without people skills, however. People are the principal substance of which the service manager's job is woven. Here's why:

First, there are the relationships with the people who are the firms' customers. It ought to be understood from the beginning that a goodly percentage of most service managers' dealings with customers are going to be difficult. The very essence of the position requires that the service manager deal directly with the most difficult of customer problems and often with the most difficult of customers themselves. Because of that simple fact, the ability to retain composure and to deal objectively with customers even under the most trying of circumstances will be a sharply honed trait in the professional service manager. The relationship between you as a service manager and your customers is discussed in detail in a later chapter.

Second, in this chapter, we'll be concentrating on the equally important and even more complex problem of dealing with the people working directly under your supervision. Ask any experienced business executive today what qualities are looked for in promotable young people, and there is an excellent chance that the list will be topped with "the ability to deal with people." If the position to be filled is that of service manager, you can be certain that this characteristic will be considered essential.

Whether or not the ability to deal successfully with people can be learned from reading books is problematical at best. There are those who insist that such talents are instinctive: you either have them or you don't. Furthermore the whole issue of human relationships in business is so all-encompassing that a single chapter in a book can deal with the subject only at a superficial level.

Nevertheless, it is generally agreed that there are basic laws governing successful relationships between people and these laws can be learned. They are not difficult to understand, and they are as immutable as the basic laws of physics taught in every high school. Familiarity with them is not necessarily going to make you an expert in human relations, but it can certainly provide you with a foundation that you can use to sharpen your skills as your experience grows.

Regardless of whether people talents are instinctive or whether they are learned, I believe that a knowledge of the ground rules can make life a lot easier right from the beginning for anyone involved in supervising the activities of others. The more effort you elect to invest in learning about this part of your profession, the more you can expect to improve on these vital skills.

Before we examine some of these principles of modern management, let's take a brief look at the world of the manager in the earlier days of this country's industrial efforts.

How We Used to Do It

It wasn't so terribly long ago that a manager or supervisor was a person to be feared and awed by subordinates. For an employee to arouse the wrath of his supervisor was a foolhardy act indeed, since it was not uncommon to be discharged on the spot for even the most minor infraction of the rules.

In those days, what do you suppose were the chief characteristics that were sought in candidates for supervisory positions? First, the supervisor was expected to be tough—tough mentally and, in some cases, even tough physically. Second, the person chosen to be a supervisor was often the most productive and highly skilled worker in the unit.

The reasons for selecting people with these credentials were very sound at the time. In some ways, our world of business was still stumbling in the shadows of the dark ages. It had not yet discovered a basic principle that is vital in modern management. It had not yet discovered the simple premise that there are *two ways* to generate productive effort on the part of other people.

Persuasion and Force

There was only one theory in use in the old days: if you wanted someone to do more or better work for you, some form of force had to be employed. Hence the tough manager capable of enforcing this principle came into his own. The tough manager could frighten his employees into working harder, while his highly skilled counterpart was expected to shame his workers into better performance. It is not hard to imagine that the supervisor who was both tough and highly skilled must surely have been much sought after. The awesome potential of good human relations in business was, at that point, largely unknown.

Some Early Pioneers

In management, as in most important fields of endeavor, it remained for a few hardy pioneers to blaze new trails to make the going a bit easier for those of us yet to come. One by one, a sprinkling of business leaders began to shed light on an entirely new principle in the employer/employee relationship; each in his own way contributed to a formula that was to provide the foundation for effective supervision as it is practiced today.

Henry Ford was one such man. Many years ago, when Ford announced to the world that he was instituting a $5 daily wage for his factory workers, the reactions were swift and harsh. Newspapers across the country wrote editorials on the subject. Most were condemnations of what was termed a foolhardy and irresponsible move. "What's this man, Ford, trying to do?" they asked. "Wreck the entire financial structure of the country? Five dollars a day, indeed. And at a time when a thousand factories could be filled with men willing to work for half as much."

Ford paid no attention to his critics. He went ahead with the $5 wage—and on to become one of the world's richest and most successful men.

At about this same time in our history, there were other men independently discovering the powers of effective human relations in business. Andrew Carnegie, the steel magnate, made a lifelong study of people, their behavior, and the powers of good human relations. He made no secret of the fact that he felt his success was a direct result of his knowledge of people. Carnegie developed an entirely new business philosophy that was itself to become responsible for the personal success of many people to follow.

One of these was Charles Schwab, a protégé of Carnegie and one of the first men in this country ever to be paid more than a million dollars in a single year for his services. In his later years, when asked to share the secrets of his success, Schwab is reported to have replied, "You can take away my factories, you can take away my machinery, and you can even take away all of my money; but, if you will leave me my men, I will build new factories, new machinery and . . . I will even build a new fortune."

Each of these men, in his own way, was saying the same thing. They were telling the world that the use of force in the business world was dead and should be buried and that the use of persuasion was the only intelligent and profitable way to deal with people.

How It's Done Today

Gradually, the world began to listen. Today, most business leaders will readily agree that the success of a potential executive rests to a major degree on the ability to "get along with people." Pulitzer Prize–winning author James McGregor Burns sums this point up well in his scholarly work *Leadership*. Says Mr. Burns, "A leader and a tyrant are polar opposites."

The Art of Persuasion

The use of the art of persuasion in management has now been refined to the point where it can be said that the executive who finds it necessary to resort to the use of authority in goal accomplishment is not a skilled professional. Such an executive has not discovered the dynamic power available through the application of good human relations. In short, the executive has not realized the simple fact that there are *two* ways to get someone to do a job well—you may use persuasion or you may resort to force—and that the more experienced we become, the more we are learning to abandon the use of force entirely in our relations with our business associates. The use of persuasion, while it may require a bit more effort and skill, is so superior, so far more productive, and so much more satisfying than the use of force that effective executives the world over recognize no other road to administrative success.

THE LAWS OF HUMAN RELATIONS

As I mentioned earlier, there are specific laws in the world of human relations, just as there are laws that govern our physical world. You are aware, for example, that if you allow a water glass to slip from your fingers and fall to a hard floor, the glass will shatter. You also know that carelessness in the form of hitting your thumb instead of the nail with a hammer will result in an immediate and painful injury. All of us are familiar with the penalties involved for violations of these elementary laws of our physical world because the penalties are immediate and can be seen, heard, or felt.

In the world of human relations, however, penalties for violating the rules are often delayed, and rarely can they be seen or heard.

Because of this, managers often go about unknowingly violating the rules at every turn. Usually, they cannot understand why their ideas are met with resistance or even hostility on the part of their subordinates and working associates. Under these circumstances, the unskilled supervisor tends to blame the people who are resisting him, accusing them of being uncooperative or disinterested. This reaction only serves to compound the problem, and the unfortunate supervisor finds himself buried deeper and deeper under the weight of frustration.

Unfortunately, such problems in business leadership are not easily resolved. The subject is demanding and frustratingly complex. As author Burns puts it, "Leadership is one of the most observed and least understood phenomena on earth."

Fortunately for us, however, there is nothing especially difficult about the *basic* rules of good human relations. In fact, most of the principles involved are made up of simple commonsense applications that most people could put to good use in any phase of their lives.

One of the most important of these is the need for you to win the confidence of your people. The manager who has earned (and earning is the only way you can get it) the confidence of the people under his direction will find the path to success an easy and natural one. The ground rules of effective human relations are such that mutual respect and confidence between a business manager and his subordinates is necessary if the objectives of the business are to be reached.

Confidence, as I use it here, can be described as a state of mind that is built up slowly between two persons, based on their mutual experiences and reactions. It can take a long time indeed to build a good confidence relationship, but it can be destroyed swiftly through even the most seemingly minor breaches of the laws of sound human relations.

Every contact that you as a manager make with those persons with whom you must work serves to either build up or tear down whatever confidence that person has in you. The supervisor who is aware of the importance of the confidence relationship measures daily encounters with her employees in terms of how well she is developing this skill in herself.

Personal Dignity

Perhaps the biggest single factor in developing confidence in others is the one most often violated and abused by the unsuspecting or unskilled administrator. Every human being, regardless of financial or social status, has a powerful and intractable instinct. This human emotion is so strong that no supervisor with even a rudimentary knowledge of his profession would dare fail to respect it. This instinct may be called the need for the *preservation of personal dignity*.

Most of us realize that no human being wants to be subjected to the loss of personal dignity. It is surprising, though, how many people are not aware of the explosive sensitivity with which this subject is regarded by others.

Every day, in every type of business, unskilled supervisors continue to erode their confidence relationships with their associates in ways that are so minor that they go unnoticed except by the person who has been offended. Every such unsatisfactory encounter serves to reduce confidence and respect until, ultimately, the employee throws up a defensive screen that the supervisor cannot penetrate. When this happens, in most cases the manager is inclined to blame the employee, who is considered uncooperative, disinterested, or perhaps even lazy. Unaware that he himself is at least partially to blame, the supervisor continues his mistakes with other employees until his entire department is affected in varying degrees.

Let's take a look at some of the ways in which you as a service manager can enhance your confidence relationship with your people and, at the same time, avoid some of the pitfalls that lie in wait for the careless administrator.

Most managers know by instinct that criticism of an employee in the presence of others is to be avoided. What many do not seem to realize is that practically *any* minor form of correction in front of other employees is considered to be embarrassing and degrading by many people.

One young fellow of my acquaintance, newly promoted as a service manager, noticed a "cooling off" in the relationship between himself and one of his department's best service technicians. It was all the more puzzling to Mr. Service Manager because of the fact that he had considered this man to be one of his closest personal friends prior to his recent promotion. Gradually, the relationship between the two men deteriorated to the point where Mr. Service Manager found his technician to be uncooperative and even hostile toward his efforts to supervise his daily work.

Finally, Mr. Manager realized that something had to be done. He wisely chose to "lay his cards on the table" by calling the technician aside in private and putting the question of what had gone wrong directly to him.

At first, Mr. Serviceman was reluctant to speak his mind, but finally, he "unloaded." It seems that Mr. Manager had a habit of greeting his technicians while they were in the building in the morning and calling their attention to minor errors in their paperwork of the previous day, asking them to make immediate corrections.

Because of the minor nature of the errors, Mr. Manager did not think of his actions as a form of criticism. However, Mr. Serviceman, who took a rightful pride in his work, did not feel that way. Each time an error was called to his attention in front of the others, he felt that his work was being publicly and deliberately criticized. In his own mind, the situation became distorted, and he became so sensitive to the criticism that he built up a strong personal resentment toward the man he felt was responsible for his embarrassment.

Once the service manager became aware of his friend's sensitive nature on that point, he never again committed the same indiscretion. In time, after the confidence relationship between them had been restored, the technician once again took his place as a productive and valuable asset to the department.

While this example may be an extreme case—since most people are not quite as sensitive as Mr. Serviceman—it is, nevertheless, a true story and serves to illustrate two points: first, it is not only the obvious sins that can cause a manager trouble. Everyone in a supervisory capacity must keep "tuned in" to each individual personality in order to avoid clashes that may weaken or destroy confidence. Second, a confidence relationship, in the form of a personal friendship, that took years to build can be destroyed in a relatively short time over a seemingly minor violation of the principles of good human relations.

The moral of this story, then, is one of the most basic rules of effective supervision: never subject an employee to personal criticism within the hearing of other persons. Public criticism is only one of many ways in which the unskilled supervisor can injure the dignity of employees, but it is one that can be relied on to produce the most undesirable of results.

Personal Recognition

Another fundamental urge that is present in all civilized human beings is the need to be recognized as an individual. No one wants to be thought of as just a number or a blank face in the crowd. In the average person, this need does not take on unrealistic proportions; rather, it is a simple desire to avoid the painful indignity of being looked upon as a nonentity by other people.

Since, in our society, a person's business life is the most significant yardstick for establishing position in the world, the need for recognition on the job becomes obvious. It is a mistake to think that those persons who occupy relatively low places on the ladder of business achievement are any more immune to the need for personal recognition than the most successful of executives. In fact, the need for recognition at the lower levels of the business world can be more urgent and immediate than at the higher levels. Perhaps this can be attributed to the fact that there is a degree of automatic recognition associated with promotions to higher-status jobs, while the rank-and-file worker must seek out self-recognition wherever it can be found.

The skilled supervisor never overlooks this desire for recognition on the part of every associate, regardless of position. He recognizes this normal human characteristic as a powerful tool that can be a valuable aid in building confidence with subordinates.

As a manager, you should make it a point to learn something about the personal life of each person under your supervision. Without becoming too personal, you can then make occasional inquiries about the parts of their lives with which you have become familiar. Of course, as with anything else, you will have to guard against the possibility of overdoing it. Some people will respond openly to your interest in their nonbusiness lives; others will not. This is simply another good illustration of the differences to be encountered in dealing with people. And you must be keenly aware of these differences so that you may react appropriately.

Many people who hold relatively modest jobs lead surprisingly full and productive lives apart from their work. Some are active in important civic or charitable affairs, and others have hobbies that qualify them as experts in unusual and interesting fields. Most of these people will experience a feeling of pride and satisfaction when the boss demonstrates a genuine interest in their accomplishments.

The most important form of recognition that you can develop, however, is recognition of the good work done for you by your people. The old axiom "a pat on the back is a lot more effective than a kick in the pants" is one that you should not forget. Regardless of how routine a job may be, the skilled supervisor will find many reasons to justify an honest compliment or an occasional word of appreciation to the person doing the work.

But Discipline Is Necessary Too

In addition to the basic obligations to his employees that each manager should respect, there are also obligations that he has to himself and to his employers. One of these is the responsibility for maintaining a reasonable discipline.

Upon being introduced to the principles discussed in this chapter, some old-line administrators will express the opinion that this sort of approach is too "soft" or that the job will never get done by "babying" the employees. If you should happen to feel that way, I urge you to discard that silly notion at once. The use of good human relations in business does not mean that the boss is neglecting the obligation to maintain proper discipline among subordinates. It means, in fact, quite the opposite: the use of these principles will make the job easier to accomplish.

The question of discipline is rarely a matter of major concern in the life of the manager who puts the principles of sound human relations into everyday practice. Employees who enjoy the dignity of equitable treatment and genuine interest seldom create disciplinary problems.

Remember persuasion and force? As a service manager, you are already in the position of having to give instructions, pass out work assignments, and make some criticisms almost every day. This giving of orders is a delicate part of the manager's job. If done clumsily, resentment and resistance are sure to result. If handled skillfully, maximum cooperation can most often be expected.

It has been said that the best way to give an order is not to give it at all. This, of course, simply suggests that direct commands are generally the least effective means of getting work accomplished through other people.

The skilled manager is one who has learned that job assignments, instructions, corrections, and other forms of order giving are best-couched in terms that are comfortable and easily acceptable to the recipients. Often, the most effective managers are those whose orders are usually expressed in the form of requests; for example, "Joe, would you mind running these over to the parts department for me?" or, "Tom, how about giving me a hand with these reports."

Realistically, of course, occasional disciplinary problems are going to rear their ugly heads even in departments being supervised by the most skillful of managers. When this happens, you can be sure that the manner in which the problem is handled will be carefully observed by other members of the group. Judicious and even-handed handling by the supervisor will serve to lessen the chances of a repetition, while inept or clumsy handling might well result in permanent damage to the morale of the entire department.

The term "discipline," as I use it here, refers to the means that are available to you for maintaining appropriate conduct and keeping order within the group of workers for which you are responsible.

Perhaps the first step in learning to handle discipline is to arrive at a clear-cut understanding of what actions constitute grounds for disciplinary procedures. For obvious reasons, there is no simple formula for accomplishing this. The wide margin of variables that can exist between one company and another, and even between departments within the same company, does not lend itself to simple rules. For example, practical joking may be considered a minor infraction in an office or on a sales floor, but it may be regarded as a gravely serious offense in a service shop full of power equipment where injury or death could result from even minor horseplay.

There are, however, certain conditions that always, or almost always, call for some disciplinary action on the part of the manager involved. The following list is necessarily general and does not include the specialized problems of individual groups or departments:

Tardiness
Quitting early
Deliberately wasting time
Wasting materials
Drinking on the job
Spreading rumors
Fighting on the job
Insubordination
Careless handling of tools or equipment
Taking unnecessary chances with safety
Falsifying records or reports
Poor attendance
Failure to report an injury
Gambling on the job
Poor customer relations
Dishonesty

The relative seriousness of these offenses will vary with the type of company involved, the department, the work being done, and other such variables. Some are obviously very serious offenses that call for full discipline in any organization; others may be considered minor under certain circumstances. It is up to the supervisor to be able to recognize every infraction and to interpret it in terms of the conditions under which the group must operate. In most organizations, it would be wise for you to consult with your own boss for counsel before attempting to deal with a serious disciplinary problem.

A word of caution here: the relative seriousness of a given infraction must never be allowed to vary with the individual involved. If the wasting of supplies in your department has been considered a serious offense in the past, you must be certain to handle the problem in the same way with every future offender. Discipline will become extremely difficult, if not impossible, to maintain if you allow yourself to develop a set of double standards.

The temptation to overlook a given offense can be very strong if the individual involved happens to be one of the more productive members of your group or just someone you like. This sort of handling, though, will be immediately noticed by others and will soon lead to charges of favoritism. If allowed to continue, such a practice will quickly undermine the morale of an entire department.

Once you have determined which infractions necessitate disciplinary action, it is your obligation to see to it that everyone understands the ground rules. Employees should never find themselves in trouble for breaking rules that they didn't know existed. Special or unusual orders should be put in writing, and employees should be encouraged to ask questions whenever they are in doubt about what is expected of them. Wherever practical, your employees should be told why any new or unusual rule has been put into effect.

Handling Grievances

Discipline, of course, can be considered as a sort of two-way street. An employee who is unhappy with the behavior of you or your company is going to feel a grievance toward you. How you handle grievances is an important part of your skills as a manager.

Few problems have the potential for more negative effects on the performance of a group of workers than discontent with working conditions, grudges against management, or unheeded grievances of any sort. The discontented employee, unless handled with skill and sincere interest, can well prove to be the service manager's most difficult problem.

Many new service managers experience their first frustrations when attempting to deal with a disgruntled worker. If this is handled in a clumsy manner, the damage done may take a great deal of time to overcome. If the wrong approach is consistently used, the resulting damage to the morale of the group or individual involved may have widespread and lasting ill effects.

There are two effective weapons in your arsenal for dealing with the problem of discontented workers and their grievances. First, an analysis of the basic needs and wants of the average employee will provide a checklist of points that will help you avoid trouble spots before they can take shape. Second, a knowledge of some of the symptoms that indicate unrest will help you recognize trouble at an early stage so that you can go to work to rectify the cause.

Practically all employee grievances are the result of a real or imagined loss of one or more of the fundamental needs that are common to all of us. For this reason, it behooves every manager to be familiar with these needs. Recognition of these requirements by the company's basic personnel policies is not enough to ensure smooth sailing for the front-line manager. It is essential that the employee's immediate supervisor see to it that these policies are visible to the worker and that they are publicized to the extent that every employee is aware of the company's interest in her welfare.

Let's consider some of the things that all of us want out of life.

THE FUNDAMENTAL PHYSICAL NEEDS

Ample food, shelter, and clothing are certainly basic among human needs. In terms of a person's job, this can be translated into the need for adequate wages.

Recreation and Leisure Time

Human beings are hard workers by nature. However, both the body and the mind must have ample time for rest and leisure activities in order to maintain top efficiency. A reasonable amount of time off every week, periodic vacations, and paid illness allowances are employee benefits long recognized as effective in maintaining both efficiency and morale at a high level.

Advancement

Although many workers have no genuine aspirations for advancement, most want to see evidence that opportunities to advance are available to them. The policy of promotion from within satisfies a basic need, provided the policy is put into visible practice and publicized on a regular basis. It is surprising to me how often employees of an organization having a promotion-from-within policy will complain about the lack of opportunity for advancement unless they are periodically reminded of promotions that have come from within in the past.

Dignity

Most people are willing to accept discipline, work under the direction of a business superior, and abide by the regulations governing their employment, provided they are not subjected to the loss of their personal dignity anywhere along the way. This is one of the requirements that *must* be respected by you as a manager. Regardless of the company's willingness to fill this need, the immediate supervisor is responsible for dealing with it successfully on a day-in and day-out basis. The manager who, either by accident or design, trespasses on the dignity of subordinates will completely nullify the effects of whatever the company policy might have to say on the matter. Even more harmful is the damage that will result to the relationship between the manager and the persons involved.

Working Conditions

There is a natural resentment among workers who feel that their employer has no interest in providing them with good working conditions. While the degree of control over working conditions will vary among service managers at different companies, every administrator should see to it that his superiors are made aware of any deficiencies that might affect the safety or morale of his own group. In addition to being as pleasant as circumstances will permit, working conditions should be safe, healthful, and convenient.

Recognition

There is a universal human aversion to being regarded as a nonentity. Regardless of one's station in life, the human ego demands recognition for its individual efforts. This is another need that is best-fulfilled by the employee's immediate supervisor. Company policies may specify that this important aspect of human relations be honored, but it remains for the employee's immediate boss to put the principle into daily practice.

Security

It wasn't so long ago that the threat of dismissal was used as a weapon to intimidate employees into what was hoped would be improved performance. Modern management principles have taught us that top efficiency is a natural partner to a feeling of job security. The employee who enjoys the knowledge that his job is reasonably secure, as long as his performance remains satisfactory, will usually strive to preserve this security by doing his best to maintain good performance.

Accessibility to Management

Employees do not like to feel that they are shut off from contact with company management at any level. Although she may never choose to do so, the average worker likes to feel that she is able to talk things over with the top brass if the need should ever arise. As a service manager, you should never attempt to discourage the feeling that top management is always available to discuss problems facing individual employees. Experience indicates that the supervisor who openly fosters this important policy is the one most likely to be chosen by subordinates when they feel the need to talk with a management representative.

Accomplishment

There is within nearly all of us a strong desire for creative expression. While our abilities to fulfill this urge may vary sharply from one individual to another, every worker likes to see tangible evidence of personal efforts. It is for this reason that job assignments that allow the worker to identify with the finished product are generally much more satisfactory than those found on assembly line arrangements where each worker contributes only a narrow portion of the completed job. This principle can be put to work by service managers in almost any type of service operation. Wherever possible, assignments that will allow the employee to take credit for the entire project (or at least a significant portion of it) are preferable to those in which each worker contributes only a small part.

These, then, are some of the most basic wants of workers everywhere. Failure to recognize them can surely be expected to cause or contribute to employee dissatisfaction and grievances. As I mentioned earlier, the inclusion of rules to provide for these needs within the company's basic personnel policies is not enough to guarantee smooth sailing in the employee morale department. It is up to the employee's immediate supervisor to transform these policies into daily reality.

As the pages in this chapter suggest, the subject of human relations in business is infuriatingly complex. It is important for you to understand that the subjects covered here are, at best, only a sort of sneak preview of the kinds of problems that anyone involved in supervising the activities of other people can expect to encounter.

It would certainly be presumptuous of me to suggest that I can make you an expert in this subject, or even that I am an expert myself. Despite a lifetime of dealing with the challenge of human relations, I find there is hardly a day that I do not learn something new or encounter a new situation. I might also mention that there is hardly a day that I don't find myself fumbling an opportunity to do a better job in some specific human relations situation. This, though, is what makes the "people business" an exciting challenge.

My basic purpose in this chapter is simply to acquaint you with a subject that you may not have given much thought to and, more important, to encourage you to embark on a lifelong effort to develop professionalism in your relationships with the people who work under your guidance. There are any number of good books available that will help you sharpen your people skills. I have listed a few at the end of the book in the Additional Readings that I feel are especially well-done.

Let me close this chapter by reminding you that I know of no other single skill that will help you more in a career as a modern service manager than the ability to motivate others to do their very best.

Chapter 3

The Magic of Communicating

Ours is a world of communication. The business world, in particular, depends on communication in all its forms for its very existence. Is it any wonder, then, that the most successful people in business are those who have learned to communicate effectively with their associates?

We all learn how to speak in our infancy, but speaking and communicating can be two entirely different things. As you may well know, it is not uncommon for a speaker to give an elaborate talk, only to find when she is finished that she has failed to get through to the group—that the point she was trying to make to her audience did not register with them. When this happens, the speaker can usually blame herself for her failure to communicate.

On the other hand, consider the eloquent facial gesture of disapproval registered by the impresario of a large symphony orchestra when he detects a discordant note. To the last person, everyone in the group understands his precise meaning. True communication has taken place without the help of a single spoken word.

A radio transmitter broadcasting the most vital news would be communicating with no one if there were no receivers tuned in to the proper frequency. True communication requires both a transmitter and a receiver, each tuned in to the other. The most articulate speaker is not communicating if his audience is not tuned in to his efforts. Yet effective communication can take place through the most simple gesture or facial expression or even an unspoken thought provided there is a receiver tuned in to the message being transmitted.

IT STARTS WITH GOOD LISTENING

While I'm using the analogy of transmitters and receivers, let me assure you that there is a huge oversupply of transmitters and a grave shortage of good receivers in the world of business communications. Most people like to talk; few of us are naturally inclined to be good listeners. As a business executive, you will need to make a very special effort to train yourself to be a good listener. Above all, try to avoid the habit of thinking of what you're going to say next instead of *really* listening to what the other person is trying to say. As a manager of people, you will be called on to do a lot of transmitting and receiving. You must learn to be skilled at both.

And Clear Instructions

One business activity that calls for precise communication is giving orders or instructions to others. Another example might be telling the boss about an idea of your own or, to pick a really tough one, turning down an employee's suggestion or request. A modern manager will find himself being called on during practically every part of his day to express himself clearly.

Although the use of words is not the only means by which we humans may communicate with each other, it is by far the most important. Since the use of the spoken word is learned so early in life, many of us take this form of communication for granted by failing to recognize its profound importance in our daily lives.

A single word can drastically change the meaning of an entire sentence. The right word spoken at the right time can close a big sale, win a friend, land a job, or make someone happy. The wrong word can lose a customer, injure a reputation, start an argument, or lose the respect of others. To be sure, the ability to select the proper words to use in our oral and our written communications is a most valuable asset.

A GOOD VOCABULARY HELPS

It has been estimated that the average high school graduate has command of approximately 25,000 words, although there are some experts who feel that the vocabulary of the average American is limited to 10,000 words. Compare these figures to the vocabulary of the average business executive who, it is estimated, has a working familiarity with at least twice as many words as the typical high school graduate and, in many cases, much more. If you are 25 years of age or older, your lifetime vocabulary is already more than 95% complete—unless you decide to do something about it!

Why all this fuss about words in a book about service management? Why are words considered to be such an important part of effective business communications?

Words are actually the very foundation not only of our communications with each other but of our very thoughts as well. If you stop to consider it for a moment, you will realize that your thoughts actually come to you in the form of words. Dr. John Dewey, the famous American educator, said, "Thought is impossible without words." William Randolph Hearst is quoted as having said, "Each of us is trying to transfer an idea from his own head into some other brain, and this is done with words."

Some years ago, Johnson O'Connor, of the Stevens Institute of Technology, came to the following conclusion after conducting a series of tests on personality traits: "An exact knowledge of the meaning of English words accompanies success in the business world more often than any other single aspect that we have uncovered."

In short, the more command you have over words, the more precisely you will be able to use them to clarify your own thinking and, thus, your ability to communicate with others. As in mathematics, a knowledge of words is an additive process; the more words we know, the more effectively we are able to think. An inferior, undeveloped vocabulary will not only prove to be a handicap in our attempts to communicate with our associates but will also act as a barrier to the full growth of our mental capacities.

In light of these facts, it becomes evident that a well-developed vocabulary is an essential working tool for the modern executive. If you find yourself handicapped by an inadequate command of the language, however, you need not be discouraged. Developing a powerful vocabulary at any age, regardless of the extent of your formal education, can be a very pleasant and rewarding pursuit. A great many inexpensive courses and books designed to develop a superior vocabulary as a spare-time project are widely available. The only qualifications for success are a sincere and abiding interest in the use of words and the patience to continue your efforts for a reasonable period of time. The chances are, however, that once you develop a taste for the study of the proper use of words, your interest in this fascinating subject will never leave you. As your vocabulary grows, you will become increasingly aware of your new ability not only to organize your own thoughts but to convey them more convincingly to others as well.

Now that we've talked a bit in general about the importance of words, let's take a brief look at some specifics. Not long ago, while he was visiting a foreign country, the President of the United States found himself in some minor but sticky diplomatic trouble. During a speech by the President, his experienced and presumably skilled translator flubbed several words in a key phrase. The error completely changed the meaning of the sentence, and as a result, the President's hosts were offended.

The whole mess was straightened out later when the error was discovered, but the damage had already been done. The speech had been carried live on radio and television in the host country, and it is likely that some of the listeners never heard the explanation.

If the President of the United States with all the resources at his command can sometimes have difficulty in making himself understood, you can imagine the risks that plain folk like you and me must face every day. Such problems in translations from one language to another are not at all unusual. A student of languages soon learns that translation is a difficult and demanding process. Subtle shades of meaning can be extremely difficult (and, in some cases, impossible) to express correctly in a language other than the original.

Be assured, however, that you don't have to be bilingual to find yourself in trouble with garbled meanings. The chances are that you're much more involved with them than you realize. Communicating effectively in plain old English is more of a problem than you may think.

WHERE DO YOU FIT IN?

What does all this have to do with you and your job as a service manager?

Plenty.

Recently, I heard an experienced business executive make a statement to the effect that the great majority of all problems in business are due to some form of misunderstanding between people. That is, someone said something he didn't mean; wrote something that didn't come out the way he intended; or in some other way failed to communicate precisely what he wanted to say.

I don't know about the rest of his audience, but he really struck a responsive chord with me. I have felt the same way for many years. In fact, my own observations have led me to believe that almost *all* business disagreements between people are due, at least in part, to some form of misinterpretation of what some person has said or written.

As I mentioned earlier, service is a people business. Today's service manager deals with people, not things. Because of this, the ability to communicate thoughts and ideas is a central part of the job of service management.

"So, what's the fuss?" you ask. "I've been speaking plain English since I was in knee pants."

Don't be too sure.

Let me share with you a few examples from my personal collection of communication clunkers. Before you've finished reading this, you're probably going to think I'm putting you on—that I made them up. I promise you that such is not the case. I have personally heard or read every single one, and these are only a few favorites from a large collection.

Here's an interview I heard just recently on the evening news. It may not be exactly verbatim, but I wrote it down immediately after I heard it, and it is substantially accurate.

Police official: We must, in light of certain revelations, accept the premise that the suspect was in possession of data and information tending in the direction of self-incrimination.

Reporter: You mean he knew things that only the police and the murderer could know?

Police official: Well, yes.

While they are openly guilty of crimes against the English language, police officials are not the only culprits. Lawyers, who should be the best communicators in our society, are notorious for cluttering their writings with unfamiliar and undecipherable phrases. I am personally acquainted with a number of lawyers, one of whom cheerfully admits that he is completely incapable of writing a *simple* declarative sentence. Here's an excerpt from a letter written by another lawyer and passed on to me:

> My client has authorized me to inform you that the sum indicated in your most recent communication is simply not viable when viewed within the context of the alleged incident.

What he was trying to say, it seems, was simply, "You're asking for too much money and we're not going to pay it." Of course, if lawyers were to speak that plainly, some people might begin to question the need for them.

Back to the White House again. The President had declared war on gobbledygook. We will, he promised, make sure that government regulations and communications are written in plain English for a change. Personally, I do not doubt for a moment that Mr. President was sincere, since he is known as a champion for the cause of plain talk. It would appear, however, that his efforts have not yet plumbed the black depths of the Washington bureaucracy.

In a recent budget for commissary operations, the Department of Defense referred to some of its office facilities as "existing administrative nonappropriated fund support structures." As far as I can tell, the phrase refers to the department's headquarters offices.

As proud as I am of my own collection of this atrocious nonsense, I must tell you of a collection that puts mine to shame. In his delightful book *A Civil Tongue*, author/newsman Edwin Newman has put together a treasure that may never be equalled. In one example, an unfavorable financial report was described as "vulnerable to negative scrutiny." In another case, an Amtrak report about arranging bus schedules to fit train arrivals said, "The [bus companies] do not like to intermode." A task force put together to see how well TV stations were dealing with public affairs reported that "there was minimal affirmative correlation found between priority social issues and station priorities."

The amazing thing about all this is that the people who write and publish this sort of drivel firmly believe that they are doing a skillful job of communicating.

Let's get closer to home. Here are a couple of paragraphs from a letter in my files written to me some time ago:

> The viability of these two programs depends upon the maintained representativeness of the sample provided by the test units. Collectively, we share the responsibility to protect the credibility of this sample.
>
> Some special programs requested by sources or though the merchandise departments may unintentionally tend to distort the representativeness of the data spectrum provided by the participating unit. Of course, our interest is to cooperate fully in the administration of these specialized programs, however, sample effect remains first priority."

This is no joke. The writer of that letter was sincerely trying to remind me of the importance of collecting accurate statistics for some surveys that we were conducting, though it took me a while to figure that out.

This is from another letter that I received:

> It is our continuing objective to enhance the effectiveness of this management tool. The disciplines realized through interfaces with other programs, and with service input expanding each month, increased dimensions of credibility and timeliness of the data can be expected.

Examples of this sort of thing can go on endlessly, of course. People who consistently try to communicate relatively simple thoughts through pompous and wordy efforts can be found all around us. My reason for stressing this subject to you in this chapter is not that I think you may be guilty of such outrageous conduct. It is simply my attempt to steer you clear of a common error young executives often make when they are told that they should sharpen their communication skills.

You may not have ever thought about it before, but I daresay that you are personally acquainted with at least one misguided soul who has concluded that learning the meaning of lots of new words—especially big ones—will enhance the search for social and business success. This is the person who is forever confusing others with the use of long, unfamiliar words. To make matters worse, the superficial manner in which this person learns the meanings of such words results in their frequent incorrect usage.

You will recall that I began this chapter by reminding you of the importance of being able to put your thoughts into the proper words. Naturally, if you are to make yourself understood, you must have command of a sufficient number of words to properly express your ideas. If you stop to think about it, it becomes obvious that a person with a severely limited vocabulary is going to have difficulty in trying to explain ideas to another person.

Translation: if you want to improve your ability to communicate with other people, improve your vocabulary.

BUT DON'T OVERDO IT

That happens to be *very* good advice. The only trouble is that it is so often misunderstood—even when given by people who are supposed to be experts in making themselves understood.

Back in the late nineteen-forties, an extensive analysis of a large number of highly successful business executives revealed only one trait common to nearly all of them. Now, please understand that all the traditional characteristics we have come to expect in the successful business executive were found in abundance in this group. Such traits as ambition, financial orientation, leadership, high physical energy, and strong determination were all represented. Each individual, of course, had a unique combination of such physical and mental characteristics. However, only a single characteristic was common to all or nearly all the personalities studied: a better-than-average vocabulary.

The results of this study were widely published at the time and, I believe, dealt an almost mortal blow to the cause of better communication.

Why?

Because countless ambitious young people (and a few authors of books) around this country drew the wrong conclusions from the information that was provided. If you want to be successful, they reasoned, you must *enlarge* your vocabulary.

Perhaps you have spotted the difference between that last sentence and the one a few paragraphs back that I described as very good advice. I talked about *improving* vocabulary, not *enlarging* it. The difference is subtle but, in my opinion, very important.

If all of this sounds confusing, just think of it this way: communicating your thoughts and ideas to other people requires that you develop a good working vocabulary. What it does not require is that you learn and use a long list of big, impressive words that most people will not recognize or understand.

If you are fortunate enough to develop a lively interest in the world of words and good communication, the chances are that you'll be hooked for a lifetime. It is truly a fascinating subject with special rewards of its own.

You may, for example, find that you have begun to admire talents that you had not even noticed before. Have you ever seen Mr. Alistair Cooke on television? If you are already one of his fans, you're probably aware of his uncommonly skillful use of the English language. Though he seldom uses any but the most familiar and basic words, Mr. Cooke has a fascinating talent for choosing precisely the correct phrase to express the subtle shades of meaning that he likes to convey.

Of course, most of us can never hope to achieve Mr. Cooke's level of accomplishment in the art of effective communication, nor is it necessary for us to do so. As a service manager, though, your efforts to improve your ability to communicate your thoughts will pay you a rich return in the form of greater personal effectiveness.

The ability to select proper words is not, of course, the only qualification for effective communication. Once this aspect is mastered, though, the rest is easier to learn.

Basically, we use our words in two different forms: the written word and the spoken word. While the rules are essentially the same, skill in one form does not necessarily mean skill in the other.

SKILL WITH THE SPOKEN WORD

William Jennings Bryan said, "The ability to speak effectively is an acquirement rather than a gift." If Mr. Bryan was right, then there's hope for all of us. Make no mistake about it. Being able to speak effectively is of major importance to everyone in management. It has been estimated that the average supervisor will speak as many as 20,000 words per day in the course of work. As a practical matter, nearly all those spoken words will have some bearing on the performance of the supervisor's department.

Talking face to face with others is a part of our everyday communications, and each day presents the manager with plenty of opportunity to improve his skills in this area. The ability to communicate orally is one of the most essential tools needed by today's administrators and as such should receive a good portion of every service manager's self-improvement time.

Skill in speaking will come easier for you if you learn to respect a few of the basic ground rules:

> Speak clearly. Clear enunciation comes only with practice and conscious effort. No supervisor can afford to have his instructions misunderstood because he mumbles or races through his sentences. Not everyone can have a beautifully resonant voice, but anyone can be understood by speaking carefully.
>
> Be a good listener. This is at least half of being a good talker. Train yourself to allow the other person to make his point without interrupting. Nothing is more humorous (and useless) than two people, each ignoring what the other is saying while breathlessly awaiting an opportunity to interrupt with his own ideas.
>
> Speak at a controlled pace. Individuals vary greatly in their abilities to digest new thoughts and ideas. Tailor-make your approach to the individual or group involved in order to improve the chances for getting your message across. If you feel that you sometimes speak too rapidly, chances are that you're right.

Almost everyone in management will find it necessary to address a group at a formal meeting or training session from time to time. There is, perhaps, no other time in which skill in the use of the spoken word is of more importance.

Most of us have had the experience of attending a lecture or speech that held promise of great interest or entertainment, only to come away disappointed and bored. On the other hand, dull programs or topics will sometimes spring to life and captivate a skeptical audience. The difference, of course, is the speaker. Some people can stand before an audience and fail to ignite even a spark of interest on the most topical of subjects, whereas others are able to thrill their listeners while talking about "nothing."

Since the art of public speaking is a topic that cannot be adequately discussed here, I will remind you of the large amount of material on the subject available at any public library or bookstore.

MAKING A SPEECH

To whet your appetite, here are a few of the fundamental rules of good public speaking. They will help to maintain interest whether your audience is two or three clerks receiving brief instructions or several hundred people in a large auditorium.

Avoid Distracting Habits

Shifting your weight from one foot to another, glancing at the ceiling or floor, making nervous gestures with your hands, and other such habits will prove distracting to most audiences, causing their minds to stray from what you are saying.

Have a Plan

Perhaps the biggest single factor in a successful talk before a group is . . . planning. Have an outline to follow. Know exactly what you want to say and how to say it.

Practice Helps

Practice your talk in advance. (But don't memorize your talk word for word. The result will sound artificial and uninteresting.)

When to Stop

When you have made your point, stop! In public speaking, brevity is a virtue that will enhance your reputation.

Voice Counts

Don't speak in a monotone. How many times have you wearily suffered through talks that were delivered in a monotonous, tiring voice that could not possibly do justice to any subject? Vary the pitch of your voice as well as the speed of your delivery. Occasionally reducing your voice to a near whisper can help to make a telling point.

Watch such technicalities as diction, pronunciation, and proper grammar. While college professors are the only speakers who are expected to be faultless in such things, consistently poor grammar or pronunciation will seriously detract from the impact of any talk.

Watch Your Language

Don't rely on colloquialisms or too much slang. While such devices may spice up a talk if used sparingly, they will only call attention to themselves if overdone.

Summing Up

Be sure to "tie the knot." Any talk worth the effort can be brought to a meaningful summary at the close. Never leave your audience dangling in midair, trying to decipher your message. The final phrases of your talk should always be designed to knit your points together into a logical and clear conclusion.

As with anything else worthwhile, skillful public speaking will not come without intelligent effort. Few people are skilled in their first attempts at speaking before groups. If you are interested in developing this particular aspect of your management abilities, you should take advantage of every opportunity you get to speak before groups, large or small. In public speaking, practice (provided there is plenty of it) makes perfect.

THE WRITTEN WORD

Then there is the written word, which can be a valuable asset or an unfortunate handicap to your efforts. The writing of memos, reports, instructions, etc., is a part of practically every manager's duties. Unskilled or clumsy use of the written word results in visible testimony to the writer's ineptitude, and it's there for the whole world to see. On the other hand, the manager who is able to make the best use of written communications has the benefit of one of the most effective tools of the trade.

All the principles that apply to the use of the spoken word are equally true in written communications, along with a few special rules that make written words even more demanding masters than their spoken counterparts. In addition to all the problems in oral communications, written words must accomplish their purpose without benefit of facial expression, physical gestures, tone of voice, and other such devices that aid the user of the spoken word to drive home a point. Even more skill is needed to communicate effectively in writing than is needed in speech.

WHY BOTHER TO WRITE?

If oral communication is so much easier, why write?

Well, the fact of the matter is that the flood of paper that inundates most businesses today makes a fast phone call or a quick face-to-face conversation a very good alternative to another piece of paper. Personally, I try to avoid a letter or written memo whenever possible. However, the complexities of today's business world and the growing demands on the time of busy executives have led many administrators to prefer certain types of facts and reports on paper.

Word-of-mouth communications require that two or more busy people arrange their schedules for a personal meeting. Some types of information must be studied or slowly digested, and this is possible only if the information is in written form. And, of course, permanent documentation is required for some types of records and reports. The recipient of a written report is able to study the information at leisure. Where great distances are involved and the matter does not justify the use of long-distance telephone, a written communication is the obvious answer.

All these things add up to an inescapable conclusion. Modern managers cannot completely avoid involvement with the written word.

I have known many service managers over the years who have purposely shied away from written communications just because they lacked confidence in their writing abilities. As I said earlier, developing any worthwhile skill calls for plenty of practice, and writing effectively is certainly no exception to this rule. The rewards to be gained by the manager who has skill in communicating in any form, however, make any amount of effort a good investment.

Aside from formal classroom training, the best way to develop your writing skill is to enlist some coaching from an experienced person. When this is not possible, a group of two or more persons can get together for self-criticism and evaluation. This can be a lot of fun and the results will be lasting dividends in self-confidence and effectiveness on the job. Here are a few basics to get you started:

> Keep it simple. Attempts to impress others through the use of big words will backfire.

Have your point well thought out before you attempt to reduce it to writing.

Keep written reports neat, precise, and courteous. They reflect your own image.

"Slant" your report toward the recipient. If your boss is the type who demands lots of supporting facts, see that he gets them. Make your case solid and airtight. On the other hand, if he prefers things brief and to the point, make your reports in skeleton form. When putting instructions in writing, keep them simple. Guard against writing over the heads of those who will be reading your report.

If it is necessary to quote facts in your communication, double-check your information. Errors in writing are much harder to justify than spur-of-the-moment comments. Always proofread everything that will bear your signature.

Choose your words with care. Don't forget that a single word can radically change the meaning of an entire sentence.

Don't leave the reader hanging in midair. Try to foresee any questions that may arise as a result of what you are writing, and answer them for the reader before they are asked.

MEETING MANNERS

Practically everyone in management is required to attend a certain number of meetings. It is in this area that many people fail to communicate to their own advantage. There can be little doubt that a great many man-hours are wasted every day through attendance of meetings that fail to accomplish their intended purpose and thus are of little or no value to anyone. Every manager owes it to himself to make certain that he understands the purpose of every meeting that he attends, and to see to it that he contributes his proper share, no more and no less, to the proceedings.

It would probably be difficult to find a business executive who has not had the unfortunate experience of attending a meeting that was verbally dominated by a single individual who had very little of real value to add to the matter at hand. Every meeting should have a leader or chairperson, whose duty is to see to it that overly talkative individuals are kept within bounds. Since business meetings are usually made up of groups of busy people, every minute is valuable and wasted time can be very costly.

Managers who must participate in meetings can communicate most effectively with the group by observing a few fundamental rules of meeting etiquette:

Only topics of interest to the group as a whole should be introduced. It is poor business to tie up several specialists by discussing subjects of no interest whatever to some participants.

If the chairperson has restricted the agenda to specified subjects, respect this request.

Don't allow yourself to go off on a tangent by introducing irrelevant or nonbusiness topics. If you're acting as the chairperson, don't allow anyone else to do it either.

Unless the meeting is highly informal, request permission or acknowledgement before speaking. When you have the floor, resist the temptation to be "flowery." Make your point as briefly as possible.

One wise executive is quoted as saying, "Usually, the most successful participants at a meeting are those who have listened well; spoken little; and left promptly."

Learning to communicate with maximum effectiveness in the variety of situations you will encounter as a modern service manager will require a good deal of sincere effort and patience. However, if your interests and efforts are genuine, your newly developed skills will make your job easier and much more satisfying.

Chapter 4
Productivity —the Big Challenge

To some people, productivity is a bad word. It seems to be burdened with all sorts of terrible implications. To many workers, it suggests that the "system" is attempting to exploit them through conspiracies designed to force them to work harder. As if that weren't trouble enough, many managers are reluctant to deal with the subject because of the fear that employees will react negatively.

That's a shame, really, because productivity isn't a bad word at all, though it is often misunderstood. The fact of the matter is that a healthy interest in productivity will usually benefit all parties involved.

All this is not to suggest that today's professional service manager can afford to be naive about the subject. Decades of labor/management confrontations over worker output have created a web of subtle problems that can be frustratingly difficult to deal with. Like it or not, however, productivity and its attendant problems will be a part of your life as long as you are a service manager. Without good productivity, no service business can expect to survive.

In his excellent book *Ten Thousand Working Days* (MIT, Cambridge, Mass., 1978), Robert Schrank, a uniquely qualified expert on the psychology of work, sometimes takes a pessimistic view of the subject. "I wonder," he says, "whether humans would work at all if it weren't for the punitive consequences of not working."

At the risk of sounding presumptuous, I must admit that my own experiences have led me to put a less harsh interpretation on that subject. Most people, I believe, have an instinctive need to do meaningful work of some sort. Given reasonable working conditions and skillful motivation, the majority of us will respond favorably. The hooker here is skillful motivation. Too many managers are woefully lacking in their ability to generate it, and many others are unwilling to try.

One supporter of this view is the much-lettered Charles Jackson Grayson, Jr. Mr. Grayson, a former presidential cabinet member, has devoted his life to a nonprofit organization which in turn is devoted to the gospel of improved productivity. The extraordinarily active Grayson has often expressed dismay at how little most companies have done to improve the productivity of their own employees. It is his feeling that improved productivity is the only real answer to America's inflation problems.

In any case, you can be sure that improved productivity is a certain answer to the efficiency and profitability problems of most service departments.

Fortunately, better productivity does not have to come at the expense of the worker; it is usually a direct result of improved working conditions and management skills. After a year-long study, one large service organization concluded that most of the things that were causing poor productivity were things being improperly done by management, not by the service personnel.

THE SERVICE FACTORY

The concept of good productivity, and the need for it, is readily apparent in a factory environment. A factory building widgets, for example, is going to turn out a better product in larger quantities if it makes use of good equipment, modern methods, and well-trained workers. The same type of factory trying to squeeze by with outdated machinery and poorly trained or poorly equipped workers and managers will turn out very little finished product in relation to the amount of money spent to run the factory—that's poor productivity. To be sure, this is an overly simplified example, but it's easy to understand and it's quite true. Not everyone, though, sees as clearly when it comes to the subject of productivity in service departments.

In many ways, your service department can be compared to a factory. The raw material going into your "factory" is the merchandise that needs repairs. The finished product coming out at the other end of the "production line" is a properly completed repair job. At the end of each workday, a certain number of repair jobs have been "manufactured." When the number of repair jobs is divided into the total cost of running the factory for that day, the result is the cost per product.

It goes without saying that if your factory is staffed by well-trained, properly motivated personnel using modern methods and efficient equipment, your cost per product will be relatively low. If, on the other hand, the opposite conditions exist, productivity will be poor and the cost of the finished product will be higher.

BETTER PRODUCTIVITY MEANS BETTER PROFITS

As a professional service manager, it is absolutely essential that you have a clear understanding of the relationship between good productivity and the financial success of your service operation. Of all the operating factors that influence financial performance, the most important is productivity. In a labor-intensive business such as service, the productivity of all employees is important, but that of your service technicians or mechanics is most important of all.

An analysis of the cost structure in one large commercial-equipment service organization revealed the following:

Technical payroll	38.60 %
Management and supervisory payroll	4.90
All other payroll	20.02
Mileage expense	5.70
Overhead, rent, heat, etc.	30.78
	100.00 %

Operations in many branches of the service industry will have a similar expense structure. As you can see, the payroll for repair technicians alone came to 38.6%. No other single classification of expense was even close in size. When you add all three categories of payroll together, you have a whopping 63.5%, nearly two-thirds of the total cost of running the business. In a smaller operation, payroll might well represent an even larger portion of the total cost. Remember, too, that the accelerated rate of labor-cost increases in our inflationary economy is almost certain to make this ratio even more dramatic in the future.

Is it any wonder, then, that the amount of properly done work turned out each day by each employee (productivity) will determine the profit or loss of the business more surely than any other single expense factor? For an illustration of the economic leverage of productivity, consider the following:

The mythical ABC Appliance Service Company employs twenty service technicians. Their average productivity is five completed calls per day. That is, the twenty technicians combined complete an average of 100 repair jobs per day. Now, let's assume that the average technician's wage at ABC is $60 per day.

$60 divided by 5 calls = $12 payroll cost per call

For the sake of illustration, let's assume that the service manager at the rival XYZ Service Company, after putting the methods discussed in this book to work, is able to increase the productivity of her technicians to a daily average of six completed calls per worker instead of five. Let's also assume that both companies pay the same wages.

$60 divided by 6 calls = $10 payroll cost per call

What all this means is that the labor costs at ABC are 20% higher than at XYZ, *even though both companies pay the same wage rates.* It is not at all unlikely that the $2 difference in technical payroll cost per call would make the difference between a profit or loss for the businesses in the examples used.

This is why no service manager can afford to be anything less than an expert on productivity. And make no mistake, service managers, productivity is your personal responsibility.

MOTIVATION

Have you ever wondered why people do the things they do? If you have, you're not alone. Since the earliest days of civilization, great minds have pondered the mysteries of human reasoning. From the observations of such philosophers as Aristotle and Plato to the clinical notes of today's psychologists, we have all the evidence we need to demonstrate that we'll probably never fully understand the complex workings of the human mind.

Don't let that scare you, though. The fact is that the basic knowledge that has been carefully gathered by those who have gone before us is relatively easy to understand. It can be put to work by any service manager in the effort to improve productivity. Fortunately, it isn't necessary to hold a degree in psychology in order to benefit from a knowledge of a few of the fundamentals of human motivation.

In Chapter 2, you read of two of the most powerful human drives—the preservation of personal dignity and the search for personal recognition. These and the other basic human drives, such as ambition, the desire for security, and monetary gain, combine to form what has been called the most powerful force on earth. There is no stopping this omnipotent energy. It can move mountains or build palaces; it can topple governments or win wars; it can and does alter the course of history.

As a matter of fact, it can be said that every advance in our material world is brought about by the unleashing of one or more of the basic human motivations. Great inventions have resulted from the search for personal recognition, and civilizations have been built around the instinct for self-preservation. Our own democratic form of government was born as the result of the search for freedom and personal dignity. Many great industries have been built through the drive of an individual seeking financial gain or power. The list could go on almost indefinitely.

If you reflect on these things, it will be apparent to you that a service manager faced with the job of influencing the efforts of other people must not tamper with the awesome force of human motivation. How much easier and more rewarding it is to learn how to harness this great energy and turn it in the same direction that we ourselves are traveling, to use it to assist our efforts rather than attempt to fight against such hopeless odds.

The science of management has been described as getting things done through other people. That, of course, is a rather simplistic description of a very complicated job, but it does get to the heart of the matter. The skill of today's manager can be measured in terms of his ability to motivate those around him to do a good job—and a good job includes consideration of the amount of work done.

As a concept, productivity may be discussed in simple terms, but it cannot be approached that way on a day-to-day working basis. Countless volumes have been written about the problems of improving productivity through motivation, and there will no doubt be many more as new techniques are learned. It is, indeed, a complex subject and there are those who will quickly tell you that they still have much to learn about it even after a lifetime of study.

A Perplexing Problem

One classic study of productivity involved a series of experiments conducted by the Western Electric Company in 1927. In what has since become known as the Hawthorne Research, carefully measured changes were made in working hours, wages, organization, supervisory methods, and physical working conditions in order to determine what effect such changes would have on the output of the workers involved.

The final conclusions were hardly what most of the researchers expected. In one phase of the experiments, productivity went up when improvements were made in lighting conditions. Before you say "that's obvious," be advised that later, when the lighting was made poorer than it had been originally, productivity rose again. Eventually, the researchers came to understand that it was the extra *attention* being paid to the test group that was influencing them to increase their output—another indication of the complexity of the subject.

Productivity, they concluded, was affected much more by certain social and psychological influences than by changes in such basic things as wages and hours. In other words, a worker's relationships with peers or the prevalent mental attitudes of the workers as a group were much more important than such likely candidates as wages and working conditions when it came to influencing productivity.

The Hawthorne Research—so named because it was conducted in Hawthorne, California—was perhaps industry's first lesson showing that increases in financial incentives alone cannot be counted on to improve productivity. Since that time, this premise has been demonstrated over and over again in almost all branches of industry.

In his scholarly book on work incentives *Money and Motivation* (Harper & Row, New York, 1955), William F. Whyte complicates the matter even further: "It is often assumed that high morale and high productivity go together. . . . If we mean by high morale only that workers are well satisfied with their jobs and think well of management, then high productivity does not necessarily follow."

Mr. Whyte goes on to point out that people may simply be happy to be part of the organization, but that such contentment will not necessarily translate itself automatically into higher output. This observation nicely puts to rest the naive notion that a manager need only be a nice guy and keep everybody happy in order to develop high productivity.

Obviously, then, there are no nice and easy formulas to tell you exactly what you will need to do to improve the efficiency of your service department. Nevertheless, many people have gone before you, and most of the basic lessons they have learned can be put to work to make life at least a bit easier for you. Provided you are willing to work at it, you can learn the techniques that will work best to improve productivity in your organization.

MEASURING PRODUCTIVITY

Someone once observed that the very first step required to solve a problem is gaining a clear idea of exactly what the problem is. As obvious as this may seem, it is surprising how often we ignore it.

In the case of productivity, that first step in an effective method for improvement must be a careful and accurate measure of where you are starting from—exactly what your productivity is now. Before you can expect to improve productivity, you must learn how to measure it accurately. I once heard the matter put quite succinctly: "If you can't measure it, you can't manage it."

You may as well know from the beginning that measuring the productivity of mechanics or service technicians is not an easy job, and there is no uniformly accepted method for doing so. There are continual arguments over whether such things as coffee-break time, shop-cleanup time, travel time, and other forms of nonproductive effort should be included or excluded from the statistical analysis when computing productivity. There is also a clear lack of agreement about the statistical handling of such things as "callbacks" and estimate refusals.

There are, in fact, a number of service managers who believe that technician and mechanic productivity is best measured not in terms of the number of completed repair jobs performed but by the amount of labor income dollars developed. There are several reasons why I do not recommend this approach to you. For one thing, such a system can be cumbersome and unfair where a significant amount of in-warranty work is involved, especially where in-warranty labor rates are different from those charged to customers. Also, in today's consumerist environment, I tend to be concerned about the temptation to perform or charge for unnecessary work. The most successful and reliable systems that I have seen and worked with for measuring and improving productivity are those that concentrate on the number of successful completed repair jobs performed by each individual. Properly analyzed in an organization using skillfully set service rates, this method of productivity review will assure both good productivity and good labor income.

Because of their lack of uniformity, published industry figures on productivity should not be relied on unless you are certain that they have been computed on the same basis as those you are using. Productivity figures developed within your own organization will be the most helpful and meaningful for you, provided that you arrive at them in a professional manner.

In some branches of the service industry, considerable progress is being made in this area. The National Association of Retail Dealers of America (NARDA) makes available to its dealer members a computerized program that provides a dependable and consistent method for measuring the productivity of service technicians. The participating service dealer sends NARDA certain statistical information each month for analysis by NARDA's computer. This results in a monthly report to the dealer containing detailed productivity data in a consistent format. The availability of the data sent in by other members provides service managers with a means for comparing the productivity of their own technicians with that of others doing similar work.

By no means, however, is it necessary for you to have the help of a computer in order to do a good job of analyzing your productivity. The manual system of record keeping may not be as convenient or sophisticated as a computer system, but it is every bit as accurate, and it can be kept simple enough to suit the needs of any service organization not ready for computerization.

Learning to Count

Let's begin our analysis of productivity in your service department with the elementary problem of how to count completed repair jobs. This may seem painfully simple to you, but bear with me for a moment.

I once heard a tale about a factory that manufactured automobiles. It seems that at the close of a particularly busy day, the manager walked into the comptroller's office and asked how many completed automobiles had been built that day. The comptroller consulted the tally sheets and replied, "525."

"That's odd," the manager said, "I just checked the cars in the storage area and I count only 499."

"Of course," said the comptroller, scribbling furiously with a pencil, "but when I subtract coffee-break time, cleanup time, and time for the training session we had this morning, we produced *at the rate of 525 cars per day*."

Such a conversation is unlikely in a real factory, of course, but you'd be surprised how close we come in some service departments. In an effort to be fair to the individual technicians, some service managers make so many statistical concessions that daily productivity of eight, ten, or even twelve jobs per day are recorded for technicians who never completed more than six or seven actual repairs in a single day in their lives. Such self-deception causes many problems for the manager who practices it. Here's a rule I suggest you paste on the inside of your hat: never include "phantom" completes in your analysis of productivity. At the end of the day, the only repair jobs that should be counted are the ones that actually were completed. Count only "those cars that are sitting in the storage area."

One of Mr. Grayson's pet peeves is what he describes as most companies lack of progress in such an elementary phase of productivity as how to measure it. He wasn't talking specifically about service departments, but he might as well have been.

In the years that I have been working with the problem of measuring the productivity of service personnel, I have developed several personal guidelines. I recommend them to you.

1. The precise method you use to count and measure completed work is not as important as is absolute consistency, provided your system is reasonable and avoids self-deceptive extremes such as those in the tale of the automobile factory. Once you settle on a formula for measuring the number of completed jobs, you must try not to alter it in any significant way. Otherwise, you will not be able to develop the statistical history needed to measure your progress.

2. Do not rely on published industry statistics unless you have some way of determining whether they make use of the same methods as you do for gathering the data involved. If your department is large, you can compare individuals or groups of individuals with others doing similar work. In smaller departments with only a few employees, you may have to rely on comparisons of how each individual is doing with respect to his or her own previous performance.

3. The time you take to compute your productivity statistics will be some of your best-used personal time. Do it promptly at the close of each month or have it done for you. You cannot hope to improve the efficiency of your service department without a clear history of the productivity of each individual involved.

4. Keep in mind that absolute numbers are not especially relevant in your productivity analysis. What you are attempting is a *relative comparison* between one individual and another, between one

group and another, or between one month and another on a consistent set of standards. This is why you should not be unduly concerned by the specific numbers sometimes publicized as industry averages. Your goal is to establish a reasonable and consistent method for measuring productivity in your own organization and then to develop a means for improving it.

With even the most simple system for measuring productivity, you will have to begin with a basic decision: will you base your computations on hours paid or on hours worked? While a case can be made for either choice, I much prefer hours worked. With this choice, such things as vacations, illness, paid holidays, or other paid absences that may vary greatly among individuals do not affect the computations. This system requires only two simple steps:

1. Compute the hours actually worked by each individual for a given period of time, usually one month. Divide that number by 8 to arrive at days worked. (Count overtime hours as straight hours even though they may have been worked at premium pay.)
2. Divide days worked into the number of jobs completed during the period to arrive at average daily productivity.

Here's how these steps might look in a typical example:

Technician Jones
Hours worked during May = 148
148 divided by 8 = 18.5 days worked
Jobs completed during May = 95
95 divided by 18.5 = 5.1 completes per day

To be sure, the use of hours *paid* in these calculations could be considered technically more correct than hours *worked*. One reason is that hours worked does not provide any accommodation for excessive absences from work, tardiness, or other such factors that are automatically included when hours paid is substituted for hours worked in the formula. It is my feeling, however, that problems such as these are disciplinary and entirely unrelated to productivity during actual working hours. Productivity is best-analyzed when it is isolated as a separate subject. Bear in mind, too, that if you are in the habit of assigning nonproductive types of work to your technicians, this will show up in your calculations. So will operating systems that waste your technicians' time.

Once your calculations are complete, they should be entered on a productivity record form for later analysis. Figure 4.1 shows a typical productivity record and analysis sheet.

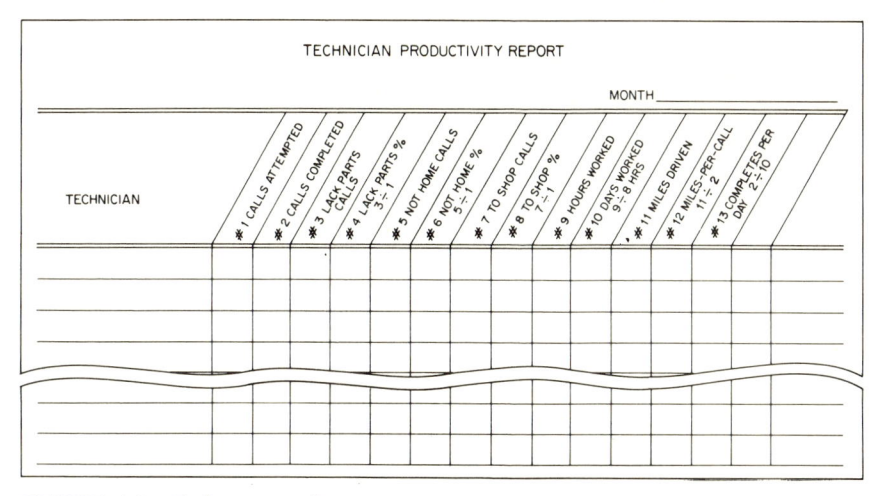

FIGURE 4.1. Technician productivity report.

OK, you have developed a good system for measuring the output of your technical personnel. Then what?

WHAT YOU CAN DO

First of all, a few words on something you can do right now that will probably give you an immediate improvement in productivity—take a critical look at the paperwork in your organization.

We in service management seem to have a remarkable tendency to proliferate unnecessary paperwork. There's probably a psychological root cause for this malady, but if so, it's beyond me. Regardless of the reasons, though, you must be ruthless in your war against the tidal wave of paper waiting to engulf you. (The larger your company, the more likely this is to be a serious problem for you. Sometimes, very small operations suffer from a lack of adequate records.)

Too Much Paper?

Start first with your service or work order. It's an essential part of every service operation. However, if you have any influence over such things, you should ask yourself these questions: (1) how much information does the repair order call for? Whether it's an office clerk or a technician who makes the entries, every line on a work order takes someone's valuable time. (2) Do you really need and *use* all of the information required? Take a careful look to see if your work order can be simplified. (3) If it's a multicopy order, are you sure that you need every one of those expensive copies? One work order I have seen was skillfully designed so that the technician had only to check the necessary boxes to provide most of the needed information. A real time-saver. A sample of a well-designed work order is shown in Figure 4.2.

Now consider the other paperwork in your department. A work order must be created for every repair job, but every other piece of paper used regularly in your operation should be under suspicion. In particular, be on the lookout for duplicate records and information within your department. You are the only one in your organization who can be entrusted with this investigation. Often, it is the conscientiousness of the best employees that causes them to create and to perpetuate parallel record-keeping systems.

Why?

One reason, I have found, is the tendency of some employees to mistrust your simple system. Because of this, they create a supple-

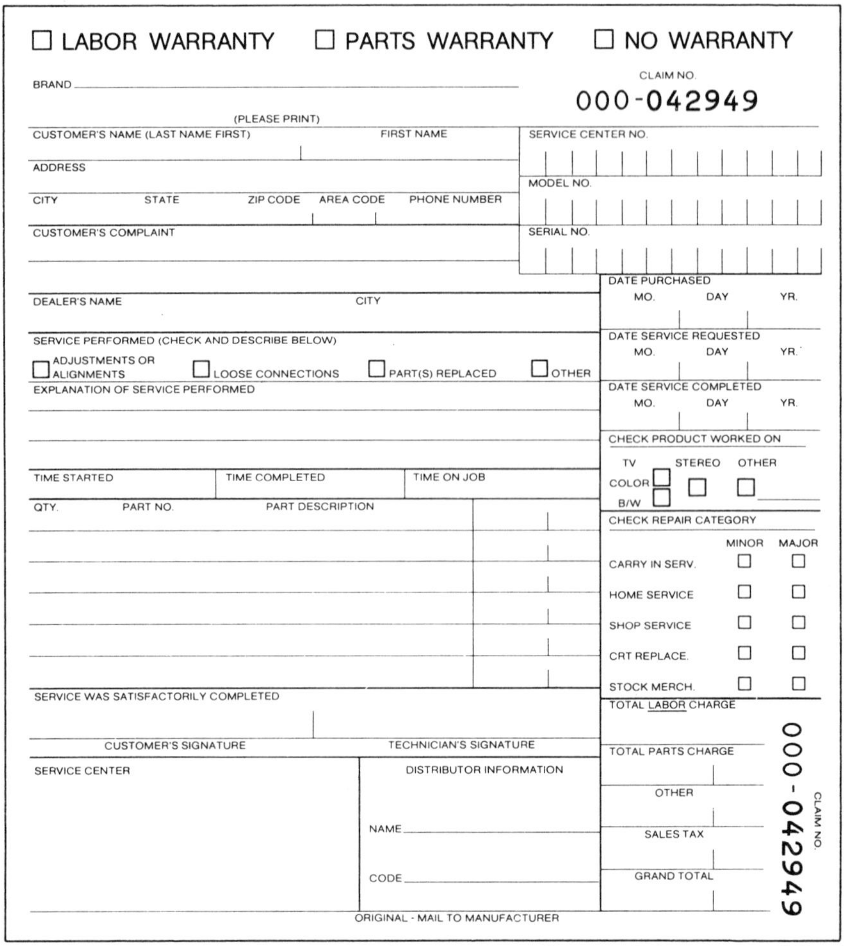

☐ LABOR WARRANTY ☐ PARTS WARRANTY ☐ NO WARRANTY

BRAND

CLAIM NO.
000-042949

(PLEASE PRINT)
CUSTOMER'S NAME (LAST NAME FIRST) FIRST NAME
SERVICE CENTER NO.
ADDRESS
MODEL NO.
CITY STATE ZIP CODE AREA CODE PHONE NUMBER
CUSTOMER'S COMPLAINT
SERIAL NO.
DATE PURCHASED
MO. DAY YR.
DEALER'S NAME CITY
SERVICE PERFORMED (CHECK AND DESCRIBE BELOW)
DATE SERVICE REQUESTED
MO. DAY YR.
☐ ADJUSTMENTS OR ALIGNMENTS ☐ LOOSE CONNECTIONS ☐ PART(S) REPLACED ☐ OTHER
EXPLANATION OF SERVICE PERFORMED
DATE SERVICE COMPLETED
MO. DAY YR.
CHECK PRODUCT WORKED ON
TV STEREO OTHER
COLOR ☐ ☐ ☐
B/W ☐
TIME STARTED TIME COMPLETED TIME ON JOB
QTY. PART NO. PART DESCRIPTION
CHECK REPAIR CATEGORY
MINOR MAJOR
CARRY IN SERV. ☐ ☐
HOME SERVICE ☐ ☐
SHOP SERVICE ☐ ☐
CRT REPLACE. ☐ ☐
STOCK MERCH. ☐ ☐
SERVICE WAS SATISFACTORILY COMPLETED
TOTAL LABOR CHARGE
CUSTOMER'S SIGNATURE TECHNICIAN'S SIGNATURE
TOTAL PARTS CHARGE
SERVICE CENTER
DISTRIBUTOR INFORMATION
OTHER
NAME
SALES TAX
CODE
GRAND TOTAL
ORIGINAL - MAIL TO MANUFACTURER
CLAIM NO. 000-042949

FIGURE 4.2. A well-designed work order *(Courtesy of National Association of Retail Dealers of America).*

mentary system of their own, "just in case." It would be natural for you to feel that this problem is not present in your operation, but please remember that it's not going to be obvious. If it were, you would have noticed it a long time ago without my reminding you.

One place I have seen this happen many times is in the logging in and out of customer merchandise in the shops. A simple loose-leaf log with alphabetical entries will do the job just fine for most types of service shops. The use of a shop log will be covered in more detail in the chapter on shop layout and work flow.

By the way, you have an important ally in your battle against unnecessary paperwork—your accountant. A good one is trained to ferret out inefficiency in record keeping. I recommend that you enlist her help in streamlining your paperwork systems. If you work for a big corporation, ask your accounting department to give you a hand.

Setting the Stage

I hope that it's clear to you now that one of the basic steps required to improve productivity is to set the stage properly. Conditions favorable to good productivity must be established by management. As obvious as this might seem, I cannot stress too strongly that most poor productivity results from management's failure to provide the proper conditions, not from the technician's reluctance to do a good job.

C. Jackson Grayson has said, "I've heard all the rhetoric about we-don't-want-to-work-anymore, and I don't believe it. The work ethic has not been lost. What has happened is that autocratic, bureaucratic organizations in business and public service have suppressed the desires and abilities of the individual to feel that he or she is contributing." In *Ten Thousand Working Days*, Mr. Schrank observes that "insensitivity to workers is turned around to become lack of motivation." Sound observations on productivity from two men well qualified to speak on the subject.

In Chapter 2, you read of the importance of good human relations. At no time will this subject be of more importance to you than when you are working to improve productivity. Dealing with this responsibility effectively requires direct, face-to-face contact with poor performers. How these meetings are handled will, to a great extent, determine your success or failure in improving group performance. When you are ready to start your work in this area, it would be a good idea to review Chapter 2 again. Better yet, get hold of one of the many books available on the subject of human relations in business. A wide knowledge and a deep interest in this subject will serve you throughout your entire business career, no matter what your position.

Over the years, I have observed that service managers with demonstrated ability to improve the performance of their employees have several things in common.

First, they are not hesitant to approach the subject openly and honestly. They are sincere in their feeling that an employer is entitled to a reasonable amount of work for the wages he pays, and they're not afraid to discuss the matter.

Second, they have developed a "bedside manner" that clearly shows their understanding of the employee's point of view. They respect the employee's personal dignity, and they show a willingness to listen to the worker's side of things.

Third, their productivity interviews are always held on a positive note. That is, an atmosphere of mutual cooperation is developed. One successful service manager I know begins productivity interviews with poor performers by asking, "Is there anything I can do to help?" And somewhere during the course of the interview he will ask, "Are we doing everything we should to allow you to do a good job?" That kind of an approach helps to dispel any notion that the employee might have to become defensive or uncooperative.

Needless to say, good producers should be afforded proper recognition. They, perhaps more than any tool at your disposal, can be a very positive influence on those who are slow to respond to your efforts. The manner of recognition best for you and your operation will depend on a number of variables.

In very large organizations, formal programs to recognize top performers can be quite effective. Plaques, certificates, and acknowledgements at meetings and dinners have all been used to advantage. In small units, individual prizes and incentive awards, such as cash bonuses or dinners, can be used. Keep in mind, however, that such awards are intended to *recognize* good productivity; you must not depend on such devices to develop it. Perhaps the clearest message in the Hawthorne Research is the discovery that incentives alone, even money itself, cannot be counted on to generate increased output. Frustrating though it may be, there are well-documented studies showing that increased financial incentives have actually resulted in decreased worker output under certain circumstances.

You will want to remember, then, that good productivity, where it exists, must be acknowledged and skillfully encouraged. If formal programs are not your style, consider the most basic approach of all: a simple "pat on the back" from time to time. The need for recognition has long since been established as one of the basic motivations of the human animal. You would be wise to incorporate this knowledge into your style of management.

As a professional service manager, you will want to make certain that your operating systems are not setting up a barrier to good productivity. Your technicians and mechanics are paid to repair things. Any time they spend on unnecessary tasks will lower their output.

One of the most common of these time-wasters is the paperwork discussed earlier in this chapter. To be sure, certain written information can be provided only by your technical personnel. For the sake of productivity, though, what is required of them should be kept to an absolute minimum. Time spent by a technician with a pencil is time that cannot be spent with his tools.

As far as is possible, your technicians should not be called to the telephone to speak with customers. Your service-call takers should be trained to handle most questions. If given the opportunity, some technicians will gladly pass the time chatting with customers while their productive work lies waiting.

ROAD TECHNICIANS

If your operation uses road technicians, you will want to streamline your check-in and check-out procedures. In this regard, one of the most important statistics you can develop is time to first call. This is the average time it takes your technicians to reach their first stop each day, from the time their workday begins to the time they knock on the first customer's door.

If you haven't been in the habit of recording and analyzing this information, you may be in for a shock. I have seen countless examples of average time to first call of well over 2 hours—20 or 25% of the workday gone before the first repair begins.

AVOID TIME-WASTERS

In the appliance repair industry, surveys indicate that only about 55% of the average technician's time is spent on productive work (about 4.5 hours of each 8-hour day). This statistic will be affected in your organization by the type of service that you are performing and by your decision as to whether or not to compute travel time as productive time. For most service organizations, I recommend that only time spent actually repairing be counted as productive time. This is covered in more detail in the chapter on setting service rates.

The actual hours worked for a full-time person will normally average about 1850 annually. Using a 40-hour week as a basis, there are 2080 working hours in 52 weeks. However, that figure is reduced by vacations, holidays, illness, and other reasons for absence. The *maximum* productive time available for the average shop technician without travel time is about 80% of the hours for which he is paid in an organization with average holiday and vacation policies.

As often as not, the problem of low productive time is caused by—or at least compounded by—disorganized, time-wasting procedures for morning check-in. Your objective for this part of your operation should be procedures that will enable fast, simple check-in and check-out. Everything that can be done for the technician ahead of time should be done. Routing should be completed and parts should be pulled and ready to go before the technician arrives.

One productivity buster that must be avoided is having technicians standing around in line in the morning waiting to be helped by clerical or parts personnel. Larger units having this problem should implement staggered starting times with intervals of 30 minutes or longer. This will permit you to get one group of technicians on the road before the next group reports in.

Another morning time-waster is the group coffee break. I doubt that there is a permanent cure for the propensity of service technicians to gather every morning at the nearest diner for an extended coffee-break discussion covering everything from the Super Bowl game to the boss's bad temper. There are some innovations, though, that have provided at least a modicum of success for some service managers.

The staggered starting times mentioned earlier can help, provided there is a sufficient interval between starting times. Otherwise, the system can backfire when late arrivals cause the early shift to opt for a second cup of coffee.

Some service companies have instituted policies that require outside technicians to complete at least one service call before taking the morning coffee break. This rule, introduced tactfully and policed properly, can be a big help in easing the morning coffee-break problem.

Another way to speed up morning check-in is to see to it that your technicians are not called on to make decisions. If the technician is having trouble with his truck, has to get information about a part, wants to talk to the boss, or just wants to gripe about the sorry business he's in, there should be a well-defined procedure for him to follow. Human nature being what it is, any loose ends that you allow in your operating procedures will surely be seized upon as a reason for socializing.

ALL TECHNICIANS

One productivity improver that is gaining in popularity is the "15-minute rule" (or the 30-minute rule, etc.). Under this system, the technicians or mechanics are given a specific time limit in which to make a clear diagnosis of the problem. If a shop technician is unable to complete his diagnosis within the prescribed time, he must consult his supervisor or service manager. An outside technician must either call in for help or pull the merchandise for shop repair. This idea provides the dual advantage of maximizing the incentive to make a prompt diagnosis and minimizing the burdensome costs of having estimates refused after several hours of work to diagnose the problem.

Speaking of diagnosis, let's spend a moment or two on the subject of test equipment. In many branches of the service business, the time spent on the diagnosis of the problem is often longer than the time spent making the actual repair. Electronics is a good example of this. In those cases where diagnosis is difficult and time-consuming, it will usually be to your advantage to provide the best and most modern test equipment available. Even a machine that costs many hundreds of dollars can pay for itself quickly if it can reduce the time needed to make a correct diagnosis or speed up the actual repair. At today's wage rates, these savings can mount up very quickly.

Let's say a technician earning $7.50 per hour wants you to buy a certain piece of equipment costing $500. She says that it will save her time on most jobs. You check with your accountant who suggests that such an item should be depreciated over a period of 5 years. That comes to $100 per year. $100 divided by $7.50 means that the equipment will have to save only 13.3 hours over an entire year in order to pay for itself. Divided by 52 weeks, that comes to only about 15 minutes per week (3 minutes per day). Of course, any time saved in excess of this means added productivity and more profits for your department.

Obviously, you must establish with reasonable certainty that a given piece of equipment will, in fact, reduce diagnosis or repair time by a measurable amount. In actual practice, most standard equipment of the latest design in your field will probably satisfy this requirement. When it comes to the best equipment and tools, that initial bite may seem painful. Over the long term, however, it doesn't pay to skimp on these items that are so essential to service success.

Training

The fact that good technical training and good productivity are natural partners should be reason enough for service managers everywhere to get on the training bandwagon. But, alas, it is not so. Even in large companies where internal training is readily available, some service managers have to be constantly prodded to participate.

I urge you not to permit yourself to fall into the habit of trying to save money by shortchanging your people on either training or equipment. Good productivity is just about impossible without a proper share of both.

It is true that time spent in training classes is time not spent on repairing things. Unlike other nonproductive time, though, good training is a profitable investment. Technological changes and new servicing techniques come at us so fast today that a skilled technician or mechanic can be seriously handicapped after only a single year without training updates. Two years or more without training and your people will surely be unable to do their work efficiently.

If you are part of one of the large national organizations with an internal training program, your training needs will be easy to satisfy. It is necessary only for you to take the initiative to see to it that your people take part in the company's prescribed training programs.

Service managers in smaller companies must keep themselves aware of the wide range of excellent training offered by manufacturers, distributors, local utilities, and suppliers. In most cases, this training is provided at little or no cost. If your company is large enough, many manufacturers will provide training on your own premises at no cost. Don't let the price fool you, though. Most of this training is as good as can be had anywhere. Trade journals, such as *Appliance Service News*, carry regular listings of available source training. A partial list of service trade journals is contained in the additional readings section at the back of this book.

By the way, do you subscribe to at least one or two of the trade journals in your field? If not, I urge you to get your order in the mail right away. I can't imagine how you could keep abreast of all the things you should know about your profession without regularly reading a dependable periodical devoted to the subject. Remember, you need training too.

Two-Man Jobs

There is one productivity buster that is so notorious that it deserves special mention. I refer to that special category of service job known as a "two-man job." I have seen countless examples of jobs requiring two workers for no other reason than tradition—it's always been done that way. If there are any jobs in your organization that regularly require two or more workers, you should carefully investigate the reasons. Sometimes, two people will be required for safety reasons. As often as not, though, the job can be done safely and easily by just one person. For heavy equipment, you will want to make use of the latest devices that enable one person to handle heavy objects. Even though it may take one worker a bit longer to complete the work than it would if he had a helper, you'll be ahead of the game whenever you eliminate the two-man job.

HOUSEKEEPING

Next, a word about the way you keep house. You may feel that cleanliness and neatness in your service department are odd subjects to be included in a chapter on productivity. If you do feel that way, please read on.

I'm not sure that I have the necessary credentials to offer an erudite explanation of why it is so, but I can assure you without a moment's hesitation that there is a direct and unequivocal relationship between good housekeeping and good productivity. I will, in fact, go so far as to say that I have never seen a meticulously clean and neat service operation that was not also efficient and profitable.

Frankly, some of the reasons for this relationship aren't really all that mysterious. A working environment where every tool, every item of supply, and every repair part is kept in place in a well-organized manner is obviously going to result in a minimum of lost motion and, thus, in high efficiency. However, there is more to the relationship than such obvious factors.

Perhaps it is at least partly due to the way we humans respond to the stimuli around us. A neat and orderly environment may well suggest an orderly approach to our work. Conversely, working all day in a dirty, disorganized place would seem certain to impose a negative suggestion on that part of our subconscious that deals with motivation.

In any case, you can add a strong plank to your productivity platform by implementing a positive housekeeping improvement program throughout your service department. Another advantage: once you have planted the seed and your people get a taste of working in a neat and clean atmosphere, chances are that the program will develop a momentum of its own. Most people are not inclined to give up a clean work area once they have enjoyed its advantages.

FINANCIAL INCENTIVES

Despite the weight of the evidence against the practice, trying to improve technical productivity through the payment of financial incentives continues to be the primary management thrust in many service organizations. I do not favor this approach because I feel that the risks clearly outweigh the advantages. There is, of course, a great temptation to try to solve the whole problem of productivity by using financial incentives as a substitute for good management. In many cases I have seen, the incentive program served only to foster careless or even unnecessary work, thereby placing management in a compromising position. Improving productivity through skillful management techniques may require more effort, but the improvements thus developed will be longer-lasting and more positive.

As I suggested at the beginning of this chapter, productivity is a complex subject with more facets than an Elizabeth Taylor diamond. Fortunately, you don't have to know everything there is to know about it in order to bring about improved efficiency in your own operation. I hope that the thoughts in this chapter will serve to stimulate ideas applicable to conditions in your own service department.

Because service productivity is such a vast subject, there are several aspects of it that I haven't tried to cover in this chapter. Such things as routing and dispatching service calls, shop layout and work flow, and repair parts inventories all deserve separate chapters of their own. We'll be talking about them in detail later on.

Chapter 5
Routing and Dispatching

On the surface, it appears to be quite simple. There are service calls to be run or shop jobs to be completed. This work must be assigned to the people who are expected to complete it.

Much easier said than done.

Remember the chapter on productivity? Well, the system you use to assign work to your technicians or mechanics (routing and dispatching) is one of the most important tools at your disposal for influencing productivity. A well-planned and consistent system for assigning the workload in your service department will have a positive effect on the efficiency of your entire organization. A poorly planned system—and I'll define a poor system—can make good productivity a practical impossibility.

ROAD CALLS

As you know, there are two basic types of repair work. There are those jobs that have been brought into your shop by either the customer or one of your road technicians, and there are repair jobs that are to be completed at the customer's home or business. Let's talk about these "road" calls first.

If your service department is the type that has road calls to run and if you are using the hoary system of routing and dispatching that has been in use since the first repairmen hopped into their buggies to run service calls, you can rest assured that you are wasting both time and money.

The Same Old System

I began my career in the service business in a small company more than 30 years ago, and I find that the very same system used to assign my daily workload then is still being used today in countless service organizations, large and small, without the slightest change. Recent years have seen the service industry grow remarkably sophisticated in most aspects of its daily operations. For some reason, though, there has been a tendency for some service managers to hang on stubbornly to that antiquated system for dispatching road technicians, perhaps because of its simplicity.

While there may be some minor variations between large and small service organizations, the basic system works like this: early in the morning on the day the work is to be done, or during the previous afternoon, the service calls to be run are placed in nice, neat piles, each of which is *estimated* to be a full day's work for the technician to which it will be assigned. A route sheet listing each of the calls will usually be included in the package. When the technician reports to work each day, he is given his neat little package of work orders and sent on his way, usually with instructions to call in for more work if he should happen to finish his calls before quitting time (don't count on it). At the end of his working day, the technician either goes home or reports back to the shop.

As I said earlier, the system is indeed a simple one, and this may well be the reason it has managed to cling to life despite its numerous and costly disadvantages. Here are some of the more serious ones for you to consider:

If you are familiar with the pithy works of C. Northcote Parkinson, you are aware of Parkinson's law: work expands to fill the time available for its completion. While we can assume that Mr. Parkinson was not thinking specifically of the service industry when he formulated his theory, he easily might have been.

Although service technicians are some of the finest and most talented people in today's business world, they are human even as you and I. As one service manager I know puts it, "Send a technician out with ten calls and it will take him 8 hours to do them; send him out with eight calls and it will take him 8 hours; send him out with six calls and it will take him 8 hours." You get the idea.

In my view, it is simply unrealistic not to expect even the most conscientious technician to relax his pace on those days when he is running ahead of his anticipated schedule. A couple of unexpectedly easy jobs or "not homes" are bound to cause a certain slowing down, even if the action is not the result of a conscious decision.

Starting a technician out with an estimated full day's work also has the disadvantage of requiring that a skilled and knowledgeable person who knows both the technical considerations and the geographic area spend great amounts of time trying to put together just the right workload for each technician. That same person's time can be spent much more profitably overseeing alternate methods of routing and dispatching.

Finally, you will remember that in the chapter on productivity I mentioned your systems should be designed in a manner that will require the smallest possible number of decisions on the part of your technical people. Decisions take time and detract from the technician's basic purpose. Giving your technician a full day's work to organize and plan requires that he use valuable time to make many nontechnical decisions throughout the working day.

All of this should not be taken to mean that I feel there is no place for the full-route dispatching system. For reasons of their own, some managers will never be comfortable with the newer variations that have been developed, or they feel that their particular types of service operations are better-suited to the older system; they may well be correct.

It is my hope, though, to convince those of you who insist on staying with the old system to incorporate the modifications that will bring it up to date, there by minimizing the likelihood of lost productivity.

SUGGESTED CHANGES

When a route sheet is used, it should always be prepared in duplicate. This will allow the use of "stop-routing." In this system, the technician is required to list on both his copy and the office copy the exact sequence in which he will make his stops. The advantage here is psychological as well as practical. Customers calling to inquire when the technician can be expected to arrive can be given an estimate based on the call sequence. Perhaps more important, both the technician and the office personnel know that the technician can be located easily by comparing the time of day to the order of stops listed and calling the appropriate customer to see if he has arrived. An experienced dispatcher can usually locate a technician with only one or two fast calls. For example, a call is made to customer number 4 and it is learned that the technician has already left. Customer number 5 says he hasn't arrived yet, so a message is left for him to call the office when he gets there. A major advantage of this procedure is that it tends to impose a structure on the technician's day, making it less likely that he will quit early if he is running ahead of schedule.

In larger operations employing a skilled dispatcher who knows the service area well, the sequence of stops can be decided during the preparation of routes. Some managers, however, prefer to have the technician do his own stop-routing on the theory that he may be more likely to stick with a sequence that he has developed himself.

Some managers using the full-route system require the technician to report in to the shop at both the beginning and the end of the working day. This is a serious error and such an obvious time-waster that there should be a law against it.

If you insist on seeing your technicians every day, you should decide whether you will require them to report in at the beginning of the day or at the end, but never both. (More and more service organizations are requiring their technicians to report to the building only twice a week. Some, not at all. More about that later.)

Finally, if you use the full-route system, you will be well advised to keep in mind the urgency of skillful preparation of each day's routes. In a large organization with a number of road technicians, the job of preparing the routes should be entrusted only to a dispatcher well trained in the fundamentals of technician productivity.

Plan Routes Carefully

One of the dispatcher's most important report cards is her ability to keep the average miles per call and traveling time as low as possible. Keeping routes as "tight" as possible requires a good knowledge of the service area and a sense of organization. Miles per call is one of the statistics that should be computed regularly so that efforts to improve performance can be accurately monitored.

If yours is a small operation, you may want to do this work yourself or supervise it carefully. As a rule, when you are using this system, the technician should not be routed with anything less than a full day's work. If it becomes absolutely necessary to do this because of a lack of calls, this should be carefully noted and every effort should be made to fill out his route as soon as calls are available. When there is not enough work to give every technician a full route, you should *never* permit the dispatcher to distribute the available work so that all or most of the technicians are given short routes in order to get them all on the road. To do so only hides the problem of insufficient work and guarantees that all of the technicians with light routes will have poor productivity for that day. Remember Parkinson's law.

As unlikely as it may seem, your absolute rule should be that only *full routes* are assembled and assigned, except that one technician may be sent out with leftover calls after all others have been given full routes. Again, when there is not enough work to route all road men fully, never stretch the workload by routing all or most of the technicians with partial routes. As logical as it may appear, this practice, especially if it is allowed to continue over a period of time, only makes it likely that the technicians will balk when asked to return to a full day's workload.

Having road technicians with no calls assigned to them—even if company policy requires that you pay them—may seem like a drastic step. In the final analysis, though, it has the advantage of forcing you to recognize that you do not have enough work for your people, rather than allowing that fact to be hidden from you by a well-meaning dispatcher. As far as road techinicans are concerned, out of sight may mean out of mind, but that will prove to be a very costly convenience.

If the work shortage is temporary, unrouted personnel can be assigned to other work (even cleanup or fixup, if necessary). If the drought lasts, you will have to take more drastic action, but you don't want the problem to be hidden from you in the meantime.

ALTERNATIVE SYSTEMS

The disadvantages of the old full-route system of dispatching can be summed up by saying that it does not allow management sufficient control to ensure best productivity. Giving a technician a full day's work and assuming that she will organize her efforts in the interests of maximum productivity may be a quick and easy system, but it is not realistic. It was in an effort to gain better control over the technician's activities that the one-call-at-a-time dispatching technique was developed.

One Call at a Time

As the name suggests, under this system the technician begins his workday with only one call. When that call has been completed, the technician contacts his office for his next call. Properly supervised, the one-call-at-a-time dispatching system will bring some important advantages to most types of service operations.

Each time the technician is ready for another call, the dispatcher will select one that is as close as possible to his present location. Often, a call will come in from a neighborhood where the dispatcher knows a technician is working. This call will be saved for that technician's next stop. When followed consistently, this method will reduce travel time and miles per call. The result not only contributes to better productivity but also helps to reduce the ever-increasing burden of rising transportation costs.

Remember my earlier reference to Parkinson's law and its application to a service technician's daily workload? One-call-at-a-time dispatching makes it less likely that a technician's working pace will be affected as it can be when he is assigned a fixed workload for the day. Under the one-call system, the technician has no idea what his workload is going to be for that day, and the hope is that this situation produces one less distraction for him to have to deal with.

The person doing the dispatching, as is the case with any modern dispatching method, holds the key to success in the one-call system. While there will necessarily be differences in the techniques used for small organizations of two or three people and large groups of twenty, thirty, or even more technicians, the basics remain essentially the same.

In order that the day's workload may be clearly analyzed and dispatched efficiently, the dispatch slips or work orders should be kept in dispatch control racks designed for the purpose. In one version, ordinary time-card racks are hung to provide vertical rows. Each of the vertical rows is labeled with a technician's name. The calls that are to be assigned to him are placed in the slots in the row under his name, in the order in which they will be dispatched. The dispatcher, of course, is able to alter this sequence to accommodate any emergencies or other changing conditions.

This procedure also permits management the option of beginning the day with full routes designated for each technician. Since the calls are actually assigned one at a time, the technician does not see the work assigned to him until it is dispatched.

Some service managers prefer to have the control racks labeled according to geographic areas so that a call can be assigned on that basis when the technicians call in for more work.

When compared to the full-route system, the one-call method obviously requires more management involvement and a highly structured system. In most instances, this investment in supporting payroll will be returned with interest. The one-call system results in a manifestly greater degree of operating control in the hands of management. Technicians are required to make a minimum of nontechnical decisions, and the whereabouts of every worker is known at all times.

Two-Way Radio

Contrary to what many service executives think, the one-call system can be operated quite satisfactorily using nothing more for communications than the ordinary telephone. To be sure, telephone communication is not as quick and easy as radio, and it often requires that the technician ask the customer for permission to use the telephone and to pay for it when appropriate. On the other hand, the telephone system does not require the significant investment necessary for the installation of a quality business-radio system.

Nevertheless, a growing number of professional service managers feel that two-way radio is a natural complement to the one-call dispatching system. In fact, the disciples of two-way radio would have us believe that an efficient dispatching system is not possible without electronic assistance.

In one way, two-way radio can be compared to limburger cheese: those who like it cannot imagine life without it; those who don't, refuse to try it under any circumstances. The analogy may be a bit strained, but the ambivalence on the subject thoughout the service industry is very real. General Electric (a company that happens to sell two-way radios) uses them extensively in their huge service organization. Interestingly, RCA (a company that also sells two-way radios) does not use them at all in most locations of its subsidiary, RCA Service Company.

As for myself, my experience and observations have led me to take both a for and an against position. That is, I believe radio to be a good investment for certain types of service operations and not for others. I also believe that radio cannot benefit any service organization that is not already well-managed and highly disciplined. Radio cannot be expected to solve problems. In the right hands, though, it can lead to valuable improvements in efficiency and productivity.

Let's pause long enough here to draw the necessary line of distinction between true business radio and the phenomenon that we have come to call "CB."

Citizens band (CB) radio is a special form of two-way radio that, as the name suggests, operates on special frequencies set aside for the general use of any citizen who obtains the easy-to-get license. Theoretically, CB is restricted to brief personal or business communications. In fact, it was conceived for just that purpose—to make two-way radio communication available for individuals and small businesses without the expensive equipment and elaborate licensing procedures required for full-fledged business radio.

In theory, a great idea. In actual practice, forget it.

Though it's been around since the 1950s, it was nearly 20 years before the "secret" got out. For the first years of its life, CB radio was almost the exclusive property of over-the-road truckers who used it on the highways as a means of chatting with each other to pass long hours behind the wheel and of warning each other of traffic hazards, not the least of which was "smokey the bear" (state troopers) waiting around the bend with their radar traps.

During a protracted truckers' strike a few years ago, the truckers' use of CB radio was widely publicized, and the general public was unaccountably fascinated by the whole idea. Since then, it seems that everyone able to scare up fifty bucks or so has installed a CB in his car, home, or both. The result in cities of any real size is an incredible mishmash of unintelligible cacophony on most channels most of the time.

Citizens band radio is not worth considering for your dispatching needs unless your business is very small and located in a city of no more than 20,000 or 30,000 people. Even then, you would be wise to listen in carefully during the hours you would be using the bands before making your decisions.

From this point on, my discussions of two-way radio refer exclusively to business radio—a service that requires comparatively expensive equipment of the type used by police departments and all sorts of commercial operations. Though it is more expensive, business radio is infinitely more dependable and disciplined than CB.

Customer Acceptance

There is at least one aspect of business radio that provides little room for argument. Even its most insistent detractors will grudgingly agree that it has undisputed customer relations value. There is an aura of professionalism that casts a favorable light on the technician who is dispatched by radio. There may be little logic to it, but most of us will admit to being duly impressed by service vehicles sporting that official-looking antenna.

It is, perhaps, for this reason that firms using radio will usually inform the world of that fact through brightly lettered announcements painted on their vehicles.

If the question of public relations value was the only issue to be considered, radio would probably be in every service vehicle on our highways. Such, of course, is not the case. The fact is that the cost of business radio is not insignificant.

Is It Worth the Cost?

It is in the search for the answer to this question that the real debate over business radio comes into full flower. The customer relations value of radio is genuine and probably significant, but it is extremely difficult, if not impossible, to place a specific dollar and cents value on such an intangible. If radio could be placed in your vehicles for $1 per month for each truck, there is little doubt that you would agree at once. On the other hand, if the cost were $1000 per month for each truck, the manufacturers of business radio would surely come upon hard times. How, then, do we determine whether the cost of radio (which falls between these two obvious extremes) can be justified for your operation?

In order to answer that question you will have to know two things: how much it will cost and what you can expect in return for the money expended. Let's talk about cost first.

Business radio requires what most people would describe as a significant investment. In addition to a mobile unit for each vehicle, a control station is needed. These portions of the total system may be purchased outright, or they may be leased. Monthly maintenance fees and rental costs for antenna towers and repeater stations make up most of the balance of the total expense.

The final cost of your system will be determined by such variables as the type of terrain in which you will operate (hilly or flat), whether the equipment will be UHF or VHF, how much area you need to cover, and whether the area in which you are located is already so crowded that you will need the newer and more expensive equipment designed for operation in the 800-megahertz frequency range. These are rather complex technical considerations, but you needn't fret over them. The people who would like to sell you a business-radio system will explain the details, and most will provide reliable advice on the various decisions that must be made to obtain optimum performance in your area.

Such major suppliers of business radio as Motorola, RCA, General Electric, and the E. F. Johnson Company have well-trained representatives who can be invaluable in this respect. In many areas, dependable independent dealers are also willing to provide consultation. As with any investment of this size, you should obtain bids and proposals from no less than two suppliers before making a commitment.

With all the variables to be considered, it would be a risky business indeed for me to try to provide you with overall estimates that would be meaningful over a wide variety of circumstances. However, the following figures may give you an approximate idea of what to expect when it comes to the cost of business radio. They were taken from an actual proposal submitted to a service organization in a medium-sized midwestern city.

Control station and accessories	$ 2,543.70
Repeater station and accessories	8,924.00
Ten mobile units and accessories	16,753.00
Installation costs	2,863.00
Total purchase cost	$31,083.70
Monthly maintenance charges	$ 180.00

As you can see, the proposal describes the estimated costs for equipping a fleet of ten mobile units with one fixed control location. Included are the costs for the outright purchase of a repeater station (needed to enable your radio signals to cover a wide area). In some cities, community repeaters can be rented on a shared basis at a considerable savings in the initial investment. In this example, renting a repeater would mean about $9000 less on the initial cost of the system, with a monthly rental fee of around $100 for the repeater.

With such an obvious cost advantage, you may wonder why anyone would want to buy a repeater if one is available for rent. The difference is one of convenience and efficiency. A rented repeater can be loosely compared to a party line on the telephone. With a rented repeater, you must be prepared to lose at least some of your technician's valuable time when he must stand by while another party is on the line. This is an admittedly simplistic description of the repeater question, but I am assuming that you will look into your local situation carefully if you decide to consider radio in your operation. Perhaps the best way to determine whether you would be satisfied with a rented repeater would be to talk with someone in your community currently using the same repeater you would be renting. As a general rule, a small organization with a half-dozen or fewer vehicles is more likely to find a shared repeater to be satisfactory than is a large organization. With a large fleet on the road, the greater need for air time is more likely to cause excessive waiting time.

In our example, the total initial investment is $31,083.70. If we assume a 7-year write-off for depreciation (your accountant can tell you what write-off period is appropriate for you), the monthly depreciation expense for the system would be $370.04. To that figure we must add the monthly maintenance costs of $180. The resulting total of $550 per month means that the cost per truck would be about $55 per month. Using an average of 23 workdays per month, we wind up with an estimated cost of business radio of

$2.39 per day per truck

Incidentally, a check with the service manager 2 years after this proposal was submitted and accepted revealed that the actual cost of the system was running $2.51 per truck per day. That kind of accuracy in proposals cannot always be counted on, of course. However, a survey of radio users indicates that this figure will usually fall within the $1.75 to $3 range, with the lower figure occurring in large fleets.

One more expense that should be factored in for any operation with more than a few trucks is dispatching payroll. In general, radio requires more office payroll than traditional types of dispatching. One manager with fifteen trucks on the road reports the need for 1½ persons to handle the dispatching chores. Other methods of dispatching for a fleet this size would require considerably fewer hours of payroll.

That, of course, is what the entire subject boils down to. If the service organization in our illustration is able to improve the productivity of its ten outside technicians enough to offset the cost of $2.51 per day per worker (plus the cost of any extra office payroll), the system will pay for itself. Using $25 as the labor cost per call, you can see just how little improvement in productivity would be needed to make radio a paying proposition in this service department. Currently, the service manager reports an improvement of one-half call per day per worker. If this figure is accurate and directly attributable to radio, the system is clearly paying its own way with a healthy margin to spare.

Will It Work for You?

Well, you already know one side of the story: radio requires a significant investment. For the other side, here are some of the advantages claimed by users of business radio:

1. Elimination of calls
2. Reduced travel time and mileage
3. More efficient handling of emergency calls
4. Increased customer goodwill
5. Better control over technician's time

6. Added personal security for the technician
7. The ability of the technician to obtain technical assistance out of earshot of the customer

Regarding item 6, one interesting new bit of technology is the pocket mobile repeater, a little device that can be carried by the technician when he leaves his truck. It enables the technician to transmit over the truck radio from the customer's home or business. This may provide additional security for the technician required to work in neighborhoods that may expose him to physical risks.

Another innovation in electronics is the so-called pocket beeper which you have seen in use by doctors and others who want to be available to their offices at all times. The simplest and most popular version can be rented for about $20 per month in most medium or larger-sized cities. When a specially coded telephone number is dialed on a standard telephone, the beeper sounds, alerting the person carrying it to call his office. This device is being used successfully in some service operations handling emergency service calls.

There is one advantage claimed by the users of business radio that deserves very special mention here. Once upon a time, the availability and cost of the gasoline used in service vehicles was all but inconsequential. Today, of course, all that has changed. Now, the productive time gained by driving fewer miles per call is enhanced even further by the resulting reduction in vehicle operating costs. Business radio in conjunction with a disciplined dispatching system can be an important energy saver.

My opinion? Under the direction of a skilled manager who is aware of the potential advantages and how to exploit them, business radio should more than pay for itself. However, it is important to remember that business radio, or any other operating system, is not going to solve problems associated with poor management. In other words, radio may well provide increased efficiency in an already well-managed operation. In a poorly managed department, radio will prove to be just another expense.

Other Alternatives

OK, but suppose you don't feel that radio is right for your organization? Are there other means for eliminating that archaic "come-into-the-shop-each-morning-and-pick-up-your-work-for-the-day" kind of dispatching that is still so prevalent in the industry?
You bet there is.

THE DAILY GATHERING

If there is one ritual that is uncompromisingly devastating to the efficient use of technician time, it is the system that calls for every road technician to report in to the service department every day. Except for the smallest of operations covering a small geographic area, the morning report-in routine should not even be considered in a modern service organization.

In addition to the social niceties that will be observed by your technicians each morning, their daily gathering will result in lost time due to such things as waiting in line to do all the things that you require before the workday can begin, looking for a parking space on your crowded parking lot, waiting until friends are ready to rendezvous for a cup of coffee, and commiserating over the loss of last night's ball game.

How to Avoid It

Alternate systems designed to avoid the morning traffic jam come in a variety of shapes and sizes. There is a system or combination of systems that can be made to work in almost any type of situation. When considering the possibilities, you must decide whether you will allow your technicians to take your service vehicles home with them at the end of the day or whether you will require them to return the vehicles to your shop. As with most fundamental management decisions, there is no clearly right or wrong answer. A survey of dozens of service firms, large and small, revealed no definite preference on the part of management.

Among the reasons cited by some service managers requiring vehicles to be returned at night are:

Security of the vehicles

Prevention of unauthorized use of the vehicles

Less chance of the theft of costly fuel

Less likelihood of technicians' quitting early in the day

These are valid considerations, especially in light of the fact that fuel and other operating expenses can only be expected to continue rising at a dizzying pace.

As you might expect, though, there are risks in having your entire fleet of trucks parked in one place overnight. A sufficient parking area must be found, and it must be provided with some form of security. One champion of the "let 'em take the trucks home at night" philosophy is John Hackett of Walton's, a well-regarded service firm in Jacksonville, Illinois. Mr. Hackett feels that sending the trucks home at night works best for Walton's. He says, "The trucks are less likely to be vandalized, the technician can take an emergency call going to or from his home, and it helps the technicians with transportation to work."

Of course, with any form of one-call dispatching, including business radio, optimum efficiency requires that the technicians begin the day's work directly from their homes.

The Drop-Off

If you prefer to allow your technicians to take their trucks home at night, your first challenge will be to find ways to offset the not insignificant expense of your decision, the second to exploit the advantages that it offers. One way to do both is to deliver the necessary work orders and repair parts directly to the technician during the evening or nighttime hours. One popular version of this idea requires that the messenger, who has a set of keys for each truck, pick up the necessary parts and paperwork near the end of the day and begin her rounds as the technician's day is ending.

Most managers who use some form of this system report that the handling of cash collected by the technicians is not a problem. In many types of service operations, the technicians actually handle relatively little cash. If allowing cash to remain in the truck awaiting pickup seems like an unnecessary risk to you, you may want to consider the relationship of the average amount of cash handled by a technician to the total value of the contents of the truck. The chances are that the money represents only a small fraction of the worth of the tools, test equipment, and working inventory in the truck at any one time.

Some companies are making good use of bank-type money bags—sturdy canvas bags secured by locks. The messenger, who leaves an empty bag each time she makes a pickup, does not have access to the keys. To protect the technician and avoid misunderstandings, the bags are opened only in the office, preferably in the presence of two persons.

At least one large service organization uses checks to handle this problem nicely. The service technician simply writes a personal check payable to the company, and deposits the cash collected into his checking account.

Two-Day Routing

But suppose you have no intention of investing in business radio, feel that one-call-at-a-time dispatching is too much trouble, and feel that you need to see your technicians on a regular basis. Is there any way for you to minimize the problem of the morning gathering?

Indeed there is. It may not present the optimum solution, but it's quick, easy, and can reduce your lost time by about one-half. To do this, it's necessary only that you prepare two-day routes for each of your technicians and require them to report in only every other day. To even out the morning check-in workload, you will want to have one-half of the technicians reporting in on alternate days. And don't forget: the whole exercise will be a waste of time if you don't give the technicians extra calls to run on the days that they begin work from their homes.

Grid Routing

Whatever basic system you use for routing your road technicians, grid routing can help to improve efficiency. Grid routing is nothing more than a system for dividing your service area into sections not unlike postal zones (except that grids usually cover smaller areas). A grid number is assigned to each small section. This facilitates the routing process, since anyone can prepare a group of calls bearing the same or overlapping grid numbers.

You can prepare your own grid system simply by taking a large map of your service area and laying out the necessary horizontal and vertical crosshatch lines to produce a series of appropriately sized squares. Each of these squares is then sequentially numbered. Once each grid has been numbered, a directory of each community or street address (depending on whether you are in a suburban area or a densely populated city) must be prepared. When the service call is taken, the proper grid number is placed on the work order to assist both the dispatcher in preparing the routes and the technician in locating the customer. It's a big job, but it need be done only once, and it can be a big time-saver for your service department.

If your service area is in or near a large city, there is a good chance that all of this work has already been done for you by one of the commercial map companies which supply grid maps and directories designed for the purpose. Two of the largest of these companies are: Hagstrom Co., Inc., of New York City and Hearne Bros. of Detroit, Michigan.

SHOP TECHNICIANS

There is a common but unfortunate belief that no formal procedure is necessary for assigning work to shop technicians. In many repair shops, technicians and mechanics are assigned work on a random basis, without prior planning. What's even worse is the shop where technicians are allowed to make their own selections from the pending work orders.

In order to achieve optimum shop productivity, it is necessary that the shop technician's workday be structured for him in much the same manner as the routing of road technicians. Shop routing is easier, of course, because the problems of travel need not be considered. However, such considerations as job priorities and individual abilities can be used in the planning of each technician's workday. These decisions, though, should remain in the hands of management. Remember, the fewer decisions you require of your technical people during the course of the day, the more time they will have to devote to the tasks for which they are being paid.

As with road calls, the basic decision of whether to assign jobs one at a time or to prepare a full day's route at the beginning of the day is largely a matter of preference. The advantages and disadvantages of each system are basically the same as those discussed in the paragraphs on road calls.

The dispatching function serves a critical role in the modern service organization. It is one of the principal means by which management's policies and priorities are translated into daily practice. It is for this reason that dispatching must be done with a high degree of professionalism, while remaining strictly under the control of management.

Chapter 6
Shop Layout and Work Flow

Have you ever visited a modern factory? If you have, you probably saw a good example of efficient work flow. Every aspect of a modern factory's design is conceived with the idea of developing a smooth, efficient, and uninterrupted flow of the manufactured product as it proceeds along the assembly line. Raw material is brought in one end of the building and the finished product flows evenly out the other.

REMEMBER THE FACTORY CONCEPT

Most service managers can learn a lot from that simple principle. If you recall my earlier analogy that likened a service department to a factory, we can broaden it a bit. The merchandise that comes to you in need of repairs is the raw material for your factory. Moving that raw material to the end of the assembly line efficiently is the objective of your shop layout.

In actual practice, it is a rare service shop that has been laid out with optimum productivity in mind; most have simply taken shape in piecemeal fashion. I have not seen many that could not be improved considerably by simple rearrangements that would facilitate the movement and storage of the merchandise to be repaired.

How about your shops? Is the factory concept in evidence? Is there a clearly defined work flow? If not, here are a few suggestions that may help. There is, of course, no single design that can properly serve the almost infinite assortment of types and sizes of service shops. With this in mind, we must deal with the general principles that may be successfully applied to any shop.

Unless the physical configuration of your shop will not allow it, your first objective should be to define the flow of work clearly—to establish the direction in which your assembly line will flow. Figure 6.1 shows in simple block-diagram form the basic elements common to all service shops.

If you are designing a repair shop from the ground up, it will be easy for you to incorporate the basic principles of efficient work flow simply by visualizing the assembly line concept. If, on the other hand, your shops are already in operation, the task becomes a bit more difficult. In either case, you should begin by laying out your ideas on paper. An experienced builder wouldn't think of starting construction without a clearly defined plan; neither should you.

The nature of your service organization will determine both the degree of difficulty and the degree of urgency for establishing a clean work flow. Obviously, efficiency in an automobile repair facility will suffer unless it has a separate entrance and exit, preferably at opposite ends of the building. At the other end of the scale, a light office-equipment repair shop will not impose such strict requirements. Both, however, will benefit from a layout designed to promote the free and easy flow of work.

An existing repair shop that must function with a single opening to serve as both entrance and exit can be arranged to incorporate the most important work-flow ideas. For example:

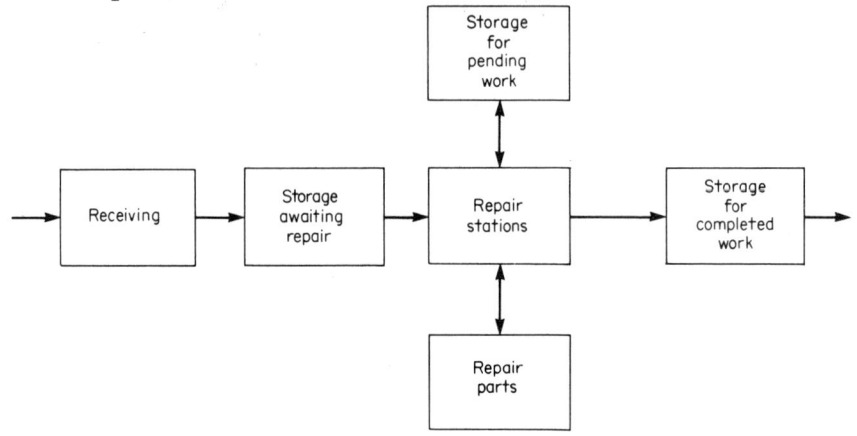

```
                          ┌──────────┐
                          │ Storage  │
                          │   for    │
                          │ pending  │
                          │   work   │
                          └────┬─────┘
                               │
                               ▼
┌──────────┐   ┌──────────┐  ┌──────────┐   ┌──────────┐
│          │   │ Storage  │  │          │   │ Storage  │
→ Receiving├──►│ awaiting ├─►│  Repair  ├──►│   for    │→
│          │   │  repair  │  │ stations │   │completed │
│          │   │          │  │          │   │   work   │
└──────────┘   └──────────┘  └────┬─────┘   └──────────┘
                                  ▲
                                  │
                          ┌───────┴──┐
                          │  Repair  │
                          │  parts   │
                          └──────────┘
```

FIGURE 6.1. Flowchart for repair shop work.

Completely separate storage areas for repaired and unrepaired merchandise.

A clearly defined direction of work flow from "unrepaired" to "repaired" areas. Where necessary, a U-shaped work flow can be utilized with the assembly line beginning and ending on either side of a single doorway.

Easy access to common supplies and tools at appropriate locations.

A logically positioned repair parts storage area.

Lighting

Once the shop's work flow has been designed and the exact locations of the work stations have been determined, it's time to think about lighting. Proper lighting, the kind that enhances productivity, doesn't happen by accident. Although its importance is obvious, lighting frequently does not receive the kind of attention that it deserves. A work area provided with well-balanced light in the right quantity is a good investment in any repair shop.

At home, the old-fashioned incandescent light bulb is king; however, for the most part, there is no place for incandescent lighting in a modern service shop. Fluorescent lighting fixtures, while they have a slightly higher initial cost, are much more energy efficient than incandescents. They produce more light per watt of consumption, and they produce a crisper illumination much closer in color to natural daylight than the warm, yellowish glow of the incandescent bulb.

Don't skimp on lighting; it's an important part of efficient shop design. In fact, according to the Better Light Better Sight Bureau, balanced lighting may actually help to conserve physical energy.

A shop work area should be illuminated with an average of about 100 footcandles for optimum results. (Footcandle is a technical term used to describe the quantity of light falling on a given point.) Precision work, such as metal machining or fine polishing and buffing, require a considerably higher level of illumination, while rough woodworking, such as sawing and planing, can be done with much less light. On the average, though, most experts agree that 100 footcandles is about right for most types of general service work.

It's unlikely that you'll be having the benefit of a professional lighting engineer to help you with your shop lighting problems, but if you're interested, you can probably obtain some valuable basic lighting information and even assistance from your local electric utility.

Work Areas

In the typical service shop, one or more individual work areas make up the heart of the operation. In an automobile shop, the work areas will be large bays, each capable of holding an automobile and the bulky equipment needed for auto diagnosis and repair. A small appliance or electronics shop, on the other hand, will utilize compact work stations. Every conceivable size and arrangement of work areas between these extremes can be found throughout the service industry— all of them serving the same purpose.

The location and size of individual work areas and the equipment each area contains should all focus sharply on the ultimate objective— optimum productivity. Just as is the case with road technicians, the system serves its purpose best when it recognizes that every minute of the mechanic's or technician's time is valuable and that not one must be wasted. The work areas should be positioned in such a way that the flow of goods through the shop is logical and efficient. Remember the assembly line concept.

If workbenches are part of the individual work stations, such details as the size and overall height of the working surfaces are important considerations. A height of approximately 33 inches will permit most people to work from a standing position when necessary without undue risk of back strain. Seats or stools of standard heights can then be chosen to provide a comfortable position when sitting.

By the way, I once met a TV shop owner who made what he felt was a devilishly shrewd decision: he removed all chairs and stools from his shop so that his technicians would be forced to work while standing. This, he had concluded, would improve productivity by preventing the lazy louts from lounging around in chairs. If this strikes you as a good idea, you weren't paying attention when you read Chapter 2.

Workbenches that are too small will obviously hinder productivity. What may not be quite so obvious is the fact that benches larger than necessary will encourage the accumulation of superfluous materials. Technicians in many parts of the service industry are notorious "pack rats." Give them a bit of unused space and they'll find some "perfectly good" parts and other junk that just might come in handy one of these days. Moral: design your workbenches to be just large enough to do the job, and no larger.

ACCESSIBILITY TO REPAIR PARTS

The time spent by shop technicians and mechanics in obtaining the repair parts they need can be a productivity disaster. In some shops I have seen, the owner or manager could retire on the value of the time lost by service personnel going back and forth for repair parts.

Except in the smallest of shops, security requirements dictate that repair parts be housed in a separate area to which service personnel do not have uncontrolled access. This is not only to minimize the likelihood of pilferage but to help in the complex job of inventory control as well.

One of the more or less standard arrangements in some types of repair shops is the separate, completely enclosed parts department where parts can be disbursed to service personnel through a window or across a counter as they are needed. In some places, auto repair shops for example, this may well be the only practical alternative because of the need for security. It is, nevertheless, the most costly system in terms of lost time. In larger shops, the parts window can be a popular spot for a quick smoke or a debate on the true meaning of life. While these things are going on, productivity can suffer. If circumstances in your shops require that all parts be disbursed in this manner, you will want to try to keep the parts window from becoming a bottleneck on your assembly line. Remember, too, this arrangement requires that every part be handled and disbursed by a parts counter person, thus adding another layer of payroll.

Bench Stocks

One compromise that is popular in many types of service shops is the bench-stock system. In its basic form the bench stock works in just the same way as the truck stock assigned to road technicians.

By assigning a basic stock of the most often used parts to the custody of each shop technician, you can cut down sharply on the time spent when each individual part must be obtained from the parts room as it is needed. As with truck stocks, the replenishment of the inventory can be done at just one specified time each day.

The technician or mechanic to whom the bench stock is assigned must be held responsible for the security of the inventory and for the proper accounting of every part used, just as the road technician is required to do. Of course, if you expect the custodian of a bench stock to be responsible for what you have entrusted to him, you will have to supply a means for him to secure the inventory when he is away from his work position. In those cases where the size and number of the parts involved are small, a simple drawer in the workbench that can be locked will usually suffice. Where the bench stock is large, a separate cabinet may be needed.

As with most innovations in our business, the bench-stock idea has not been joyfully embraced by everyone. There are service managers who feel that the time saved by the system is offset by the bother and expense of issuing and maintaining individual bench stocks. On the other side of the fence are the managers who say that they could not imagine an efficiently operated shop without the use of bench stocks. The fact is there is no single position that is correct for all shops. The important thing is that you acquaint yourself with all the plusses and minuses and adopt the system that suits the particular circumstances in your shop. Keep in mind that the objective is to reduce the time spent by your technicians in obtaining parts without unnecessarily exposing your inventory to risk of loss or theft.

Location of Parts Department

In small shops, there will usually be very few options concerning layout and the positioning of various activities. As shops grow physically larger, however, the placement of key elements with respect to each other and to the flow of work takes on increased importance. Ideally, you will locate your parts department as close as possible to the technicians who will be drawing parts from it. In large operations with two or more separate repair shops, the parts department should be in a position central to the shops so that it will be equally accessible for all.

Once the value of efficient access to repair parts is understood, any number of innovations suitable for a particular set of circumstances will suggest themselves. Economy TV, a service company in St. Petersburg, Florida, uses a wonderfully ingenious system for getting parts to its bench technicians. When a technician needs a part, she calls the parts room on the shop intercom. The part is then placed in a dumbwaiter equipped with a tripping device that automatically unloads the part when it reaches the shop. The technician need then move but a few steps to retrieve the part.

STORAGE AREAS

In shops where merchandise is left for repair, the storage areas for new work and for finished work awaiting customer pickup should be clearly separated. In shops laid out to conform to the assembly line concept, this requirement will be met automatically. If the volume of your shop is sufficient, a third storage area for merchandise awaiting estimate approval or parts on order will further reduce the time spent in locating individual units.

In even the smallest of service shops, a random mixture of merchandise on storage shelves will create an unwieldy assortment guaranteed to waste valuable time whenever an individual piece of merchandise must be located.

SHOP RECORDS

The finishing touch of professionalism in a modern service shop is a record-keeping system that is basic and simple, and yet allows quick access to the current status of every piece of goods in the shop.

There are, of course, an almost infinite variety of shop record-keeping systems designed to accommodate specialized requirements. My own favorite, one that I feel can be adapted to satisfy the needs of almost any shop, is nothing more than an alphabetically arranged loose-leaf binder with pages made up to accept the basic information needed.

For this type of record, illustrated in Figure 6.2, you will need columns to show when the item was received and when the work was completed. In between, you will need columns to show the date the work was assigned and to whom. Some shops will require columns to indicate holding for estimate approval and parts on order. Large operations will also benefit from a column to show the bin number where the merchandise is being held.

With this type of log, customer inquiries can be answered quickly, simply by looking up the customer alphabetically and noting which column shows the latest entry. If only the first column contains an entry, the item has not yet been assigned to a technician.

While different types of service shops may require some variations on this basic theme, the idea is to keep it as simple as possible. I continue to be amazed at the elaborate, time-wasting systems found in use in some shops.

Only the medium- and larger-sized shops need to maintain a shop log at all. Small shops holding relatively few items of customer

SHOP CONTROL LOG								
CUSTOMER'S NAME	DATE IN	MDSE.	MFR.	SERVICE TECH	DATE PART ORDERED	DATE EST. GIVEN	DATE COMPLETE

FIGURE 6.2. Shop control log.

merchandise at any one time may bypass the shop log entirely. In low-volume shops, the work order itself is all that is needed for keeping track of customers' goods. Under this system, the simple rule is that the work is permitted to be in one of only two places: while the merchandise is being worked on, it is with the technician. At all other times, it must be retained in a centrally located file or pending-work rack, preferably close to the telephone. If parts have been ordered or an estimate prepared, the information is noted directly on the work order.

Caution: only the smallest of shops should operate without a control log. Larger operations will lose much more valuable time looking for records and answering customer inquiries than would be needed to maintain a simple log.

CARRY-IN SERVICE

All aspects of shop design and the flow of work through the shop should come together in such a manner that the productivity of each mechanic or technician is enhanced. These are physical considerations that you will have to evaluate carefully to make certain that you are using just the right combination to suit the particular needs of your shop.

There is one aspect of shop design that is more conceptual than physical, but it is of great importance in service shops where customers carry in their own merchandise for repair. I'm talking about service while the customer waits.

I can clearly remember my attitude a number of years ago toward customers who expected their appliances to be checked while they waited. Such an intrusion, I felt, was intolerable. After all, didn't they know that interrupting a technician in the middle of a job would cause inefficiency? They would just have to leave their merchandise and wait their turns like everyone else. In looking back, I'm still embarrassed over my professional myopia—though that same attitude was prevalent in our industry in those days.

As a modern service manager, you should know that service while the customer waits is a shrewd business philosophy that benefits both the customer and the service organization, and as the saying goes, "you can't hardly find that recipe anymore." Consider the following: every piece of merchandise serviced while the customer waits is a piece of merchandise that:

- does not have to be logged in and out of shop records
- will not take up precious storage space

- does not have to be located when it's time to fix it
- will not have to be placed in storage after it's repaired
- cannot become a piece of unclaimed merchandise
- will not have to be stored while attempts are made to get the customer's approval of an estimate
- will not require telephone calls or post cards to let the customer know when it's ready

In short, merchandise serviced while the customer waits can be handled more quickly, more efficiently, and at less cost to you than merchandise handled in the conventional way. Add those benefits to the inestimable value of the customer goodwill generated in the process, and you should become an immediate and permanent convert.

Many service managers I know have come to feel so strongly about the value of service while the customer waits that they want every customer to have the service whether it's requested or not. As one manager puts it, "I'll do anything short of tying the customer down while we check his merchandise."

I can assure you that you won't have to go that far. In today's business environment, many customers find it hard to believe that they can actually get repairs of any kind on a do-it-now basis. If you provide that service, your customers will become your best advertisements.

Fortunately, service while the customer waits can be provided without any special design considerations in most types of service shops. However, if you are laying out an original plan or remodeling an existing shop, you may want to include provisions that will allow you to enjoy the maximum benefits of this important service philosophy. The requirements are simple enough: a comfortable spot for the customer to relax in while waiting for repairs and, in certain types of shops, a separate entrance that will allow the customer to bring the merchandise to be repaired right up to the spot where the work will be done.

HOUSEKEEPING

In Chapter 4, I spoke of the direct relationship between good housekeeping and good productivity. There is no place that I know of where this principle is better-illustrated than in repair shops. The most carefully thought-out shop design will not fulfill its potential if it's cluttered with junk not essential to the business at hand. The temptation to save odds and ends that "might come in handy sometime" is one that many shop technicians just can't seem to resist.

As service manager, you will want to set very high standards of housekeeping and be prepared to see to it that they are observed. Once you get the momentum going, you'll probably be pleasantly surprised. When technicians get used to working in a neat and clean environment, most will not want to give it up.

Here's a rule that you may want to adopt: the repair shop is to contain only (1) customers' merchandise, (2) tools, equipment, and supplies directly related to the work being done, and (3) repair parts that are *in the inventory*. Nothing else!

If you want to test your shop housekeeping quotient, try removing *everything* that doesn't fit into one of those three categories. If you find that you need another room to store what you have removed, go back and read this chapter three times as your punishment.

Chapter 7
Repair Parts Inventories

I remember a telephone call I once received from a business associate. He had attended a meeting conducted by one of my staff assistants the previous day. "I just wanted you to know what a helluva good man he is," my caller said. "Anybody who can talk for an hour and a half on a subject as dull as repair parts and keep his audience interested *has* to be a good man."

Somehow, as I set out to discuss repair parts with you, the memory of that call keeps intruding on my thoughts. Perhaps because the person who made the call expressed an opinion about repair parts that is widely shared by service managers throughout our industry.

THE ORPHANS OF THE SERVICE BUSINESS

Repair parts are indeed the orphans of the service business; not because they merit that status, but like Rodney Dangerfield, they just don't get the respect they deserve. The fact is that repair parts may well be the most underrated asset in our business.

Your inventory of repair parts serves two separate purposes in the successful operation of your service department. While these functions are interrelated, each is important in its own right and we will discuss them separately.

First, your parts inventory serves as a support arm for the technical services you perform. Most types of service organizations perform work that is heavily dependent on the use of repair parts. Having the right parts at the right place in the right quantity is what parts management is all about. You don't have to be in the service business to understand the frustration that develops when a repair job must be delayed for the lack of a needed part. Just ask any customer who has waited (often too long) for a service technician to show up, only to be told that a part not carried by the technician is needed for the repair. While the customer *and* the technician are suffering from the frustration brought on by "lack part-itis," the service organization must bear the costs of lowered productivity. Referring to the world of business, someone once said, "Nothing happens until somebody sells something." In the service business, we might paraphrase that old chestnut by saying, "Nothing happens if you don't have the part you need."

Second, your repair parts inventory is direct and measurable—it makes (or should make) an important contribution to the profits of your service department. It's natural to think of the service business as dealing primarily with labor charges. The truth is, though, that most types of service organizations must make significant investments in the parts inventories required to support their work. This inventory can be the source of additional profits, thus justifying the investment, or it can be a serious—even terminal—drain on profits.

We'll talk about the direct financial aspects of the parts business a little later on. Let's look first at repair parts as a vital support function for your service department.

LEVEL OF SERVICE

Ideally, of course, your parts department would supply a 100% level of service. That is, every repair part would be on hand every time you needed it. Obviously, that objective is impossible to meet because it would require that you stock an infinite number of parts (which would require an infinite amount of money).

On the other hand, you could completely eliminate the need for an investment in inventory by maintaining a 0% level of service. This is also unacceptable; the need to purchase each individual part as it is required would cost far more money than the maintenance of a reasonable inventory, not to mention the incalculable loss of customer goodwill that would result from such a policy.

The object, then, is to develop a repair parts inventory that provides a level of service somewhere between 0 and 100%. The precise point at which that figure should fall depends on such things as the nature of your service operation, the urgency of your parts needs, the cost of the parts you use, and your own interpretation of all these factors. A business providing repair services for medical equipment or a fleet of jet airliners will demand a higher level of service than would a business that repairs stereo sets (although I know a few stereo owners who might challenge that hypothesis).

Let's say that for your purposes you have set 90% as your objective for level of service. Here's how you can find out how you've been doing: for a given period of time, count all repair jobs for which a part was required. For the same period, count all calls for which the required part was on hand in your inventory. Then divide the number of parts-on-hand-calls by parts-needed calls and the result is your level of service.

$$\frac{\text{Parts-on-hand calls}}{\text{Parts-needed calls}} = \text{level of service}$$

Is 90% a reasonable objective for your level of service? In most types of service operations, it probably is. Experience in various parts of the industry sets 95% as about the highest level attainable within the constraints of economic reality. And remember, 95% is the *highest* practical level. Most service operations have to settle for something less than that.

If you do road calls as well as shop calls, you may want to calculate your level of service separately for each. In most cases, road calls will be handled at a lower level of service than that of shop calls because of the practical limitations on the amount of inventory that can be carried in a service truck.

A review of the arithmetic involved in calculating level of service will make it apparent that an increase beyond any given point will require an increase in inventory. In actual practice, this will usually be a geometric progression; that is, a small increase in level of service will require a disproportionately large increase in inventory. This relationship has been used in many computer programs to determine optimum inventory levels. When shown in graph form as in Figure

7.1, the impracticality of service levels beyond 95% becomes readily apparent.

THE 80/20 RULE

Another relationship that has shown a surprising consistency has resulted in what is now called the 80/20 rule in parts usage. That is, 80% of your parts requirements will be met by about 20% of the stock-keeping units in your inventory. This is another good illustration of the price that must be paid in inventory investment in order to reach the higher levels of service. Conversely, any decrease from the current level of service will permit a reduction in inventory. How, then, do we determine the optimum level of service?

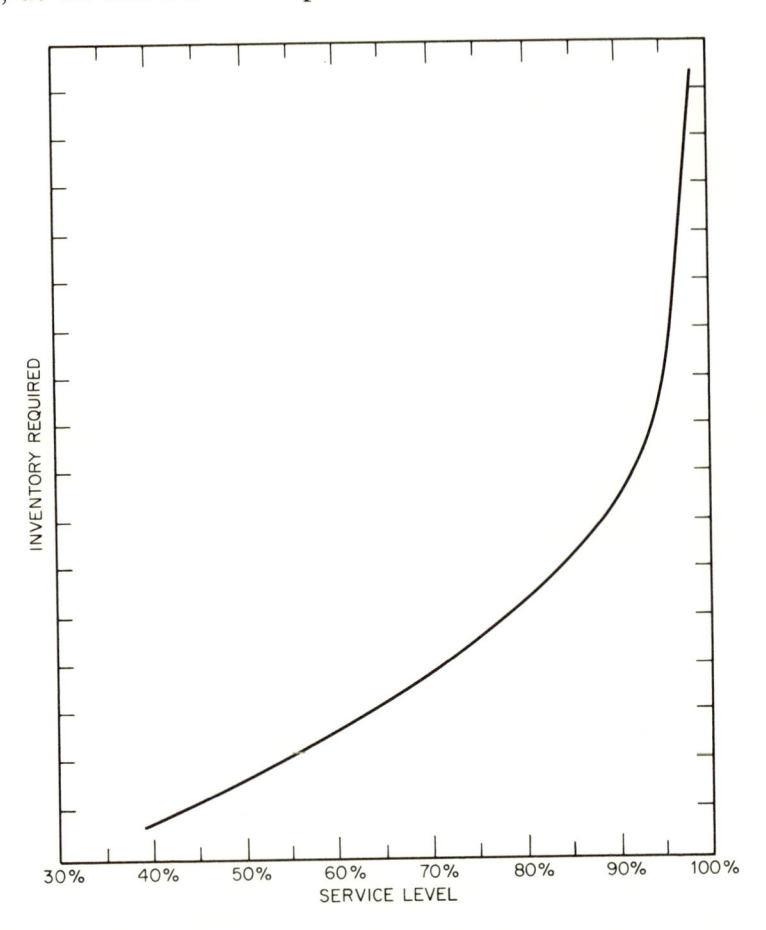

FIGURE 7.1. Service-level graph.

HOW MUCH INVENTORY?

Unfortunately, customer satisfaction is a subjective consideration that does not lend itself to precise measurements, and it must be balanced against practical financial limits if the business is to survive. And so, in a practicing service organization, inventory level of service will be weighed against another parameter: inventory turns.

Probably the best way to determine how much inventory is optimum for your business is through the measurement of turnover. As the name suggests, turnover simply measures how many times the average part in your inventory is used (turned over) in one year. In general, a range of three to five turns per year will be encountered in well-run parts departments. Many experienced managers consider four turns as the optimum figure. This will vary, of course, with the requirements of desired service level and the nature of the inventory. Using four turns as your objective, the formula for optimum inventory is

$$\frac{\text{Cost of parts sold}}{4} = \text{optimum average inventory}$$

Unless your present parts management is better than average, this formula applied to your sales for the past 12 months will probably show that you are carrying too much inventory. If, on the other hand, your actual inventory is far less than the optimum shown in the formula, your level of service is low and may be affecting both technician productivity and customer satisfaction.

This same formula can be transposed to give you a means for measuring how well you are doing in meeting your objectives for turnover:

$$\frac{\text{Costs of good sold}}{\text{Average inventory}} = \text{turnover}$$

To determine average inventory, add the *cost* value of inventory on hand at the beginning of the period being measured to the *cost* value at the end of the period; then divide the total of these figures by 2.

Please note that the formulas in this chapter specify cost value of inventory, not selling value. Actually, selling value could be substituted without altering the results, as long as you do not attempt to mix cost and sell in the same formula. However, generally accepted accounting practices call for the use of cost values when working with inventories, and I also recommend that you stick to that rule. It simplifies things and lessens the chances for errors.

To illustrate how the formula works, let's say that the cost of parts sold for the past year was $88,000, and that your average inventory during the same period was $25,200:

$$\frac{88,000}{25,200} = 3.49 \text{ turns}$$

For periods of less than a full year, the answer must be multiplied by the appropriate factor to get the annual rate. For example, if the figures used were for a 6-month period, the answer must be multiplied by 2 to arrive at the effective annual rate of turnover; for quarterly sales, the answer must be multiplied by 4.

Turnover

Turnover is a highly regarded means for evaluating the effectiveness of parts management. If you have a parts manager responsible to you, you would be well advised to review his turnover performance on a regular basis. If you're the one responsible for parts performance, you may want to tear out this page before your boss sees it. *Poor turnover means lost profit dollars.*

A turnover less than optimum means that you have invested more money in your inventory than needed to support your requirements. A turnover significantly higher than the optimum figure may seem desirable at first blush, but hold on. When you relate it back to service level, you can see that having too little inventory can be at least as bad as having too much.

If you've been paying attention up to now, you know that the optimum size of your parts inventory is determined through careful consideration of the level of service you would like to provide, balanced by the rigid restraints of your purse strings. Calculating the amount of money that you can afford to invest in your inventory is just a matter of applying the basic formulas in this chapter to your own records. Once you have determined *how much* to buy, however, you still have the job of deciding *what* to buy.

WHICH PARTS?

Using the history provided by your records of last year's sales and a careful application of the formulas for optimum inventory, you could wind up with a theoretically correct inventory that would put you in big trouble. The *size* of your inventory is, of course, vitally important.

The cruel fact is that computing how much inventory to buy is kid stuff compared to the job of determining specifically which parts to buy and in what quantities.

Record keeping does not rank very high on the list of favorite activities for most people, but when it comes to inventory control for repair parts, an accurate set of records is an absolute must. There is no other way to fulfill the requirement mentioned in the opening paragraphs of this chapter: the right parts in the right place in the right quantities.

HOW TO KEEP RECORDS

Specifically, your parts operation must include a system that will record the use of each part you carry and the parts that you must special-order. Only then can you determine the demand for any given stockkeeping unit (SKU). As I pointed out earlier, once you have determined how much you can afford to invest in your inventory, you must then make certain that you select the fastest moving SKU's for stocking.

There are, of course, an infinite variety of record-keeping systems in use to supply this information. If you are part of a large corporation, you will almost surely have the advantage of a computer program for inventory control. Because of the amounts of detail required to do a good job, many smaller companies are turning to time-sharing computer arrangements available commercially or through trade associations such as the National Association of Retail Dealers of Amercia (NARDA).

As with most record requirements, though, there are perfectly adequate manual systems that have been around since long before the first computer arrived on the scene. The so-called perpetual inventory system can be kept quite professionally by simply entering the necessary information on a control card designed for the purpose. Figure 7.2 shows a sample inventory control card. Normally, a separate card will be maintained for each SKU.

In the final analysis, it makes no difference whether your system involves a sophisticated and complex computer program or entries on ordinary 3 × 5-inch index cards, as long as it provides you with the information you need to make well-informed managerial decisions.

Repair parts control cards specially designed for manual inventory control entries are available from such companies as VISIrecord Systems of Worcester, Massachusetts, and Acme Visible Records of

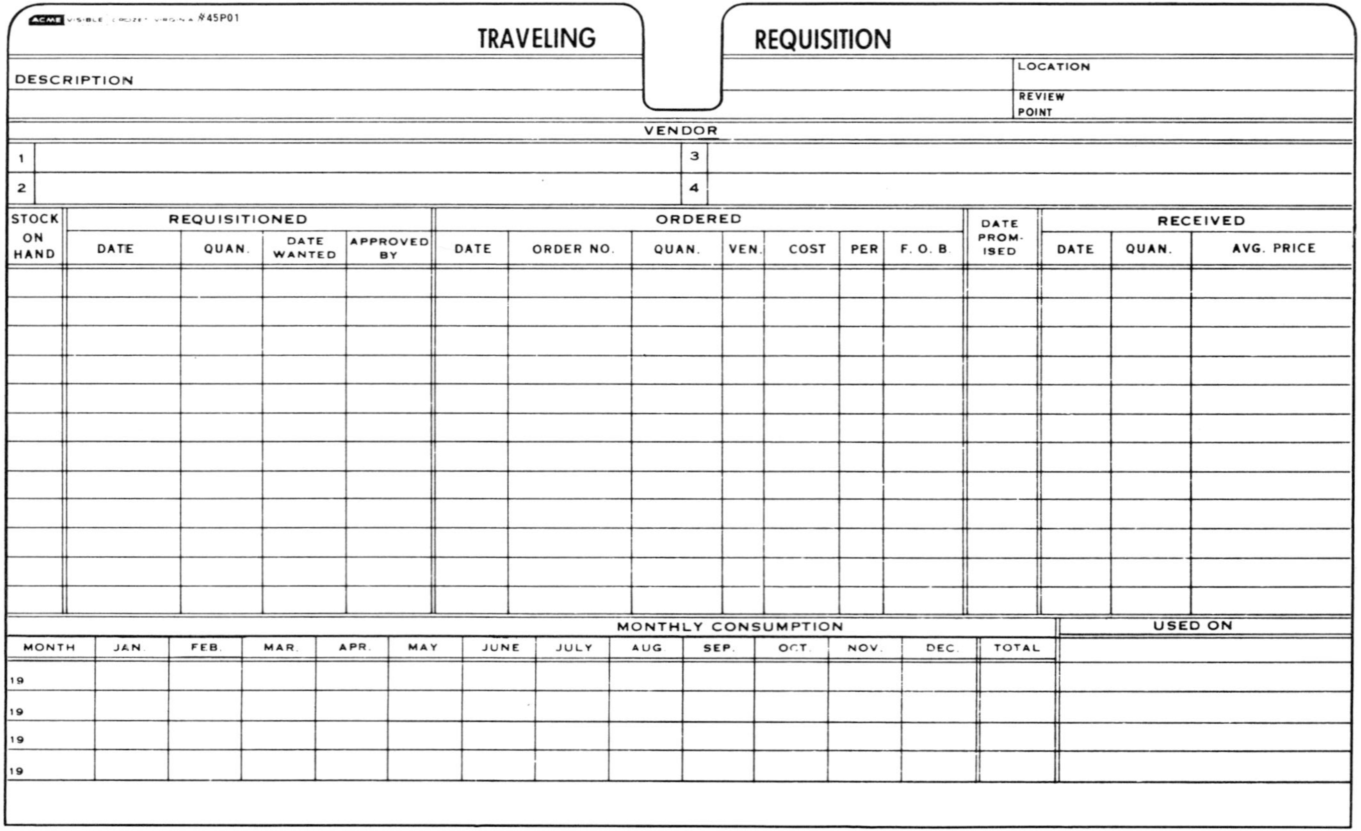

FIGURE 7.2. Inventory control card. A typical record card used for control of repair parts inventories. (*Courtesy of Acme Visible Records, Inc.*,

Crozet, Virginia. Acme Visible's line includes special cabinets designed to provide ready accessibility to each card in the system.

Normally, an inventory control card for parts will carry the part number, source of manufacturer, cost, and columns to record usage on a monthly basis:

- Number on hand
- Number sold current month
- Number sold last month
- Number sold prior month

This sort of arrangement allows you to see 90 days (one-quarter of a year) usage at a glance. Average annual usage can then be calculated simply by multiplying this figure by 4.

If there are parts in your inventory that are subject to sharp seasonal fluctuations, this will have to be interpolated into your figures on an individual basis. This problem is handled automatically in some of the more sophisticated computer programs incorporating seasonal forecasting methods.

The purpose of all this, of course, is to provide you with the information you need to identify the specific parts that you should be carrying in your inventory. If you have set four turns as your goal, you will stock every part that moves at least once every 3 months. In actual practice, an average inventory turnover of four will permit you to stock some parts that move less than four times because many parts will turn over at a much faster rate. Accurate records will help you to make sound decisions on which of the slower-moving parts you can carry while still maintaining your average turnover objective.

INVENTORY DELETIONS

Another purpose of the perpetual inventory system is to single out SKUs that should be eliminated from your inventory because they are no longer moving at the required rate. Since optimum inventory size is fixed by formula, any parts with little or no movement that are allowed to remain in your inventory take the place of parts that you should have on hand.

Once these obsolete parts are identified through your records, they should be marked down (removed from your inventory both physically and in your records). Policy in larger companies will usually require that parts marked out of inventory be immediately destroyed or discarded. Of course, any parts that may be returned to your supplier for credit should be sent back. More on this later.

If your company policy permits, parts marked out of inventory can be held. However, when such parts are sold, proper business and tax considerations require that the entire selling value be taken as income (zero cost).

Many professional managers, though, frown on the practice of retaining any merchandise once it has been marked out of the inventory. Repair parts held on the premises after they have been officially removed from the inventory records can be a temptation for employee pilferage. Also, the fact that some parts are in the inventory and some are not can lead to errors and confusion in record keeping and inventory control.

OUT-OF-STOCKS

Now that you know how large your inventory should be and specifically which parts you should stock, you must see to it that those parts are on hand in sufficient quantities when they are needed. An empty parts bin is just as bad as no parts bin at all.

Keeping parts in stock is done through a disciplined ordering system based on the proper order quantity (OQ) and minimum quantity (MQ). Let's talk first about minimum quantity.

MQ is simply the point at which it is time to place an order. The MQ may be written on the control card, on the parts bin, or on both. Let's say that the MQ assigned to a given part is eight. When the parts clerk notices that the quantity in the bin is down to eight, an order is promptly placed. If the MQ has been properly determined, the replenishment stock will normally arrive before the on-hand quantity reaches zero, thus avoiding an out-of-stock condition.

The formula for determining MQ will depend on your own objectives and on the average time it takes to receive parts after they are ordered. Let's assume that your records show an average of 2 weeks from the time parts are ordered until the time they are received. In this case, you may decide to establish a 2-week supply as your reorder point (MQ), or you may prefer a 3-week supply to provide a safety factor.

Depending on the nature of your inventory and the number of sources from which you order, you may well have a number of different lead times for establishing MQs. If, for example, you order many or all of your SKUs from a local distributor who provides dependable next-day service, you may well operate with a 1-week supply, or less, as your MQ on those parts. If, on the other hand, the bulk of your parts are ordered through company channels or out-of-town sources, you will need to establish MQs related to your experience with order life cycles.

The other half of your professional reorder program is the calculation and proper use of the order quantity. Once your MQ signal has told you that it's time to reorder, you must decide on the proper quantity to order; this is your OQ.

One basis for determining OQ makes use of a figure known as "insight." Insight is simply the total of the quantity on hand plus the quantity on order. Managers striving for four inventory turns per year often establish a 3-month supply as the insight for a given part. Using our earlier example of 2-week minimum quantity, that would leave a 10-week supply as the order quantity. Thus your insight at reorder time would be the 2 weeks on hand plus 10 weeks on order, or an insight of 12 weeks.

Remember, since MQ and OQ are based on actual usage, they must be calculated separately for each part. In actual practice, you may have a number of different order life cycles from widely varied sources and manufacturers.

The precise mathematics of MQ and OQ should not be considered inviolable. Special circumstances, such as seasonal fluctuations, may call for you to massage the figures from time to time. Bending the rules a little now and then is perfectly OK as long as it is done to permit the flexibility that would be lacking if you followed the rules rigidly without regard to changing circumstances.

For example, the frequency of ordering very low priced items must be considered in light of the cost of preparing an order, receiving it, placing the parts in bins, etc. Careful consideration of these costs may lead you to conclude that the cost of carrying a 1-year supply of some low-priced items would be less than the expense of ordering them four or five times throughout the year. In such a case, you may want to establish a 1-year supply as your insight. Some examples of this type of part would be nuts, bolts, inexpensive gaskets, and the like. Please remember, though, that this procedure must be an *exception* to your normal practice. Too much inventory can cause a lot of red ink.

A totally different type of problem is the SKU that is very large and bulky, requiring a disproportionate share of the space available for your inventory. In deference to the harsh demands of the real world, you may well decide to stock a smaller quantity of this type of part than your formula calls for.

There are, of course, an infinite variety of methods and combinations of methods for the proper maintenance of repair parts inventories. The fact that so many different systems survive can probaly be viewed as proof that there is no one approach ideally suited for all types of service operations.

What really matters is not the specific manner through which you establish your MQ's and OQ's, but that you *understand* the principles behind the simple arithmetic involved and that you apply these principles in the manner that best serves the needs of your own organization.

Let me digress here long enough for a little reminder: you would do well to remember that your efforts to establish a professional inventory control system will be for naught if you and your people do not observe your reorder points and order quantities with meticulous care. If a parts order is not triggered as soon as the MQ is reached, a costly out-of-stock condition will usually result.

As obvious as the above suggestion may sound, I'm afraid that it is honored more in the breach than in the observance thereof. (My apologies to the Bard.)

One simple system that can help to keep you on the straight and narrow is the divided parts bin. It requires only that each parts bin or container be divided into two sections. The smaller section contains the minimum quantity: the rest of the bin holds the balance of the stock. When it is necessary to take a part from the MQ section of the bin, it's time to reorder.

STOCKING THE TRUCK

Normally, every part that is carried in your trucks is also carried in your regular bin inventory. Seldom, if ever, though, will every part in your bin inventory be carried in your trucks. Working up the proper subassortments to carry in your trucks, then, is a kind of spin-off of the basic job of selecting inventory.

The principles of good inventory control are precisely the same as those for stocking service trucks, except that the need for good records and careful control is even greater for stocking the trucks than for your regular inventory. Your service technicians' time is the most valuable commodity that you will deal with as a service manager, and the waste that occurs when an outside technician needs a part not carried in his truck is compounded by traveling time and expense.

The place to begin inventory control in service vehicles is in the vehicles themselves. A neat and orderly set of bins and shelves is an absolute requisite if top efficiency is to be expected. Every day, in the best of families, service technicians write "lack-part call" when the needed part is in the truck all the time. A disorderly hodgepodge of parts scattered about in a service truck is a standing invitation to customer dissatisfaction and lost profit opportunities.

Maximum productivity from your truck stocks requires that all parts bins be numbered and that the placement of parts in these bins be standardized. Many service managers also provide each road technician with an up-to-date printed list of the parts carried in the truck. These procedures not only minimize the chances of overlooked parts but also make it a great deal easier to keep accurate records.

For the most part, the fastest-moving parts in your shelf inventory will be the most likely candidates for your truck stocks. However, you cannot rely on that rule of thumb to do the job for you. The work performed on outside calls will be different enough that parts usage in trucks should be analyzed separately.

Because the parts carried in your service vehicles are a part of your total inventory, they will have to fit within the limitations imposed by your overall policy on service level and turnover. You will want to remember, though, that a lack-parts situation on an outside call will usually be considerably more costly than it would be on a shop repair.

For years, four turns per truck per year was a familiar standard for stocking service vehicles. Today, with the cost of lack-parts calls climbing at a breathtaking rate, many service managers are lowering their requirement to as few as two or even one turn per year per truck. Where truck inventories seldom exceeded $1000 a few years ago, inventories of $3000 and more are not uncommon today.

The basic purpose of truck stock inventories is to keep lack-parts calls to a practical minimum, consistent with the cost of carrying the inventory. In some types of service operations, a goal of 5% or less lack-parts calls is not unreasonable. However, a figure of 7 to 10% probably represents a more realistic objective for most organizations.

Lack-parts calls cost money. So does maintaining an inventory. As one service manager puts it, "It costs you money if you have inventory—it costs you money if you don't have it." Some managers are losing *both* ways (by having lots of the wrong inventory).

Industry studies indicate that the average cost of maintaining an inventory of repair parts runs a little better than 2% per month (about 25% per year). This is the cost for interest, taxes, overhead, insurance, obsolescence, and other cost-of-doing-business factors. What it means is that a part that sits on your shelves for 1 year has actually cost you 125% of its original cost. Any parts that sit on your shelves for 4 years have cost you at least double what you originally paid for them. Obviously, these costs must be measured against the expenses incurred as a result of lack-parts calls in order to determine a reasonable level of service for your truck stocks.

PROFITS FROM THE PARTS DEPARTMENT

In order to generate a respectable profit from your investment in parts inventory, it is necessary only that you buy right and sell right. Buying right is what we've been talking about in this chapter up to now. Here are a few more tips on buying:

Beware of package deals. Your suppliers have the same inventory problems that you do. When they find themselves with obsolete or slow-moving merchandise, they can unload it on you by putting together tantalizingly attractive package deals. But what does it matter how cheaply you may have purchased a supply of parts if they remain on your shelves unsold, accumulating expense to the tune of 25% per year?

Take every opportunity to return surplus parts to your sources or suppliers for credit. Make it a point to learn the exact surplus returns policy of every supplier with which you do business; then be sure to take advantage of every chance to purge your inventory of unwanted SKUs. Cleaning out your inventory this way gives you the double benefit of a full or partial refund plus the room that is created for inventory that will sell.

Selling Right

Just as the amount of inventory that you buy must be carefully calculated, so must the amount you charge for those parts when you sell them to your customers. Careless, unprofessional pricing of repair parts is a common malady in service organizations—one that is responsible for the loss of untold profit dollars.

In order for you to do a professional job of pricing your repair parts, you must have a clear understanding of the basic terms involved and their relationships to each other. The ones you will be working with most often are:

Markup

This is a term often confused with the term mark-on. If you pay $1 for a part and sell it for $2, your markup is 50%—not 100%. Markup simply expresses the difference between the cost and the selling price *as a percentage of the selling price.* Stated differently, cost of the goods plus markup equals selling price.

As you can see from the definition, *100% markup is not possible unless your cost for the item is zero.* Yet you will frequently hear complaints about the merchant who gets "100% markup" for her goods. The mark-on (a seldom-used term) in the example above is 100%.

Cost Of Goods

This is the actual price you paid for the goods plus any direct buying expenses such as transportation costs.

Gross Profit

This is the difference between the cost of the goods and the selling price, less any allowances or returns. The gross profit in our example is $1.

Net Profit

This is the final profit remaining after all other applicable expenses have been deducted from gross profit. The chances are that you will have to be satisfied with a determination of gross profit for your parts operation. Computing true net profit for a specific department or portion of a business is an extremely complicated affair. It requires that all expenses for the business be precisely prorated, and this can be a nearly impossible task for anyone other than a qualified cost accountant. True net profit for the entire business, of course, is easy enough to compute. It is simply all expenses subtracted from *all* income.

These descriptions are necessarily brief and lacking in some important details. Your accountant (or a member of the accounting department if you work for a large company) will be able to round out your knowledge of these basic accounting terms. As they are presented here, however, they will be all you'll need to understand the fundamentals of pricing.

The most common pricing error for parts is the simplistic "across-the-board" markup. This approach requires that all parts, no matter what their price range, be priced at double their cost (or some other fixed multiple). This is a self-defeating system, particularly if you have a parts manager whose effectiveness you are trying to measure through his ability to generate gross profit for the business.

If you always set your selling price by doubling the cost, your gross profit will always be 50% no matter how carefully your parts manager buys. In fact, if your parts manager is an especially shrewd buyer, you will actually make less profit.

Let's say your firm has been paying $4 for a given part and that you have been selling it for $8. In this case, your 50% gross profit amounts to $4. Now let's say that your conscientious parts manager has found a supplier who will sell that same part for $3. Your system of doubling the cost will result in a selling price of $6. That same 50% gross profit now amounts to only $3. Remember, dollars go in the bank, not percentage points.

There is nothing wrong with setting an *average* 50% markup as your objective for your parts business. It is, in fact, a widely accepted figure. However, the word "average" is an important key.

Some parts, by their very nature, may appropriately take much higher markups than others. For example, parts costing less than a dollar or so may require markups of 60, 70, or even 80% because of the ratio of handling expense to selling price. Conversely, very expensive components such as TV picture tubes, refrigeration compressors, or electronic modules can be handled quite profitably with less than your average markup.

In many branches of the service industry, repair parts are assigned recommended selling prices by the manufacturers. While you may not agree with these figures, they will often serve as dependable parameters for setting your own prices.

A final word about pricing repair parts. Because of the public's universal dislike of paying for intangibles such as labor, too many service managers have given way to the temptation of charging unrealistically high prices for parts in order to present the appearance of low labor rates in the final bill to the customer. In addition to the serious moral, ethical, and legal implications of this practice, it's simply a lousy idea.

As a service organization, you have two separate products to sell: skilled labor and repair parts. Each must stand alone in a truly professional organization. Parts and labor are made up of separate ingredients, and the pricing of each must be based on sound business principles.

Chapter 8
Setting Service Rates

Perhaps you work for a large company and, thus, have no direct responsibility for determining the rates that will be charged to your customers. If so, you may congratulate yourself on your good fortune and skip this chapter. At the same time, you may want to extend sympathies to your boss when you ask him to read it. Setting service rates is a thorny business.

Of course, there are a number of owners and managers of service businesses who feel that they have solved this problem quite nicely: they simply find out what the fellow down the road is charging and set their own rates accordingly. If you adopt that system, you may discover that the trouble with it is that the other guy set his rates the same way. Thus, you and your competitor may find yourselves traveling the road to financial oblivion together.

IT MUST BE DONE WITH CARE

Setting the price to be charged for labor is a vital part of the service business; it must be done professionally.

As you saw in Chapter 7, determining how much to charge for parts is a comparatively easy job. Every part in your inventory came to you at a known cost. Arriving at the proper selling price is just a matter of applying your predetermined markup to the cost. In many branches of the service industry, markup and recommended selling prices for repair parts fall within fairly narrow ranges.

By comparison, determining how much to charge for your labor is a considerably more exacting task. When one of your mechanics or technicians completes a repair job, there is no invoice to tell you the precise cost of the finished product; yet this cost must be known if you are to establish the proper selling price.

And that's not all.

Even after you develop expertise in determining your costs for labor and overhead, your pricing dilemma will be just beginning. Factors that have no bearing on your own costs will rudely inject themselves into your calculations. For example, that fellow down the street. What he charges for his services will inevitably place limitations on those labor rates that would have solved all of your income problems. Such are the joys of our free enterprise system.

After you have learned how to deal with all the tricky variables so that you are able to set your rates at precisely the correct level, you will be ready to face the toughest part of the equation—your customer.

Service Is an Intangible

No one—absolutely no one—enjoys paying for intangibles, and service is one of the least tangible items available in our marketplace today. That last automobile you bought may have left a permanent scar on your financial hide, but the decision to buy it was your own free choice. Now you have several thousand pounds of steel and shiny chrome that you can show off to your neighbors. When you pay the labor charge for a repair job, all you can show for your money is the same article you had before the repair became necessary. The skill and time spent in completing the repair have but a fleeting existence. They cannot be seen, heard, or held in the hand. What means, then, is available to the purchaser to measure their true economic value?

Despite these problems, or perhaps because of them, your ability to set the proper prices for your labor will be one of your most important skills as a service manager. Service is a business that buys and sells the labor of skilled technicians and mechanics. In today's marketplace, the price that must be paid to obtain such skills is high. Once you have paid the price, you must resell at a rate that will allow a reasonable profit but will not be so high as to make you noncompetitive. Learning to do so is easier said than done.

There is a tendency for many service firms to set rates on the basis of past practice or what the competition charges. These are certainly valid considerations, but they cannot stand alone. To be sure, this may appear to be an easy way to solve a tough problem, but please don't let yourself be tempted.

Setting the correct level for your labor rates is a chore that will demand a certain amount of your valuable time, and it will never be quite finished. Once you have dutifully done a careful job of computing and analyzing your costs and determined the proper level for your rates, some of the original conditions will change, requiring you to decide whether or not an adjustment is justified. There is no reason to shy away from the job, though. It may seem a bit troublesome at first, but it will give you a valuable insight into the financial aspects of your business that you can acquire in no other way.

NO EASY FORMULA

One of the early lessons that you have no doubt already learned in this matter is that there is nothing even approaching uniformity in either the setting of labor rates or the manner in which they are described to the customer. Service in the customer's home or business, for example, has given birth to a dazzling array of ways to quote service rates. There are trip charges, visitation charges, basic charges, hourly rates, flat rates, ad infinitum. Shop work is not much better, with some firms using flat-rate pricing, others time and material, and still others some combination of these. Obviously, then, there is no one format for labor charges with which everyone agrees. Score another point for the free enterprise system.

In this chapter, I will describe the most popular of the systems in use, make my suggestions, and then step back to allow you to make your own decisions. In the meantime, let me urge you to make an inflexible policy of these two rules:

1. Once you have chosen a basic system for computing labor rates, be absolutely consistent. If you find that you must constantly make "horse sense" adjustments to make your prices "come out right," the system is not right for your business, or you're not using it properly.

2. Adopt a system that will make it easy for you and your employees to quote your rates to your customers in such a way that they will clearly understand, in advance, any minimums for which they are obligating themselves.

There are some very good reasons for rule number 2, not the least of which is the effect that such a policy will have on your reputation for integrity. The use of a format designed to disguise true labor rates may seem very tempting when you see a competitor apparently making profitable use of such a scheme. Over the long haul, though, a policy of clearly defined charges will bring the repeat business that is essential for survival. In case you haven't noticed, it's those service firms with questionable ethics that disappear with predictable frequency. Also, you should be aware of the rapidly increasing legal ramifications involving disclosure laws. More on this in a later chapter.

THE HOURLY RATE SYSTEM

Let's talk first about the original and still popular format for service and repair charges, the hourly rate. As with every other system for setting service rates, the hourly rate (or time-and-material) method has both advantages and disadvantages. From the viewpoint of the service dealer, it can be quite attractive. It assures the company of a known income for each *productive* hour of its technicians. The charge to the customer is computed simply by applying the fixed hourly rate to the time spent on the job.

Of course, this system can produce some interesting inequities. An inexperienced or inept technician can take much longer than necessary to complete a given job. In such a case, the customer pays a premium to underwrite on-the-job training. The dealer, in turn, is protected against such troublesome circumstances as a broken or frozen bolt or a difficult-to-reach corner that can greatly increase the time needed to do an otherwise simple job.

With all these advantages accruing to the service company, one might well assume that knowledgeable consumers would be opposed to the hourly rate. Well, some are and some are not. There is at least one advantage to the customer that is considered important in some quarters. Under the hourly rate, the customer has the use of the technician's time for the full period charged for. This is viewed by many people, both in and out of the service industry, as a sort of discipline that tends to keep things on the up-and-up. Perhaps this is why the hourly rate retains such wide popularity.

Let's say that you have chosen the hourly rate for your service department. Congratulations, you have completed the easiest part of the job. Now, how do you decide exactly what your hourly rate should be?

This is perhaps a good time to remind yourself that service is a product. As a service manager, you are buying and selling skilled labor. In order for you to know how much you should charge for your product to generate a fair profit, you must first know exactly how much that product is costing you.

The first part of that cost is obvious enough. For each hour that is worked by your technicians, you must pay them their hourly wage rate. This, of course, is only a part of your expense for producing a completed repair job. (This fact is usually not understood by the consumer and, too often, not even by the technician.) All the other costs of doing business must be added to your technical payroll in order to determine your full cost for each hour of technicial productivity. One popular method for doing this requires that you determine your overhead ratio (or burden ratio, as it is sometimes called). Here's how:

Select a period of time upon which to base your calculations. In order to get a representative picture of your business costs, you should use a minimum time period of 3 months; 6 months would be much better. If your business has been around long enough and your records are complete, a full year's data would improve accuracy.

For the period selected, you must now add together all expenses for the business *except technical payroll.* Be sure not to overlook any expenses in this step. Include managerial and supporting payroll, occupancy costs, advertising, depreciation—everything that is not direct technical payroll. The only exception is expense that is exclusively and directly attributable to the parts portion of your business: cost of parts, payroll devoted exclusively to parts, etc. This portion of your expenses is taken into consideration when you compute the markup on your parts sales.

Once you have determined your total overhead expense, divide that figure by the total technicians' wages paid during the same time period (be sure to include any paid vacations, holidays, or illnesses). The result will be your overhead ratio.

Depending on the size, efficiency, and nature of your service business, your overhead ratio may be as low as 0.8 or 0.9 or it may run as high as 1.5 or even higher. If your overhead expenses were exactly the same as your technical payroll, your overhead ratio would be 1. Get the idea?

From the standpoint of efficiency and profitability, you obviously want a low overhead ratio. More about that subject later on.

Determining Costs

Let's examine some figures from the hypothetical ABC Service Company.

| Total overhead expense for the period | $13,875 |
| Technical payroll for the period | $12,600 |

13,875 divided by 12,600 = 1.1

ABC's overhead ratio of 1.1 means that for every $1 paid to technicians, an additional $1.10 is needed to pay for overhead costs.

The next figure we need is the *average* hourly wage paid to technicians. Let's say ABC pays one technician $8 per hour, another $8.50, and a third $9. The average wage for the three workers is $8.50. Assuming that their technicians average an 8-hour day, the average daily rate is

$$\$8.50 \times 8 = \$68$$

In other words, on the average, ABC pays its technicians $68 for a day's work.

We have already determined that ABC has operating expenses amounting to $1.10 for each $1 paid to technicians (an overhead burden of 1.1). In order to get the average total burden for each technician, we need only to add his average daily wage to his average daily cost burden.

Average daily wage	$68.00
Average daily cost burden	74.80
	(68 × 1.1)
Average total burden	$142.80

That total of $142.80 represents the average cost to ABC for each technician working a full day. Put another way, it is the technician's break-even point. If ABC's technicians averaged $142.80 per day in labor charges to the customer, the company would break even on labor.

Of course, that's not the idea. The goal is to establish rates that will generate a fair profit. If the service manager at ABC has set a 10% labor profit as her goal, she must divide her break-even point by 0.9 to get the figure.

$142.80 divided by 0.9 = $158.67

Now we're getting to the heart of the matter. Using the figures above, we know that each technician must generate service charges (or credits in the case of in-warranty work) of about $159 per day in order for ABC to make a 10% profit on labor. Computing the hourly rate is now a cinch. All we have to do is divide $159 by 8. Right?
Wrong.
To do so would be to assume that each technician is going to do productive work for the entire 8-hour period for which he is paid. That, of course, doesn't happen. There are such things as coffee breaks, travel time, training time, shop cleanup, paperwork, and time that mysteriously just disappears. Studies in the appliance repair industry, for example, indicate that only about 55% of the average technician's 8-hour day is spent actually doing repair work. That comes to a little less than 4½ hours. In some especially efficient operations or in other branches of the service industry, that efficiency figure may run as high as 75 or 80%. Rarely, however, will it go higher. For the purposes of our illustration, let's say that ABC's technicians are productive 70% of the time. That would work out to 5.6 hours per day and would place ABC among the leaders in efficiency.

$159 divided by 5.6 = $28 per hour (rounded off)

For each full hour spent on the job by a technician, ABC must charge $28. Usually, this will be broken down into quarter-hour or tenth-of-an-hour increments. In this example, each quarter hour would be billed at $7.

Let's review the things you'll need to know in order to apply the hourly rate formula to your service department.

1. Average hourly wage for technicians

2. Your overhead ratio

3. Daily break-even point for each technician

4. Average productive time of technicians

5. Your profit objective on labor

The first three items are easily obtained from your records. Item 4 will take a bit of additional effort on your part. Remember the chapter on productivity? If you were paying attention, you know that the more nonproductive time spent by your technicians, the higher you must set your labor rate in order to reach your profit objective. If the nonproductive ratio goes high enough, your hourly rate will no longer be competitive and you'll find your customers going elsewhere.

PRODUCTIVE-TIME RATIO

In reading back over the example used, you will see that the productive time of your technicians is a factor that must be known. You must not hedge on this step. If you don't already know the productive-time ratio for your techs (or yourself, for that matter), be prepared for a shock.

In order to compute productive time, you'll need to analyze the actual time spent on jobs and compare that time to the total hours paid over a representative period of time. Don't use industry averages or guesswork for this step—it's too vital to your financial success.

Reducing the nonproductive time of your mechanics or technicians as discussed in the chapter on productivity will allow you to charge a lower rate to your customers, to enjoy a higher profit margin, or, better yet, to have some delightful combination of both.

It may be painful for you to learn the actual productive-time ratio for your operation, but you must be completely honest in your calculations. For each day analyzed, add up the time actually spent on each job and express that time as a percentage of the total time for which the technicians were paid. For example, suppose that one technician averaged 5 hours of productive time for each 8-hour day worked:

$$5 \text{ divided by } 8 = 62.5\%$$

In some types of service operations, the true productive-time ratio can be hidden by practices such as failing to deduct coffee breaks and lunch hours from long jobs. This, of course, would be not only misleading but downright dishonest if the customer is paying an hourly rate.

The hourly rate formula as discussed up to this point is complete for shop repairs where the work is brought in by the customer. In service organizations that dispatch technicians to the customer's home or business, the time involved in travel must be taken into consideration.

Travel Time

Whether to include travel time as productive or nonproductive time in your calculations is an important decision, since it will affect the computation of your hourly rate. There are two distinctly different schools of thought on the subject. Personally, I feel that travel time is best-viewed as simply another of the nonproductive tasks that must be done by road technicians. These would include check-in time, coffee breaks, and other things not relevant to the actual time required to complete a repair job. Proper use of this approach in computing the hourly rate makes it easy to compensate for the average time spent driving from one call to another.

The most common way in which this is handled is through the use of the minimum charge for road calls. (This charge is sometimes called a basic charge, trip charge, visitation charge, etc.) In recognition of the additional expenses involved in road calls, this system puts an extra charge "up front" to cover them.

Using the rate of $28 per hour from our earlier example, one method for charging for home calls would be to charge $14 (one-half the hourly rate) as a minimum charge for home service and to have this charge cover up to the first quarter hour in the customer's home. After that, the rate of $7 per quarter hour would apply.

Some dealers prefer a fixed trip charge covering only the time and expense for getting to the customer's home, with no time for repairs included. There are any number of variations on this theme, each with its own set of advantages and disadvantages. The method you choose is not important as long as your decision is based on the exact knowledge required to compute your labor rates properly.

In some branches of the service industry, it is customary to compute travel time as part of the time spent on the job. This approach is seen most often in highly specialized, low-volume service operations, such as medical or industrial equipment, where a given technician may be required to cover a very large geographic area. It is not unusual to find service organizations of some types covering an entire state from a single location. Under those conditions, charging for the time spent traveling to the job is the only practical method.

However, for most service operations located in typical urban areas, I do not recommend this approach. While it does permit the dealer to charge what appears to be a lower hourly rate because of actually charging for nonproductive time, the average labor charge to the customer will come out about the same under either system in areas where travel time between calls is reasonably consistent. Defending the practice of charging separately for travel time to suspicious customers and, possibly, consumer agencies could be a time-waster. Also, there is no incentive to the technician to minimize travel time if it is considered to be productive work.

There is a workable compromise for service organizations that do the great majority of their calls in a compact area but must handle an occasional long-distance run. It is necessary only to define the "regular service area" on a map. Calls outside of this area are subject to an additional charge for each mile beyond the boundary.

FLAT-RATE SYSTEMS

The flat-rate system for labor charges poses an entirely different concept. With flat rates, the labor charge for every type of repair is calculated in advance and remains the same regardless of the time required to do the individual job.

Proponents of the flat-rate system point out several advantages over the hourly rate system. On the surface at least, there would appear to be advantages for both the customer and the service dealer in this approach.

From the customer's standpoint, flat rates offer good insurance against surprises. With a specific charge assigned to each repair job, the customer can be told precisely how much the repair job is going to cost before the work is actually done.

The service dealer, too, enjoys some advantages in flat-rate pricing. Every completed repair job results in a known and fixed income, and there is the additional benefit that accrues as the result of the technician's not having to spend time making a record of starting and quitting times and computing time spent on the job for the customer's receipt.

As you might imagine, preparing your own table of flat-rates is no mean task. The job requires an immense amount of statistical analysis and, for all practical purposes, may be beyond the means of all but the largest service organizations.

At least two different means have been put to use to solve this problem in recent years.

In one system, only a handful of individual prices need be set. All repair jobs are classified as either home or shop, and each of these is further identified as major or minor. Fixed rates for each of these classifications are based on overall averages. In some cases, a few additional prices may be added to cover such things as complete overhauls, picture-tube replacements in TV sets, and compressor replacements in refrigeration equipment. This is the simplest form of flat-rate pricing, but it is also the least professional and may be the most difficult to defend against flat-rate critics.

Another format that began in the automobile industry and is gaining in acceptance in other fields is the commercially prepared flat-rate manual. A sample page from a typical manual is shown in Figure 8.1. This form of manual offers the small service firm the advantage of a

CB/Communications Receivers

⑪ Component Removal and Replacement Time—Cont.

Connectors
- 2/4 connections 5
- 5/9 connections 10
- 10 or more 15

Controls PC HW
- Single .... 5 ... 10
- Dual .... 10 ... 15
- Triple .... 15 ... 20

Control/Switch Comb'o
(Control Time +
Switch Time)

Crystals 5
Dial drives .... TP

Diodes
- Single 5
- Multiple 10

Fuses (one or more) 5
Fuse holders 10
Hardware .... TP

I.C.'s
- Plug In (each) 5
- Wired In
  - 4/16 10
  - 17/28 15
  - 29 or more 20
- Interlock 10

Jacks .... TP
Knobs (one or more) 5

Lamps
- Plug In 5
- Wired In 10

Mechanical Parts
or Assemblies .... TP
Meters 15
Microphones .... TP
Miscellaneous parts ... TP
Modules (each) 5

Receiving Tubes
- 1 5
- 2/5 10
- 6 or more 15

Relays
- 1/4 connections 10
- 5 or more 15

Resistors (each) 5
R/C Networks 10

Sockets
- 2/6 connections 5
- 7/10 connections ... 10
- 11 or more 15

Speakers (each) 10

Switches
- 2/6 connections 10
- 7/10 connections ... 15
- 11/20 connections .. 20
- 21/30 connections .. 25
- 31 or more 30

Terminal Strips
- 2/6 connections 10
- 7/10 connections ... 15
- 11 or more 20

Thermistor 5

Transformers
- Audio output
  - 2/4 connections ... 10
  - 4 or more 20
- Driver 10
- IF 15
- Power
  - 2/6 connections ... 10
  - 7/10 connections .. 15
  - 11 or more 25
- RF 15

Transistors
- Signal type 5
- Power type 15

Tubes (see receiving)
Tuner replacement 20

TP = Time Price. PC = Printed Circuit. HW = Hand Wired.

⑫ Warranty Tags and Forms (each) 5

FIGURE 8.1. Sample page from a typical commercial labor pricing manual. (*Courtesy of Sperry Tech Inc., Lincoln, Nebraska*).

much more extensive and detailed analysis than could be developed locally. There is also a certain psychological advantage in having the customer see your technician referring to an "official-looking" manual for prices.

An example of this type of flat-rate pricing guide is the *Sperry Tech Labor Pricing Guide,* developed for the radio-TV service industry by the Sperry Tech Company in Lincoln, Nebraska. One of the most widely used flat-rate manuals in the automobile service industry is *Chilton's Professional Labor Guide and Parts Manual* published by the Chilton Book Company in Radnor, Pennsylvania. Another leading auto manual is *Motor Parts and Time Guide* published by the Hearst Corporation in New York City.

You will want to keep in mind that all commercial flat-rate manuals provide only *time* requirements for each repair job. Their use still requires that you compute and establish your own *hourly rate* in order to determine the actual charge to the customer.

A Word of Caution

While it is true that the flat-rate system of labor pricing is becoming widely used in the service industry, you will be well advised to remember that not everyone is enchanted with the idea. It is in the auto repair field that the concept came into its own, and that is where the sharpest criticisms have been aimed. Pricing from the "book" is so widespread in auto repairs that shopping around for the best price on a given repair job may well net the customer nothing more than six identical estimates and some extra miles on the odometer.

Whether they are right or wrong, critics of flat-rate manuals for auto repairs claim that the average mechanic can and usually does complete jobs in less time than the manuals list. One well-known consumer organization claims to have performed its own repairs on a wide variety of autos and compared the actual times spent with the times listed in one of the most widely used manuals. The test, it is said, showed that the times listed in the manual were, on the average, 25% longer than the times actually spent by the mechanics during the test. In fairness, this could mean that the mechanics used in the test were simply 25% faster than the average—or it could mean that the times listed in the book do not represent a realistic expectation of the times needed by reasonably competent mechanics to do the work.

In any case, you will want to keep yourself aware of the obvious risks and the criticisms that may be an inherent part of some flat-rate systems. If the times used in the listings have not been scrupulously and accurately computed, the flat-rate system can indeed become unfair to the customer.

In one form of work incentive program, the mechanic is compensated not for the hours worked in a day, but for the hours *billed* in a day. The risks here are plain. Despite the best intentions of the employer, a mechanic or technician on this system would obviously benefit personally for charging for more hours than those actually worked. Despite its apparent attractiveness, I do not think it to be a wise form of operation.

Investigations and lawsuits against auto dealers alleged to be involved in this practice have taken place in recent years in California and Wisconsin. While automobile dealers have been the primary targets of interest in this issue so far, any type of service organization could become involved at any time.

Naturally, the people who publish flat-rate manuals for the service industry stoutly maintain that the times listed in their manuals coincide with the results of careful studies that are periodically updated from experience on the "firing line." If you prepare the averages within your own company exclusively for your own use, you can control the methods used and, thus, the accuracy of your listings. If you use a commercial manual, you must rely on the integrity of the publisher to protect you.

Properly administered, the flat-rate system for labor pricing is a practical and reasonable option open to the service dealer. It is the dealer's responsibility, however, to administer the system in such a way that the customer is treated fairly. It is, after all, comforting for a customer to know exactly what a repair will cost even before any work is done. Whether a customer receives a fair deal is less a matter of the choice of pricing systems than of the integrity of the dealer involved.

If you are using or are planning to use some form of flat-rate pricing, there is one simple check that will help you to satisy yourself of its fairness: jobs that require more time than listed should be in evidence as often as jobs that are completed in less time. Remember, the basic premise of flat-rate pricing is that the customer pays for the *average* time needed to complete a given repair. If the average time is accurately computed, neither the customer nor the dealer need have any surprises.

As with the hourly rate system, flat-rates are usually based on the time required for the actual repair. When the work is to be done at the customer's home or business, an appropriate rate must be established to cover the expenses involved for travel.

OTHER SYSTEMS

There are, of course, other systems for establishing labor rates. The ones we have discussed here are among the most popular and widely used in the industry. However, if you have your own ideas, that's fine. Devise a system to suit your own requirements but please be sure to do it professionally with full knowledge of the economics involved. Unfortunately, there are still countless service managers who feel that the type of computations discussed in this chapter are too much trouble. For many of them, a simple rule of thumb is all that is needed to do the job.

Let me emphasize that I do not favor such an approach, but if you insist on taking a shortcut to set your rates, I will pass along the one I have encountered most often: the hourly rate is equal to 3½ to 4 times the technician's average hourly wage.

CHARGING FOR ESTIMATES

There once was a time when many, if not most, service organizations proudly proclaimed "free estimates." While there are still many who do, the practice is becoming less prevalent as the economics of the service business make every minute of the technician's time more valuable.

In the final analysis, you will have to decide whether or not you will charge your customers for preparing estimates. You may feel, as some service managers do, that such a service is expected of you by most customers and should be provided at no charge. Dealers with a lot of walk-in customers with portable or low-cost merchandise often opt to provide free estimates and simply factor this into the expenses of doing business. More and more service managers, however, are hedging when it comes to estimates requiring extensive diagnosis. This is especially evident in branches of the service industry where diagnosis is often the greater part of the total repair time. In my opinion, a workable compromise in tune with today's conditions is a policy that allows for free estimates when they can be provided quickly and easily, but stipulates an estimate charge where significant amounts of time and effort are necessary.

An interesting development in this connection is the increasing amount of state and municipal legislation requiring that every customer be provided with a detailed, written estimate. This type of "consumer" legislation virtually dictates that every customer bear the cost of this additional work even where the customer does not feel it to be necessary.

INFLATION

As long as we continue in the inflationary spiral that has been part of our economic world for more than 30 years, it will be necessary that you thoroughly review your operating expenses on a regularly scheduled basis. As costs continue to rise, it becomes necessary to increase the rates charged to your customers.

The so-called rule of 72, long used by economists, provides a quick and simple way to demonstrate how rapidly your expenses can climb. To use it, simply divide the current inflation rate into 72. The result is the number of years it will take, if that rate remains constant, for costs to double. For example, let's assume a 6% inflation rate:

$$72 \text{ divided by } 6 = 12$$

That tells you that costs will double in 12 years if a constant inflation rate of 6% persists. At 12% inflation, costs will double in six years. At higher rates, it is obvious that expenses must be reviewed quite often if you are to be aware of how much it is costing you to do business.

Of course, as with most other things in the service business, it's not quite that easy. Increasing costs cannot always be passed on to your customers. Such things as poor productivity or poor management of general expenses usually cannot be offset by simply raising your prices. Competition can be a marvelous disciplinarian in this matter.

MODERATE OR PREMIUM RATES

As a closing note, let me remind you that the increasing militancy of consumer organizations makes it more important than ever for service dealers to use a pricing system which is understandable to the customer and which satisfies the "disclosure" legislation that is being enacted in more and more communities around the country.

In my view, a service dealer has every legal and moral right to set his labor rates at any level that he wishes, as long as the customer is made fully aware of how much she is paying and exactly what it is for. You cannot cheat a customer simply by charging high prices. If your prices are too high for the service you are rendering, the wonderfully effective forces of the free enterprise system will soon provide a solution to the problem—your customers will simply go elsewhere.

In actual practice, the odds are that setting your prices too high is not likely to be a problem for you. Industry experience clearly shows that a service dealer is much more likely to be guilty of charging rates insufficient to generate a satisfactory profit than of setting them too high to be competitive. In his book *Service Shop Management Guide* (Sams, Indianapolis, 1976), Dick Glass says, "I have never heard of a service dealer being forced out of business because of too high hourly rates. Many have failed, however, due to too low hourly rates."

There are, of course, many service dealers who follow the practice of charging premium prices for what they consider to be premium service. While my personal preference is more moderate, I know of no consumer organization or government agency that will dispute this right, so long as the customer is not misled and the rates are set forth in a clear and straightforward manner.

The modern, well-run service organization provides a professional service to its customers. In doing so, it is entitled to charge rates appropriate to the service rendered.

Chapter 9
Selling Service Contracts

Service contracts (sometimes called maintenance agreements or service agreements) are very big business. When you consider the many hundreds of companies in perhaps a score of industries engaged in the selling of service contracts throughout the nation, it's not difficult to accept the estimates that place total volume well into the hundreds of million of dollars every year.

Service contracts are sold to consumers on automobiles and on such domestic appliances as television receivers, laundry equipment, and dishwashers; to doctors and hospitals on medical and diagnostic equipment; to businesses on computers, data processing terminals, and electronic cash registers—and that's just a partial listing. Quite a scorecard for a product that didn't even exist prior to World War II.

While history does not afford us the exact moment of birth of the modern service contract, it's generally agreed that the high technology ushered in by the introduction of television provided the catalyst needed to bring the concept to full flower.

GENESIS

Circa 1948. Although the first experimental television receivers were in operation before World War II, it wasn't until the postwar technology boom got underway that commercially practical sets were made available to the general public at reasonable prices. The brand new industry was enjoying a spectacular growth rate, and television sets were being gobbled up by anxious consumers almost as quickly as the manufacturers were able to produce them.

The television receivers of those days were a far cry from the modern, solid-state sets that provide such relatively trouble-free performance for today's consumer. The sets of the 1940s and early 1950s were large and cumbersome, and they broke down with distressing frequency. As a result, the rapidly growing industry could not seem to provide qualified technicians in sufficient numbers to properly maintain the sets that were being sold.

Yes, there were tens of thousands of radio repairmen who provided a ready-made nucleus for the new profession of TV technician. The trouble was that television service required advanced electronics training and expensive shop equipment. Training and equipping a staff of technicians was a costly proposition, and the volume of service work was still unpredictable enough to make it a risky investment for many would-be service dealers.

From this dilemma came the service contract idea. If enough customers were willing to commit themselves in advance for the maintenance of their sets, the service company would have the revenue needed to build a professional service organization, and the customer would be assured of service by competent technicians. The idea was a good one, and it caught on quickly. Before long, the logic of the arrangement was applied to other types of home appliances and commercial equipment; thus, the modern service contract was launched on the road to the service hall of fame.

There were problems, of course. Some companies got into financial difficulties after collecting large sums from their customers. Worse, some unscrupulous operators set up service companies just long enough to sell contracts which they had no intention of honoring. By and large, though, the new product served the seller and the consumer well enough to survive its growing pains and emerge as a solid and dependable mainstay in the service industry.

SHOULD YOU BE SELLING SERVICE CONTRACTS?

Today, the pie is a gigantic one, and if you're not in on the action already, it's logical for you to ask whether you should be getting a piece of it.

Well, maybe yes and maybe no.

The plus side of the ledger has lots of entries. The initial income can be significant, but that's only the beginning. An effective service contract program ties the customer to your service organization and provides you with a predictable source of continuing income from renewals. Because of the compounding effect resulting from a successful renewal program, service contract income can grow at an astounding rate. In many service organizations, contract income provides the financial foundation for the entire operation.

The service manager for one manufacturer of medical equipment says flatly that his service organization could not support itself financially without service contracts, since demand service produces a net income of only about 2%.

If your service load tends to fluctuate on a seasonal basis, a large number of outstanding service contracts will help smooth out the peaks and valleys. Customers holding service contracts tend to call for service as soon as the need arises, whereas demand customers will often put off service if the item is not essential or if it is "out of season." Also, some contracts include preventive maintenance provisions, and this facilitates a carefully planned program to smooth out the workload fluctuations. These are no small considerations, since a smoother, more predictable workload makes for a more efficient operation and better productivity. Finally, service contracts can be a powerful tool for developing customer goodwill. There is something psychologically satisfying about having someone respond to your need for service and then ask for nothing more than your signature when the work has been completed.

If the land of service contracts is so bountiful, you might well ask, why isn't everyone in on the act? What are we waiting for?

Well, it's not as simple as that.

As you learned earlier, assigning the right price to repair parts requires a bit of work, and working out the right price for your labor is a lot more difficult than that. Well, you can add those two jobs together and multiply by 10, and you may have some idea of the work required to establish a pricing schedule for service contracts.

FULFILLMENT COSTS

The problem is centered around the fact that you cannot determine the correct selling price for a product until you know what the product is costing you; and finding out how much a service contract is costing you is a very big job indeed.

The basic principle of a service contract is that the customer pays the *average* price for maintaining a product of a given type and age. In order for you to determine that average, you must maintain accurate records of the service required throughout the life of a representative number of contracts. You will need to know the total cost of both parts and labor for fulfilling all the contracts analyzed. Only then can you determine the *average* cost.

And don't forget, this process has to be repeated for each type of product to be covered, by age of the product. For a firm servicing a number of different types of merchandise from different manufacturers, the possible combinations of product and age could run well into the hundreds or (heaven forbid) the thousands. Of course, this step could be greatly simplified by lumping a number of products or ages together, but this can be risky. You might well sell a lot of contracts before you realized that some were seriously underpriced. To make matters even worse, you don't have any records to study until you start selling contracts, and you can't start selling contracts until you know what to charge for them—catch 22.

Well, everyone has to start somewhere, and you wouldn't be the first if you decided to launch your program by trading on the experience of another firm already in the business. In fact, to be painfully honest about it, I don't know of any other practical way to get started. You may even find, if you ask, that *they* got started the same way.

If you decide that service contracts are for you and that you're going to appropriate someone else's prices, please keep one thing uppermost in your mind: selling service contracts will place a deferred financial responsibility directly on your company, and the prices for the contracts you sell must be based on your own experience if you are to avoid significant financial risk. For this reason, you must accumulate the necessary data to enable you to calculate your own prices at the earliest possible time.

You will also want to keep in mind that practically everyone with experience selling contracts agrees that they must be sold in reasonably large numbers if the program is to be successful. Since the premise of the contract idea is centered around the average experience, contracts must be sold in sufficient quantities to ensure a representative group. Otherwise, the luck of the draw prevails, and a string of heavy losses could be your only reward. Contracts sold in depth spread the risk over a larger number of customers, thus increasing the chances that the average statistics will prove valid. The larger the number of contracts sold, the more dependable the averages.

HOW TO SELL THEM

Service contracts wear many faces, and the methods used to sell them are equally diverse. Obviously, selling an $80 service contract on a domestic television set is not the same as selling an $11,000 contract on a piece of medical diagnostic equipment worth $100,000 or more.

Regardless of these differences, though, there is a common thread running through the fabric of available sales techniques. Since the basic premise of the service contract is that the purchaser pays the average cost of maintaining the product, it presents a unique selling challenge.

A special sale price, one of the most effective selling techniques for most products, has very limited application in the sale of service contracts. Instead, the seller must concentrate on the proven reasons why consumers buy contracts, and slant the selling techniques to highlight them. Identifying a need and then providing a product or service to fill that need form the basic premise behind all successful selling. Service contracts are no exception.

Many years ago, one of the most successful salespersons of all time coined a phrase that summed up his personal selling technique. Elmer Wheeler said, "Sell the sizzle, not the steak." His message, of course, was that the customer's mental attitudes and emotions are more important to the sale than are the specific features of the product being sold. Nowhere, I believe, is this philosophy more meaningful than in the sale of service contracts.

In their book *Service Management Principles and Practices*, Instrument Society of America, Pittsburgh, Pa. 1978, authors William H. Bleuel and Joseph D. Patton, Jr., address the same point in a different way: "The concept of utility suggests that the customer ultimately purchases a benefit, not just a product. The customer purchases what the product will do for him rather than a collection of parts. An individual purchases an automobile for transportation and a television for entertainment."

The technical specifications in the contract are important, of course, but years of experience have taught us that the customer who buys a service contract is actually buying peace of mind—the transfer of responsibility to the seller of the contract. Every successful contract sales program I have ever seen was built around an understanding of this important concept.

The underlying motivation is a major factor not only for the seller to a domestic consumer concerned about avoiding large, unexpected repair bills for appliances but also for the seller to a professional or business user concerned primarily about the consequences of excessive downtime.

Points of Persuasion

Here, then, are the principal points of persuasion that should be incorporated in your sales materials and training:

- Peace of mind—let us do the worrying.
- No unexpected repair bills.
- Guaranteed service when you need it.
- Service tomorrow at today's prices.
- Protect your investment.
- Budget maintenance costs in advance (an important feature in an inflating economy).

There are four basic methods of selling service contracts in use today: at the point of sale of the product through mail solicitation, through telephone solicitation, and by the technician who services the product. The nature of the product itself will usually determine the most effective sales methods to use.

For obvious reasons, a contract selling for thousands of dollars is not likely to be bought solely as the result of a direct mail solicitation. Transactions of this type require face-to-face selling and no small amount of sales training.

Direct mail programs, though, can be very successful in the sale of contracts on domestic appliances or relatively low-priced office equipment, especially if your company is already known to the customer. Mail programs in conjunction with telephone solicitations provide the nucleus for many of the most successful renewal programs in operation today.

In *Product Service Management* (American Management Association, New York, 1972) Thorton P. Masten suggests:

> Where budget limitations restrict the use of professional advertising techniques, other means of carrying the story to the potential customer can be explored. Both sales and service personnel can leave flyers or brochures with potential customers as they carry out their regular tasks. . . . Correspondence to potential customers or even unrelated matters can include enclosures touting contract maintenance. Almost any means that result in contact or communication with the would-be customer can carry the contract message.

A sample of a service contract sales letter is shown in Figure 9.1.

PHILADELPHIA ELECTRIC COMPANY

2301 MARKET STREET

PHILADELPHIA, PA. 19101

(215) 841-4950

MARTIN F. GAVET
VICE-PRESIDENT, GAS OPERATIONS

June 1979

Dear Customer:

As a purchaser of PE's Residential Gas Heating Service Contract you are probably well aware of all the assurances it provides for the reliable maintenance of your gas house heating equipment. And, if you had to call on us for service help during the past year, I'm certain you found PE servicemen to be prompt, courteous, and efficient.

But now that it is time to renew your contract, the enclosed information detailing the benefits and broad coverage of the contract can help to remind you of exactly how valuable this protection is, especially during these inflationary times.

Speaking of inflation, we've managed to hold down the additional cost of the contract. It's up only $2, and at $36 per year (or less than a dime a day), I'm sure you'll decide it's still a very good bargain.

And - at this low cost, the plan continues to provide for the adjustment, replacement, or repair of those items covered by the new agreement and includes most parts and labor necessary to correct your heating problems. If your heating system is either hot water or steam, I once again remind you that there is an additional flat rate service charge for the draining and refilling of these systems if required for the repair or replacement of contract-covered parts.

I would also like to remind you that in many areas qualified contractors offer annual service contracts, too. More and more homeowners are recognizing the value of service contract plans, and that's why I'm reasonably certain you'll want to renew your contract which is available only to PE gas house heating customers.

Don't miss out on this opportunity to continue coverage on your gas furnace or boiler. Complete and return the signed application with your check, money order, or credit card number (Master Charge or VISA accepted) for the contract cost of $36 per heater. If you have any questions, please refer to the enclosed information and call the number listed for your area.

Cordially,

M. F. Gavet

FIGURE 9.1. A well-written service contract renewal sales letter. *(Courtesy of Philadelphia Electric Company).*

The Best Time To Make The Sale

In almost all cases, though, the best time to sell an original service contract is at the point of sale of the merchandise itself. The customer is in a buying mood, and protecting her investment with a guaranteed service program is a logical concept to advance. Also, a trained, professional salesperson is more likely to close the sale than would be a follow-up telephone call or direct mail solicitation. You will want to remember, too, that a contract sold at the same time as the merchandise will almost always be the least costly way to make the sale.

With certain types of merchandise, the service technician can be an extremely effective sales agent. As a technical expert, the technician's opinions carry a lot of weight with most owners of appliances or complicated equipment. There is one pitfall here, though, and you should avoid it very carefully if you decide to sell contracts through the efforts of your technicians. An overly aggressive technician can easily alienate the customer who feels that the repairman is neglecting his primary responsibilities in favor of his contract-selling attempts. Careful training of the technician to avoid overzealousness is one consideration. Another is an incentive set high enough to encourage a selling effort, but not so high as to serve as a distraction to the primary purpose of the technician's job.

Regardless of the selling methods you employ, the benefits to the purchaser must always provide the basic thrust. And don't forget, "Sell the sizzle, not the steak."

SELLING RENEWALS

If there is one aspect of the service contract business that sets it apart from all other income-producing activities, it's the selling of renewals. Like the biblical bread cast upon the waters, service contracts have the ability to multiply in the most delightful way.

Many products, once they are sold to the consumer, effectively remove that customer from the market for a good many years. The proud purchaser of a new hot water heater, color television set, or office copier isn't likely to be looking for a replacement anytime soon. Not so with the buyer of a service contract. At the end of each year or other coverage period, the owner of a service contract automatically becomes a prime new prospect. In some industries, renewals run as high as 80 to 90% of expirations.

At that rate, it doesn't take much imagination to recognize that a steady supply of original contracts plus an effective renewal program will produce a nucleus of income that will compound annually at an ever-increasing rate. The original contract, then, is really only the introduction to the contract business. It is in the sale of renewals that you can realize the full economic potential of this facet of the service business.

The sale of renewals begins with a most important advantage: your prospect is already your customer. If you have done a good job of fulfilling your responsibilities under the original contract, the customer will be far more receptive to your selling efforts than would be the case if he were a stranger. Perhaps this is why simple direct mail solicitations have produced consistently dependable results for many different service organizations.

In the general mail-order business, a return of 2% or so would be considered acceptable for an unidentified direct mail solicitation (a random mailing to any mailing list). In contrast, some service firms enjoy returns of 40% and even more for their direct mail renewal letters. When this type of sales effort is combined with a well-coordinated telephone follow-up to the customers who do not respond, the results can be spectacular. This combination of direct mail and telephone selling of renewals can be used in either sequence. There are advocates of the method that calls for a mailing first, followed by a telephone contact to the prospects who do not respond. Other managers, especially those whose direct mail response has been low, argue that the reverse sequence makes more sense. That is, telephone first and mail only to those prospects who cannot be reached by telephone. As one manager puts it: "If I'm only getting a 10% response to my letters, that means I have to go to the considerable expense of mailing to 100% of my prospects, and then follow up by telephoning 90% of them. Why not just telephone 100% and eliminate the cost of the mail program?"

As these examples would suggest, it is my feeling that the best sequence to use depends entirely on the results of the mailing program. An effective mail campaign that produces consistently high returns is probably the least expensive way to sell a service contract (except sales made at the time of the original merchandise sale). However, a direct mail effort producing returns of 10% or less should be overhauled or abandoned in favor of a phone-first program.

Direct Mail Programs

Generally speaking, the design of direct mail programs calls for professional help. Very few people are blessed with a natural talent for writing effective advertising copy, though most business persons seem to feel that they can do the job quite nicely. The fact is that copywriting and graphic design are very demanding skills that are best left to the experts.

Experiments over the years have proved that modifications of the most subtle kind in direct mail packages can produce startling changes in the rate of response. Changes in the color of the paper or envelopes used, slight changes in wording, the size or style of type, the number of colors, and even the day of the week that the package is received have all been proved to affect the rate of response to direct mail campaigns. In view of this, it isn't surprising to learn that many a potentially good mail-order idea has been scuttled on the basis of poor response to an ill-conceived and poorly executed sales package.

Of course, if yours is a small company venturing gingerly into the service contract market for the first time, you may be limited as to the amount of outside help that you can afford in the beginning. If you find it absolutely necessary to design and prepare your own mail program, you will want to boost your chances of success by observing the tried and proven fundamentals of successful direct mail selling.

Mr. Al Bernatavicius of the Philadelphia Electric Company has worked on a number of successful service contract sales letters. His advice to anyone facing the task is direct and simple: try to understand the concerns of your prospect and try to identify with those concerns. When you compose your letter, try to "talk" to the recipient in the same way that you would talk to her in person.

Mail-order expert Cecil C. Hoge, Sr., offers this advice: write in the style you usually write. Read your own letter carefully. Make sure it includes the points you want to get across. Be sure it has an introduction, body, and conclusion. Keep sentences and paragraphs short and to the point. Start with a very short paragraph to key interest. End the same way to hold your point. . . .

It's no coincidence that most direct mail experts voice similar philosophies. Despite the sophisticated nature of the world we live in today, people still respond most favorably to sales letters that are sincere and avoid the use of overblown superlatives. Simple, easy-to-understand language is a must. Because of this, my personal preference is for letters written in the first person. This "me-to-you" approach lends itself beautifully to the directness and simplicity characteristic of the most successful advertising in any medium.

Another point you will want to remember is the absolute need for high-quality printing and paper. If your budget restricts you to nothing but an inexpensive mimeographed sheet or offset reproduction of nonprofessional copy, then I urge you to abandon the program entirely and look for another way to generate your service contract sales.

Your direct mail piece is your personal salesperson, and it represents both you and your company. The use of cheap materials and unprofessional printing and design is one way to guarantee a disappointing direct mail effort and a waste of your money.

As an absolute minimum, you will want to include at least one insert with your sales letter. While this may be an overly simplified explanation, it is generally agreed that the brochure accompanying the sales letter should explain and describe the *product*. The sales letter should concentrate on *why* the prospect should buy your product. To save the expense of a separate reply coupon, you may want to print it on your brochure. Finally, don't forget a postage-prepaid business reply envelope. Your local printer or post office can explain how these work.

In total, then, a direct mailing should contain a minimum of three pieces: a sales letter, a descriptive brochure, and a business reply envelope. When you put it all together, you may want to remember the observation of one advertising expert who says: advertising must create a favorable attitude toward the product, arouse the intent to buy, and provide the motivation to buy.

That's a tall order, isn't it?

If it all seems a bit baffling, you may want to consider the advice of Mr. Hoge. He says that a complete education in direct mail techniques is yours for free if only you will study the pieces you receive in the mail almost every day. The techniques of some of the highest-paid experts in the world are there for you to analyze and study at your leisure. I would add just one thought to that very valuable advice. I suggest that you pay particular attention to any direct mail package that tempts you to buy. If it works on you, it will probably affect others the same way.

As a final thought, you may want to ponder the almost universal byword in the direct mail industry—test. With today's soaring prices of postage, printing, paper, and professional assistance, you surely don't want to invest a small fortune in any mail program until test mailings have established its value. To paraphrase an old chestnut, the three most important things in direct mail selling are test, test, and test.

WORDING THE CONTRACT

The exact wording of your service contract is extremely important, and it would be irresponsible of me not to strongly urge you to obtain the help of a good attorney in drawing up the form. Your service contract will be exactly that—a legal contract. And in such documents, what you do not say can be just as important as what you do say.

The laws regarding contracts in general are complex and often will defy logic as far as the layman is concerned. I believe that the best way for you to begin would be to obtain several samples of service contracts being used by companies in the same industry as your own. (A typical contract used by the RCA Service Company is shown in Figure 9.2.) Study them carefully and then decide what features and limitations you wish to incorporate into your own. Only then will you be in a position to explain to your legal representative what you want to say.

Here are some suggestions:

Keep it simple. Lawyers are not known for their fondness of simple language and uncomplicated syntax. For the purpose of both making it easy for your customers to understand your contract and demonstrating your forthrightness to consumer agencies, you should insist that the final language in the contract be kept as simple as possible while still fulfilling the necessary legal requirements.

Decide whether you will include preventive maintenance checks as part of the contract and, if so, whether such calls will be made automatically at *your* convenience or only at the specific request of the customer.

Decide which exclusions and disclaimers you want to include, and make certain that they are precisely spelled out. Most agreements exclude damage due to such things as willful neglect or misuse as well as fire, flood, or other "acts of God." There may be others that you want to specify such as maintenance that is normally the responsibility of the user.

Be careful here, though.

Keep It Simple

Many people are suspicious of painfully elaborate wording in contacts, and rightfully so. Too many of us have had to learn the hard way that often "what the large print giveth, the small print taketh away." Your contract will do you more harm than good if it creates such an impression.

If service is to be performed on the customer's premises only during normal working hours, the contract should contain that stipulation. If the customer will be required to bring the merchandise to your shop, this condition must be clearly stated.

Another important consideration for any contract is the cancellation provision. You will have to decide what your policy will be for contract buyers who decide to cancel before the contract has run its course. Requests for cancellation may be due to the customer's perception of your failure to live up to your responsibilities; or they may be due to less troublesome circumstances, such as the customer's moving away from your area or selling the merchandise covered by the contract.

Service Agreement

RCA Service Company
A Division Of RCA Corporation
Cherry Hill, New Jersey 08358

RCA

Codes For RCA Use Only

Please note that the terms of this agreement are contained on the application and both sides of this page. Please read them carefully.

Issued To:

Service Agreement Number

Retail Installment Contract Number

This agreement has been issued in conformance with the terms and conditions of the order submitted by you.

If this agreement specifies that servicings are to be available through service calls at your premises, your address as given above shall be considered the premises at which service will be provided unless a written agreement specifies a different location.

In consideration of the services performed or available hereunder, you agree to pay the amounts prescribed in your order and specified below. If this agreement has a Preferred Flat Rate (PFR) servicing provision, you also agree to pay the specified PFR charge as required by the Service Plan you selected.

Instrument Covered By This Service Agreement / **Coverage Period**

Description	Model Number	Number of Months	Starts Mo Day Yr	Ends Mo Day Yr

Servicing Specifications

Location Where Service Will Be Performed	Service Plan	Plan Number	Service Coupons	PFR Charge
Your Premises (We will make Service Calls) / Our Service Branch (You deliver and pick up)				

Cash Price

Service Agreement Gross Price	Allowances	Net Price	Non-Service Agreement Repairs	Taxes	Total Cash Price

Deferred Payment Plan

Cash Down Payment	Unpaid Balance Of Cash Price/ Amount Financed	**Finance Charge**	Installment Payments	Total of Installment Payments	Deferred Payment Price

RCA Service Company
A Division of RCA Corporation

R. J. Sokolowski
Division Vice President

Important: This Agreement Should Be Available For Inspection When You Require Service

For Services under this agreement, please contact our local Service Branch. Its address and telephone number are as follows:

If your address changes, please notify the above Service Branch immediately so we can make all necessary adjustments or transfers of your records as provided in Paragraph 7 on the reverse side hereof.

FIGURE 9.2. A typical service contract. *(Courtesy of RCA Service Company).*

In any case, I recommend that you allow your customers to cancel a contract at any time without the need for any explanation. Such a policy can be a powerful sales tool, and it adds mightily to your firm's credibility.

One popular cancellation provision stipulates a pro rata refund for the unused portion of the contract. With this arrangement, you will probably want to reserve the right to subtract the retail value of any service already performed under the contract from the amount of the refund due.

In general, I recommend that you establish liberal provisions in your wording that do not dwell unnecessarily on relatively minor exclusions. I have seen contracts that spell out each exclusion in such painful detail that the positive features of the included coverages were all but obscured. Ideally, the language of your contract will protect your firm from unreasonable demands or legal risks while providing a foundation of benefits that will attract the potential buyer.

The benefits of a successful service contract program are undeniable. I know a number of service managers who state flatly that their service organizations could not survive in their present form without the income and the peripheral benefits that come from the sale of contracts.

Nevertheless, anyone embarking on a service contract program should do so only with a clear knowledge of the legal and financial risks involved. With this in mind, you will want to get to know your accountant and your legal representative quite well before you sell your first contract. Your accountant can set up a record-keeping system that will keep track of the deferred obligation represented by the unexpired portion of all outstanding contracts. She can also help you by analyzing fulfillment costs and retail selling prices. Through all of this, your lawyer can provide counsel on important legal ramifications that must be considered before you begin selling contracts, not afterward.

Chapter 10
Selling Your Service

The telephone is a noble instrument, but it can be a very cruel master for service managers. When it rings on a regular basis, everything looks rosy; when it stops, many service managers can do little more than sit around wringing their hands waiting for business to pick up again. The trouble with that manner of doing busines, of course, is that expenses go on whether or not the telephone happens to be in a cooperative mood. As a professional service manager, you will want to break that dependency by developing programs designed to ensure a steady flow of income dollars into the business.

In this regard, there is a high statistical chance that you are sharing a handicap with a considerable number of your peers. A goodly portion of today's service executives have reached their positions of management responsibility by coming up through the service ranks. In following this path, it is very easy to get a superb education in the skills needed to run a *service organization* and a very poor education in the skills and insights necessary to run a *profitable business*.

I have known many service managers who could have risen easily from merely good to world-class status if only they had developed the financial instincts that are the mark of business champions. In a later chapter, we'll take a look at the broad range of considerations that go into the makeup of a successful service department from the business standpoint. In this chapter, we'll stick to ideas you can use to increase the income flowing into your business.

Let's talk first about the basic product offered for sale by your organization—repair service. It's not difficult to get an argument going among service managers as to whether or not it's possible to "merchandise" repair service. Those who argue that it is not, in my opinion, have missed the point entirely. It's true, of course, that advertising and sales promotion cannot create a need for the repairman, nor can they instill a desire for the product on the part of the prospective buyer. For these reasons, many of the traditional forms of advertising can be a complete waste of money for the typical service organization. But these facts simply serve to illustrate the need for a custom-tailored approach to the job of developing extra business for your service department.

THE FIRST STEP

Make no mistake about one thing: without any qualification whatever, the best form of advertising—the best way of all to build growth in any service organization—is customer satisfaction. On the surface, this chapter may not seem to be the place to be discussing that subject. In actual fact, a deliberate and consistent policy of guaranteed satisfaction fulfills all the requirements of a good advertising and sales promotion program.

To begin with, such a program, just like advertising, calls for a financial investment. A liberal policy of customer satisfaction will mean that you will frequently spend money and make allowances that are not mandated by ordinary legal or ethical constraints. And as with any good advertising, the money thus spent will eventually produce a net return for the company.

It is unfortunate that so many of today's businesspersons do not honestly understand the positive economic influence of a customer for whom a special effort has been made—or the devastating negative economic influence of a single customer who has been treated poorly. As I mentioned in chapter 1, a national survey of 100 major American corporations revealed that the average cost of acquiring a new customer was $118.16, while maintaining an existing customer cost only $19.76.

You get the idea. The first and most important building block in any program to increase your business and help it to grow is a policy designed to make certain that you do not lose even one customer unnecessarily. Every satisfied customer not only is the equivalent of a cash asset but also serves as a walking, no-cost advertisement. And word-of-mouth advertising is far more effective than any form you can buy on the open market.

Assuming that your management skills have resulted in a service organization that knows how to hang on to the customers it already has, we can now explore the possibilities of generating additional business. There are two: getting new customers and generating additional income from the customers you already have.

BRINGING IN NEW CUSTOMERS

Every business, no matter how superbly it may be managed, will lose a certain percentage of its customers each year. Approximately 20% of the American population moves each year; and of course, both the products to be serviced and the people who own them wear out and die at a regular rate. As a result, a certain number of new customers must be found just to keep you even. Growth of the business requires an even heavier influx of fresh blood. It is this requirement that is addressed by your advertising program.

Yellow Pages

One of the first decisions that every service manager must make is whether to use the Yellow Pages, and to what degree. There are some interesting opinions on the subject. While the overwhelming majority of service organizations will be found nestled comfortably in their local Yellow Pages, not every service manager is satisfied with the number of customers who "let their fingers do the walking."

Lately, too, there has been an increasing tide of criticism of the Yellow Pages by consumer groups and by industry associations. Consumer advocates in a number of cities are working with local telephone companies in an effort to screen out misleading ads. Unfortunately, many of the ads under fire represent the service industry.

One apparently widespread practice of unethical servicers is to take out a number of ads under different names, thus making it difficult for the customer to know the true identity of the firm with which he is doing business. The use of multiple phone numbers and "phantom" addresses is designed to attract customers who believe they are patronizing neighborhood firms.

Ma Bell and the company that handles the Yellow Pages have also been under fire for failing to screen ads that falsely imply technicians have received special training for certain brands of appliances, and for printing ads that make unauthorized use of company logos.

Consumer groups, however, aren't the only critics of the ubiquitous Yellow Pages. Industry trade organizations, such as the Oregon Professional Electronics Association (OPEA), have also had their say. OPEA representatives have challenged the claims of local Yellow Pages officials concerning the effectiveness of the Yellow Pages in attracting new customers. OPEA is conducting its own continuing survey to help resolve the question for its members.

In Denver, Colorado, a decision by Yellow Pages officials to allow half-page ads has some service organizations fuming. The previous policy of limiting ads to quarter-page size, say the critics, kept a reasonable lid on Yellow Pages advertising costs. Now the competition to maintain a dominant position will cost a great deal more money, they feel. The owner of one appliance service company in Denver called the half-page ads "nothing more than a rip-off by the phone company." Other firms called them "profit stealers" and "nowhere near as useful as word-of-mouth advertising." Similar Yellow Pages controversies are in evidence in other parts of the country.

But like it or not, the Yellow Pages are going to be around for a long time. As one appliance service dealer says, "Yellow Pages are the most important advertising I do. I use all of the space I can get." If your competitors are taking out ads in the Yellow Pages the chances are that you'll want to be right in there with them.

Harry Raker of the Raker Corporation, an appliance service firm near Baltimore, Maryland, expresses a different view toward Yellow Pages advertising. He uses no display advertising at all—only bold-faced listings under all of the categories serviced by his firm. He says, "I believe that it is necessary to be listed in the Yellow Pages so that your own customers can find you. If they don't see you in there, some customers might feel that yours is a fly-by-night type of operation."

Regardless of conflicting opinions such as these, the odds are that you will decide to make an appearance of some sort in the Yellow Pages. If you do, here are a few thoughts that will help you prepare your ads.

If you decide that display ads are right for you, don't automatically assume that the largest available ad will bring you the largest possible return. Display space in the Yellow Pages is an expensive form of advertising, and you must contract for it a full year in advance. Because of this, you will want to make certain that the space you sign for is sufficient to do the job, and no more.

Realistically, if your book already carries a number of quarter-page or half-page ads under the same classifications in which you will appear, a tiny ad may be lost in the crowd. You'll have to make a judgment call in such cases.

When preparing your ad, be sure to identify the needs of your potential customers. Who are the prospects? What are they looking for? What are the reasons that they should come to you for service instead of your competitors? Select those aspects of your organization that meet the needs of most customers and feature them in your text.

Don't Mislead

Be sure to avoid exaggerated claims in your copy. Superlatives that do not accurately describe your firm may eventually damage your reputation and cost you valuable customers.

I also urge you to resist the temptation to invent such brilliant names as AAAAA Service Company or Aardvark TV in order to obtain first-place listings. This practice, along with the use of multiple names, not only is a hopelessly transparent ploy of questionable effectiveness but, in the eyes of many people, will mark your firm as a good one to avoid.

You might, in fact, find yourself in a fix similar to that of Dr. Nathan Feigelman, a dentist in Newport, Rhode Island. The very first dentist listed in the Newport Yellow Pages was Dr. Aaron A. Aaron, supposedly a partner of Dr. Feigelman's. However, the directory was the only evidence that Dr. Aaron ever existed. Dr. Feigelman denied any wrongdoing, but the Rhode Island Board of Examiners in Dentistry was unmoved. The board voted to suspend Dr. Feigelman's license until he changed his phone number and disassociated himself from the elusive Dr. Aaron. At the time of this writing, Dr. Feigelman has appealed the decision, leaving the matter unresolved.

As for your ad, try to make it stand out. Your copy should be clear, brief, and to the point; yet it should contain all the necessary facts. Make use of open space and type that is readable and aesthetically pleasing. Your local Yellow Pages representative can be a big help in preparing copy and designing your layout.

Make sure that your ad is under the right category. Try to anticipate where a potential customer will look for the type of service that you offer, and make sure that your ad is there. You may find that you should be represented under more than one heading.

If there are brand names or well-known company names associated with your organization, be sure to feature them. But make certain that you have obtained the necessary approvals lest you find yourself the featured attraction in a lawsuit.

As for results, don't guess. Follow the lead of OPEA and take your own survey. The only way you can be certain whether or not your Yellow Pages advertising is bringing in a sufficient number of new customers is by keeping your own records. One service-firm owner told me that he had a special telephone number exclusively for use in his Yellow Pages ads. That made it easy to keep track of all calls resulting directly from the ads. The results, by the way, were so poor that he discontinued his display ads.

Bear in mind, however, that despite experiences such as that one, the almost universal use of the Yellow Pages by the service industry indicates that a good many people are sold on their effectiveness.

OTHER FORMS OF ADVERTISING

Because of the wide range of types and sizes of service organizations, it is virtually impossible to generalize on the effectiveness of the standard advertising media. While a huge international supplier of office copiers, let's say, might well be able to justify a full-page advertisement in the *Wall Street Journal* extolling the virtues of its service division, a local appliance repair company may find that even a small ad in the local newspaper will not produce enough business to justify the expense. As with Yellow Pages advertising, the *only* certain answer to the question of whether a specific form of advertising is cost-effective for your firm depends on careful testing and the keeping of accurate records.

While large metropolitan newspapers do not seem to be a viable medium for use by smaller service firms, many service managers report excellent results from ads placed in local weeklies. This form of advertising is relatively inexpensive and is automatically targeted to the advertiser's service area. Also, a weekly paper has a longer life span before it's discarded, thus increasing the probable exposures for your ad.

Direct Mail

In Chapter 9 the use of direct mail in the sale of service contracts was discussed. New customers can also be developed through the use of direct mail, but the job must be done in a professional manner.

Uncle Sam's mail service offers some unique advantages to the advertiser. For one thing, it permits focusing on a specific group of prospects—residents of a given city or neighborhood, for example. It also allows the exercise of considerable latitude in the configuration and treatment of the advertising message.

RAKER CORPORATION
The Appliance Professionals
10635 York Road • Cockeysville, Md. 21030

Attached is an unbelievable coupon. We are giving you — completely FREE — an $18.00 service call. Any additional work will be completely up to you. We hope the coupon will encourage you to call us and we can demonstrate our appliance service ability. In the future we want you to join the many customers that already use us year after year.

No doubt our yellow service trucks are a familar sight in your neighborhood. Our growth has been steady for years as more and more people have found what we offer:

1. Very efficient appliance service at fair prices.
2. Service on **all** major appliances.
3. 100% guarantee on all work.

Our secretary in the Cockeysville office can answer questions or give you up to the minute truck scheduling. Each radio-dispatched truck is well stocked enabling us to complete most repairs immediately. For replacement equipment we have fast delivery on Maytag appliances.

We go to great lengths to satisfy and keep our customers. I'm sure that if you use the coupon and try us you will join your neighbors in becoming another one of our regular customers.

Very truly yours,

Harry D. Raker

FREE SERVICE CALL

$18.00 VALUE

RAKER - *The Appliance Professionals* - 666-8030

Limit one to a customer - covering one appliance   Expires 6/30/79

FIGURE 10.1. One example of a consistently successful direct mail promotion letter. *(Courtesy of the Raker Corporation).*

The direct mail letter and coupon shown in Figure 10.1 consistently produces a return of about 2% in an unidentified mailing. This develops new customers at a cost of about $20 each, which includes the cost of the printing and postage as well as the cost value of the free service provided. Remembering the statistics quoted earlier, I would call that a bargain price for a new customer.

Another form of direct mail used by some service organizations is the referral letter. In one form of this effort, existing customers are given a coupon which, when redeemed by a new customer, entitles the new customer to a discount and the customer who made the referral to a special gift or rebate. Reports from several service managers using variations of this program were mixed. As with any other type of advertising program, limited tests and carefully kept records are the best way to determine effectiveness.

NEW BUSINESS FROM OLD CUSTOMERS

I mentioned earlier that service advertising cannot create the need, or even the desire, to purchase the product. There is one important exception to that statement: preventive maintenance.

With certain types of products—industrial machinery, for example—preventive maintenance (PM) is such a firmly established concept that it no longer needs to be "sold." Any product that causes a serious financial loss when it is inoperative will probably be given the best preventive "medicine" available without the need for much prodding by the service company.

On the other hand, products that cause only inconvenience when they malfunction can present a lively market for PM, but the idea must be sold to a sometimes skeptical owner. Home appliances, automobiles, office equipment, medical and diagnostic equipment, and all sorts of production machinery are excellent targets for PM advertising. If they are to be convincing, however, your PM advertising and promotions must clearly identify the reasons why an owner should spend money to service a product that is operating satisfactorily.

Be advised that this can prove to be a most difficult assignment for some products—relatively inexpensive home appliances, for example. Although I have seen a number of successful PM promotions aimed at color television receivers and home heating/cooling equipment, I know of no similar successes with campaigns aimed at radios, record players, and the like.

As the price tag on the product goes up, selling the idea of PM becomes easier. In any case, promoting the idea of PM is best limited to your present customer list. It isn't likely that you will find much success in selling the idea of a PM checkup to people who are strangers to your firm.

The basic idea behind the PM checkup must be stressed in your advertising. (See Chapter 15 for some sample letters.) For the most part, you will want to concentrate on these two themes:

1. A PM checkup now may eliminate or minimize costly downtime in the future.

2. Pay a small amount for a PM checkup now to avoid inconvenience or larger repair bills in the future.

Depending on the product involved, you will want to focus on either one or both of these two points. And don't forget, a great big reason (in addition to increased income) that you should consider promoting PM work is that it helps to even out the workload. Concentrated PM promotions during your slow season can help keep your technicians busy and thus improve year-round efficiency and productivity.

By the way, your technicians, if properly trained and motivated, can be developed into an excellent source of additional PM business. The technician called out to repair a customer's automatic clothes washer can provide some sound reasons for doing a PM check on the dryer at the same time. An office copier or window air conditioner needing service in an office building will often mean that others in the same building are prime candidates for PM treatment. Most customers view technicians as experts and tend to respond to their recommendations. This is a fact that neither you nor your technicians should overlook. An added advantage to both you and the customer is that a technician already on the scene means a lower price to the customer and a higher profit margin to you.

Another quite obvious but often overlooked form of advertising designed for existing customers is the simple, self-adhesive sticker. These dandy little advertising gems are available in a virtual plethora of materials, sizes, designs, and price ranges. They are intended, of course, to remind your customers of who you are and how they can reach you. Your technicians should be trained to attach a sticker to every product serviced and to say that it's been placed there for the customer's convenience. One firm that supplies these stickers is NEBS, Townsend, Massachusetts, 02746, whose catalog is free.

YOUR IMAGE

In this real world that we live in, it is not facts that influence us as much as our perceptions of facts. Translation: it makes no difference how professional your service organization may be; what matters is how professional your customers perceive it to be. For this reason, an important part of your program to sell your service should be a conscious effort to upgrade the appearance of those parts of your operation that can be seen by your customers.

Let's begin with your technicians or mechanics. Do they look professional? Countless surveys have clearly shown that customers tend to link appearance with the perception of professionalism.

That's not hard to understand, is it? Can you imagine how unsettling it would be if you were to board a commercial airliner only to be met by a captain who was bleary-eyed, badly in need of a shave, and wearing a uniform that looked as though it had been slept in?

On a similar but less dramatic level, I'm sure that you would not welcome into your home or office a technician who was dressed in grimy, ill-fitting clothes and carrying a sloppy assortment of tools in a burlap bag. While it's not likely that your technicians present such an extreme assault on the senses, it is possible that a sharpening of your standards for neatness and grooming could improve the overall perception of your service operation.

In this regard, you may want to consider the value of having your technicians outfitted in appropriate uniforms. Why it should be so, I can't tell you; but I can assure you that a technician in a crisp, neat uniform is automatically afforded an extra notch or two of professional status in the eyes of the average customer. If you decide to put your technicians in uniform, you will want to check with the proper agency in your state with regard to the laws on the subject. In most states, if the employer mandates the use of uniforms, all or part of the cost must be borne by the employer. In at least one state that I know of (New York), state law further requires that the employer bear the expense of laundry and maintenance. Despite these added costs, many of the most highly regarded service organizations in the industry consider uniforms to be an indispensable part of their image.

And what about the trucks that represent you? Are they dirty, dented, and afflicted with fading or chipped paint? If so, you would do well to have your name removed from them at once. Your trucks are the most highly visible part of your service image. As such, the money spent to keep them "squeaky clean" and sharp looking will prove to be one of your most astute investments. One estimate places the number of customer impressions from trucks working in a metropolitan area at one million per truck per year. If you want a good example of this philosophy in action, I refer you to United Parcel Service. Have you ever seen a dirty or damaged UPS truck on your neighborhood streets?

If your service operation is of the type that is visited by your customers, please don't neglect that prize opportunity to enhance the public perception of your organization. It is appalling to me that more service managers do not seem to grasp the dramatic impact of a service shop which doesn't look like the stereotype that most customers have come to expect.

Yes, when it comes to impressing your customers, neatness counts. And impressing your customers is the best way of all to sell your service.

Chapter 11
Controlling Expenses

There is a story about a gentleman whose wife lost her credit card. "I'm not reporting it to anybody," he said. "Whoever found it is spending less money than she did." Now I can't vouch for the accuracy of that story, but the subject itself couldn't be more timely.

Regardless of its type or size, every business incurs expenses from the moment of its birth until the day its doors are closed forever. How those expenses are managed will help to determine how much time separates those two dates.

Later on, in Chapter 13, we'll be discussing control of expenses that are common to all businesses. Here, we'll concentrate on those costs that are either unique to or have a special influence on service organizations.

TECHNICAL PAYROLL

A service department, by definition, is a labor-intensive business. In a very real sense, a service manager is in the business of buying and selling skilled labor. Since the cost of that labor is the largest single expense in a service organization, it should be the object of your most intensive management efforts.

In the final analysis, there are only two basic factors that determine what your costs for technical payroll will be: the rate of wages you pay and the amount of satisfactorily completed work performed by your technicians.

The first of those items is basically a noncontrollable expense. Assuming that you are paying competitive wage rates in order to attract and hold high-caliber technicians, there is little you will be able to do to affect them.

It is in the amount and quality of the work performed by your technicians that your expense control skills will receive their severest test. Technical productivity, more than any other operating variable, will help shape the total cost structure in your service department. Every minute spent by your technicians in activities other than repairing merchandise is suspect. The higher the ratio of nonproductive to productive time, the higher will be your total expense ratio.

It is because of the heavy influence of technical productivity on economic results that I have devoted three separate chapters to various facets of this subject. In your review of technical productivity as it relates to expense control, I suggest that you invest enough time for a thorough review of Chapters 4, 5, and 6. Together, they constitute a broad look at the techniques that can work toward keeping your technical payroll under professional control.

OTHER PAYROLL

Not to hurt anyone's feelings, but the fact is that your technicians or mechanics are the movers and shakers in your service organization. Like the salespersons in a retail store, they are the only ones who can ring the cash register. All other employees (the service manager included) are supporting personnel. It is their job to do those tasks that will allow the technical people to spend all or most of their time repairing things.

That's obvious, of course, but what is not quite so apparent is the answer to the question of how many and what type of supporting people are absolutely necessary for optimum performance. The decision is a crucial one.

The whole question of supporting, or behind-the-scenes, personnel is fraught with danger for the unsuspecting service manager. Most of us have read about the gaggle of people who are involved in the production of TV shows and movies. For every person who appears on the screen, there are five, or ten, or fifteen who work behind the scenes. If you're like me, the only thing you know about show business is what you read. We, then, can only assume that all those people are absolutely necessary for the show to go on.

The trouble is that there are very few businesses that require more people behind the curtain than on the stage, and service is not one of them—or it shouldn't be. In actual fact, though, it isn't at all unusual to see a service organization that employs more clerks, parts handlers, typists, supervisory personnel, and telephone operators than technicians. I hope this never happens in your service department.

This danger is least in small operations. For obvious reasons, it is unlikely that a service operation employing three technicians is going to have four or five supporting people. As the organization grows, though, the rationalization for adding people grows right along with it. Once a service department reaches ten, or twenty, or forty technicians, the specter of empire building will be an unrelenting threat to the service manager's efforts to keep a rein on expenses.

Because the structure of a service organization will vary widely depending on its size and the specific industry in which it is involved, there are no neat formulas or even guidelines to tell the service manager exactly how many supporting people are needed to get the job done. In other words, it's up to you to cast a gimlet eye on every man-hour of payroll spent on nontechnical activities. What this means, of course, is that you must take a step or two backward and make an objective analysis of every single facet of your operating procedures. Never mind that you designed them yourself and that everyone always looks busy. Remember Parkinson's law? As long as there are people around, the available work will conveniently expand just enough to keep them all busy.

How about your files? Do they contain papers that you will probably never need? Filing costs money, and so do the papers that are being filed. How about your parts inventory? Is there duplicated effort in your record keeping? Is every person cross-trained to do all the nontechnical jobs in the office? These and hundreds of others are the types of questions that must constantly be asked by today's service manager. Because payroll, both technical and supporting, makes up the largest piece of the expense pie in a service department, any system or procedure that interferes with the efficient use of any employee's time must become the target of your vengeful wrath.

SUPPLIES

There are a number of ways in which a service organization can view the problem of expendable supplies.

One way is to take a cavalier approach to the whole subject. A "technicians need supplies and they won't use any more than they need so why bother to keep track" sort of philosophy is one that I frequently see in practice, especially in smaller service operations. In my view, such an approach to business not only is intolerably wasteful but also displays a dangerous lack of understanding of the human equation.

Forgetting for the moment any questions of employee honesty, consider only the well-known and easily demonstrable fact that the lack of discipline in a business structure will inevitably be reflected in the conduct of the individual employees.

Set a Good Example

If management, through its actions, implicitly suggests that the expenses involved in the purchase of tools, supplies, or equipment are not worthy of careful scrutiny and security measures, then it can be expected that the employees will come to regard these expenses with a conspicuous lack of respect. From there, it follows that careless disregard and waste will become the rule and not the exception.

I hope that you will not interpret my comments here to mean I am suggesting that you establish a police-state sort of atmosphere which would subject your employees to the indignity of having to account for each paper clip or dab of soldering paste. Such an extreme approach would be at least as damaging as no control at all. What I am recommending to you is a professional approach to the very real management problem of imposing reasonable controls on expenses.

For example, does your accounting system allow for separate entries for the cost of expendable supplies, and a means for reconciling your stocks on a periodic basis? If not, your accountant can easily make the necessary provisions.

Be advised, though, that paper control is, at best, only half the job. Physical control of supply materials is no less important than is control of your regular inventory of repair parts. I have seen many service organizations with remarkably thorough systems of control over parts inventories, and no control whatever over the use of expendable supplies.

In one refrigeration service company I visited recently, I found an open storeroom for supplies that included a shelf full of silver solder at a time when a 1-pound roll of the stuff was selling for about $75. The techs were simply allowed to help themselves whenever they were in need. Later that same day, the service manager loudly bemoaned the fact that *inflation* was causing his expenses to rise at a staggering rate.

Fortunately, few service managers are likely to be quite that naive. However, it is not at all unusual to find an accounting system that provides for scrupulous record keeping and protection for capital equipment, such as test equipment and electric tools, while completely ignoring expendable supplies. This in spite of the fact that the full annual depreciation of tools and equipment in many service organizations is less than the amount spent for the purchase of supplies in a year.

Naturally, the size of your operation will be the principal factor in determining the type and extent of control appropriate for your supply inventory. There is one simple system, though, that can be incorporated into any service department, regardless of size, type, or configuration. All that is necessary is that each supply item be assigned an identification or stock number, placed in your parts department (or other secure area), and disbursed in the same manner as any repair part. A simple record should be kept of each disbursement so that unusual usage can be detected.

This idea won't work, of course, if your parts inventory is located in a nonsecured area with uncontrolled access by all technicians or mechanics. In that case, though, control of your supply expenses will be the least of your worries.

Paper and Printing

One inescapable expense in every service organization worthy of the name is the cost of the repair or work order itself. Since at least one work order must be created for every repair job, this is a permanent expense that will grow in direct proportion to your workload.

While an attractive work order is a definite plus, it can become a burdensome expense if discretion is not exercised in its design. Of primary concern is the number of copies. In case you haven't checked lately, multicopy, self-carbon forms can be outrageously expensive.

How many copies of the work order do you really need?

One for the customer's receipt; one for your accountant or accounting department; one for your permanent customer file—that's three copies. Perhaps the nature of your company's operations is such that you require more, but I suggest that you review the need carefully before you accept that decision. Isn't it possible that one copy could be made to do double duty?

Before you answer, you will want to remember that many well-managed service organizations make out quite nicely with a work order consisting of the original and one copy for the customer's receipt. In the case of in-warranty work, the receipt copy is used to support claims. In those exceptional cases where additional copies may be needed, the copying machine is put to work.

One of the curses of modern business is the so-called paperwork explosion. Shouldn't you take steps to make certain that your service department doesn't get added to the list of victims?

By the way, are your work orders serially numbered? If not, I hope that you will make the necessary arrangements for your next order from the printers. Loosely controlled, blank work orders are an unacceptable risk for a professional service manager. When your orders are numbered, it is easy to implement operating procedures requiring that every service order be accounted for—*every* service order, no exceptions.

Remember, too, that all other forms of printed supplies are expensive, and rapidly becoming more so. Not-home tags, shop tags, and any other items that are custom-printed should be carefully controlled to make certain that they aren't winding up as bookmarks or scrap paper.

THE TELEPHONE

As I observed earlier, Ma Bell's invention can be an invaluable friend to a service manager—it can also be an unnecessary and persistent drain on your profits. In theory, your friendly telephone company can be depended upon to advise you conscientiously on any number of ways in which you may reduce the cost of your phone service while improving efficiency.

Don't you believe it.

This is not to suggest that Ma Bell's children would engage in any form of deliberate deception. It is simply a recognition of the cold reality that most of the telephone company representatives with whom you will come into contact are paid to sell (or at least help to sell) telephone service and equipment. Despite their best intentions, such an arrangement is not likely to result in dedicated efforts to find ways to lower your telephone bill.

None of this should be taken to mean that you should ignore telephone company recommendations—quite to the contrary. There is a whole world of technology out there today that can make your telephone system—even if yours is a small operation—a powerful ally in the efficient operation of your business. Obviously, you won't be able to benefit from features available to you if you aren't told about them. Realistically, though, you must keep your relationship with your telephone company reps in its proper perspective. While you may be given valuable advice on how a telephone with push buttons can improve the efficiency in your office, you cannot expect that your benefactor will dwell on the fact that each and every button on each and every instrument will result in an increase in your bill each and every month.

As is the case in most situations of this kind, the more firsthand knowledge you have in your possession, the more likely you are to reach the best decision. While you will probably never become an expert in telephone communications, chances are that you can benefit from a bit of fundamental knowledge and a few suggestions. Don't hesitate to ask you local telephone company for their recommendations concerning your telephone needs. They employ trained experts who can tell you about innovations that you may have never even heard of, and some of them may well prove to be valuable assets for your service operation.

However, as one major telephone user told me, after the recommendations have been made, be sure to ask the representative three important questions:

1. Exactly how will the proposed changes benefit my business?
2. What other alternatives are there for accomplishing the same objectives?
3. How much will the change add to my cost for telephone service?

At this point, it's up to you to listen carefully; take nothing for granted; use the in-depth knowledge of your own business that only you can bring to the matter; and make the final decision for yourself.

Among the developments that may or may not be cost-effective for you are such things as:

- Foreign exchange lines that permit customers living outside your immediate calling area to call you, or you to call them, for a flat monthly fee
- Wide area telephone service (WATS), otherwise known as 800 or toll-free service, that allows free incoming calls from a wider area up to and including the entire United States
- Intercom systems that utilize your telephones
- Automatic call directors that replace older switchboard-type systems
- Automatic monitoring devices that count incoming calls or busy signals and play recorded music or announcements for customers who must wait

- Touchtone service, available in most urban areas, that allows numbers to be "dialed" much more quickly than the standard dial system. If your people place a lot of outgoing calls, the extra expense may be worthwhile.

Among the free services offered by most telephone companies is training for your people who use the telephone as part of their jobs. It's good. Take advantage of it.

By the way, if you are starting a new business or opening up a new branch, you don't have to settle for the first telephone number offered to you. It is generally recognized that a "good" telephone number (that is, one easy to remember) is an asset to a service-type business. While such considerations as the size of your company and how long the exchange in your area has been around will affect the availability of such goodies as 123-4567 or 555-5000, go to the boss, if necessary, to see what numbers are available.

The Equipment Audit

If your service operation is large enough to require a number of different instruments or push buttons, or any of the special features or hardware offered by your phone company, you should become familiar with the equipment audit—it may save you money.

Every phone company has thousands of pieces of equipment and a staggering assortment of services to keep track of. Despite the companies' best efforts, errors are unavoidable. One of the most common is billing for equipment that has been removed or never installed in the first place. For a large telephone user, errors of this kind can be very costly.

At your request, your local Bell company will perform an audit of the equipment on your premises and compare the results with your current billing. Normally, the company can be depended on to do this job quite conscientiously. If errors are made in the company's favor, a credit will be issued to you. A branch manager for a large service dealer once told me that an audit of this type resulted in a retroactive credit of $6,000 for his operation. You don't have to be a large telephone user in order to benefit, although the larger and more complex your phone system, the more likely that errors will turn up. In any case, ask your phone company for an equipment and service inventory on a periodic basis. It's good insurance, and you can't beat the price.

As a final thought, you may want to remember that it is no longer mandatory that you use Bell System equipment exclusively in your phone system. The long-standing monopoly enjoyed by the Bell companies has been declared invalid. This has resulted in a host of alternative equipment and systems being made available by many different manufacturers and specialists in communications. While considerable savings may result for some users, it is best to shop and investigate carefully before you buy or sign a contract to lease. Despite her faults, Ma Bell turns out a reliable product and, in most areas, service is top-notch.

ENERGY

While every service business consumes energy in its various forms, most service managers are especially dependent on gasoline to power their service vehicles—and gasoline, as you are so painfully aware, is a mighty expensive commodity these days. If your service organization does not require motor vehicles for running outside service calls, chalk up one point for your good luck. If you do operate your own cars or trucks, the cost of gasoline deserves your most careful scrutiny.

If your fleet is larger than eight or ten vehicles, you may want to consider having your own pump and underground tank installed in order to benefit from the so-called tank-wagon prices enjoyed by big users. It may surprise you to learn that in the good old days, before the 1973–1974 oil embargo, your friendly local gasoline wholesaler would have been happy to install pumps and tanks at his expense, just to get you to buy your gasoline from him (sob!). Today, if you want the job done, you'll have to pick up the whole tab yourself, and it's no small expense.

The smallest-capacity tank suitable for this purpose runs about 1000 gallons. However, in order to qualify for true wholesale prices, you'll need to be able to accept delivery in full-tanker load quantities, and the average tanker you see making deliveries around town holds about 8000 gallons. That means you'll need a 10,000-gallon tank (and a hefty cash flow) in order to qualify for those tidy little discounts given to commercial service stations. If your fleet is large enough, however, and you feel that a wholesale arrangement may be possible, you may want to ask a couple of dealers for quotes. Once you have the prices in hand, you can have your accountant figure out the yes or the no of the economics. If you do, be sure to remind old Scrooge of the comfort that would come from having your own allocation of the stuff.

There is, of course, an endless parade of expenses that demand attention from every service manager. In this regard, every facet of your business must come under scrutiny, right down to the last paper clip. Given today's tax structure, the easiest way to increase profits by $1 is to spend $1 less.

Chapter 12
You and Your Customer

WHAT IS A SERVICE MANAGER? WHAT DOES HE DO?

The answers to those questions, of course, will depend on whom you ask, and when. You can be sure, though, that no matter where or when you ask the questions, the answers will be widely dissimilar, influenced heavily by the personal experiences of those who were asked. And you can bet that the answers given today will be vastly different from those you would have heard 25 or 30 years ago. Today's service manager is perceived a lot differently than was his predecessor prior to the post-World War II technological boom.

It was only natural, I suppose, that few people were willing to accord professional status to service managers while the industry itself was still in its awkward, formative stages. Gradually, though, as the demands placed on service personnel became more stringent, it followed naturally that the management of the service activity grew into a more exacting discipline. Then still another dimension was added. Consumerism, as we have come to call it, introduced an element that demanded even more skill if the delicate relationship between the consumer and the supplier was to be kept in balance.

These forces working together in a sort of synergisitc way have helped to shape service as both an industry and a profession. The trouble is that all this moth-to-butterfly evolution has produced a lot of overblown descriptions of what we do in our jobs as service managers. Recently, for example, I read the following description in a trade journal: "A service department must be conducted like a fine orchestra. Every person does his thing in harmony with others in such a fashion that it is pleasing to the listener, for this is the purpose of the music."

Beautiful isn't it?

My first reaction was unabashed admiration for the writer: such graceful prose—almost poetry. I wished that I were able to write with that sort of majesty. But then, after the glow wore off, I realized that the whole thing was just an exercise in semantics. It doesn't say anything. Like gossamer wings and Chantilly lace, it's mostly form with very little substance. What does it mean? What does it have to do with how a service manager does his work? Couldn't the metaphor apply equally well to a football team? A building construction crew? A communal love-in?

Frankly, I believe that our profession is better served when we stick to a straightforward description of the tough, two-sided job responsibility that is the lot of every service manager today: first, we must satisfy the customer. Second, we must exercise all the usual management skills required to run a profitable business.

Let me note here that I am quite aware that even the casual browser could hardly fail to note that the greater portion of this book is devoted to the blatantly mercenary task of turning a profit. In the interest of effective communication, let me hasten to explain that this should not be taken to mean that I view the fiscal responsibility as more important than the ability to satisfy customers.

Perish the thought!

IT'S THE CUSTOMER WHO COUNTS

The wide diversity of topics that make up the business side of things requires what might appear to be a disproportionate use of space. The truth is—and this might well be the most important point within these pages—that the very foundation of the service industry rests on the premise that customer satisfaction is the ultimate objective. Without it, there is no service profession. Unfortunately, not all our associates have a clear understanding of that simple philosophy. As a result, there is something less than universal admiration for our efforts out there in that harsh world. And not without cause.

It can be discouraging for someone dedicated to professionalism in our industry to observe the way customers are sometimes treated by service personnel. I'm sure that you have seen, as I have, employees of companies, large and small, behaving in an incredible fashion when confronted by an indignant customer.

It's easy to blame the employee under these circumstances—to assume that he or she simply doesn't care. My own experience has convinced me that this is usually not the case. A poor understanding of the principles of good customer relations can usually be traced directly to management's failure to set appropriate standards and to follow through with adequate training. Most of us who must work for a living instinctively learn to respond to the boss. When we find out what our employer expects from us, we learn how to deliver.

Consider the case of young John Wanamaker. A devoutly religious man, Wanamaker opened his now-famous department store in Philadelphia in 1851—10 years before the outbreak of the Civil War. From the first, Wanamaker made it clear that customer satisfaction was to be the hallmark of his organization. He communicated this premise not only to his potential customers but to his employees as well. In a period in our history when caveat emptor ("let the buyer beware") was the byword of the day, many of Wanamaker's contemporaries declared that he must surely be mad. The store, they predicted, would perish under the weight of such a philosophy. Customers would take advantage of the firm, and Mr. Wanamaker would lose everything. There's no need to recount history here. We all know the success of Mr. Wanamaker and others who established customer satisfaction as the cornerstone of their businesses. As simple as that premise is, though, it is unsettling to see the number of people in business today who appear not to understand the principle involved: then, as now, the way to make a business successful is to see to it that its customers are satisfied.

There you have it. The service manager, as well as the entire service organization, owes his existence to the necessity of satisfying customers. It's as simple and as complex as that.

That was a rather long introduction to arrive at an obvious conclusion, but you might be surprised at how many of our associates do not yet have a firm grasp of that fundamental principle of our profession. A doctor's job is to minister to patients; a house painter must paint houses; a writer must write; and a service manager must satisfy unhappy customers.

There are, of course, many levels of responsibility within which a service manager must function. Direct customer contact may seldom, if ever, be a part of the life of the service manager responsible for an organization of hundreds or thousands of employees. At the other end of the scale are front-line managers who must deal with unhappy customers may times every day. Most service managers will find their own direct customer-contact activity falling somewhere between these two extremes.

It is important to understand, I believe, that it makes not one whit of difference whether a service manager works directly with customers every hour of the day or functions only as an administrator over others who do. The foundation of his responsibility remains the same—to see to it that the people who do business with his firm are satisfied. That is, after all, why he was given the job.

Perhaps all of this smacks of laboring the point. I hope not. But if it does, I plead not guilty on the basis of the number of service managers I have known who do not have a clearly defined idea of what they are supposed to be doing—or what they should be teaching their employees. Let's talk about some of these things.

WHO'S LISTENING?

I once heard a friend of mine observe, "The trouble with the world today is that everybody is talking and nobody is listening." I got to thinking about that later, and I had to admit that there's a lot of evidence to support my friend's theory. You may have noticed, as I have, that there are precious few good listeners around these days. Most of us can't wait for the other person to finish talking so that we can explain the facts as they really are.

Research has shown that we spend, on the average, about half our waking hours listening. Yet we retain only about 25% of what we hear. That's not too surprising when you reflect on the fact that there is no attempt during any part of our school years to teach us how to listen.

Being unable to find someone willing to listen is frustrating enough in our personal lives, and it is absolutely intolerable when we are paying customers trying to communicate with people whose jobs we are supporting.

I am well aware that my plaintive comments here are not going to bring about the slightest improvement in this universal state of affairs. However, if I can convince *you* to brush up on your listening skills, I will have made a positive contribution to your development as a professional service manager—and will have made life a great deal easier for you in dealing with customers.

Customers Want to Be Heard

The simple fact of the matter is that an outrageous amount of customer alienation is due directly to the fact that *no one was willing to listen.* Recently, a major executive in the service industry told me that his professional skills were multiplied manyfold (and his career enhanced) when the value of just listening to what customers had to say finally dawned on him. "I could not begin to estimate the number of customer problems I have been able to 'resolve' just by offering the customer a chance to talk while someone listened," he told me. "Once I made that remarkable discovery, facing tough customers was no longer an experience to be dreaded."

All this may sound too neat and comfortable to be true—one of those convenient little aphorisms that is taught in classrooms but has no application in the real world. I can assure you that such is not the case. Here is a suggestion: the next time you have to deal with a customer who has a problem, either on the telephone or in person, say that you'd like to help and ask the customer to please tell you all about it.

Then, just sit back and listen.

- Do not interrupt.
- Do not attempt to set the facts straight.
- When the customer pauses for breath, do not take over. In fact, leave the burden to keep the conversation going entirely on the customer.
- As the time between pauses grows longer, do not lose your resolve. Make certain that the customer is completly "talked out" before you say a word.

The Value of Silence

There is sound psychological reasoning for not rushing into the breach when the customer pauses. Silence can be unnerving, especially for the person who has been invited to make his point. By refusing to "help out" during those pregnant pauses, you will be maintaining control over the conversation while actively demonstrating your interest in hearing everything the customer has to say.

If you will resolutely adopt this listening technique, you will find some pleasant things happening. To begin with, most customers will instantly become easier to deal with. Nothing more than an opportunity to release frustration on someone who displays a willingness to listen will often turn a tiger into a pussycat. This approach can be counted on to soothe the savage breast even more effectively than a Montovani record or a double martini.

But the benefits have only begun. Once all the customer's hostilities have been vented, it's time for you to speak. What you say at that precise moment will be crucial to the outcome of your adventure. I have but one recommendation:

"What would you like us to do?"

If that sounds like an invitation to disaster—an opening for an outrageous demand—relax. It doesn't work that way. Far more often than you are likely to imagine, the customer who is all talked out will ask for something less than you would have offered. If you've done your listening job well, the customer has been emotionally drained by the talking experience. Since you have shown no hostility and have, in fact, lent a sympathetic ear to the problem, there is no reason for the customer to place you in a difficult position, and most will go out of their way to avoid doing so.

Try it. It works.

BROKEN PROMISES

Every survey involving repair service that I have ever seen has listed broken promises as a major source of customer dissatisfaction. While broken promises are not always the most frequent complaints, they are often the cause of the most bitter feelings on the part of the customers who were affected. I'm not exaggerating, and most of us will not have to look any further than our own experiences to prove it.

Have you ever waited at your home or office all day for a sorely needed repair technician who never showed up? Or have you ever gone to a repair shop to pick up your automobile or appliance at the promised time only to be brushed off by an aloof employee with the casual comment that "it isn't ready"?

If you have, it isn't likely that you will ever forget the incident, no matter how long ago it may have happened. Experiences like that are among those that are especially galling in this impersonal society of ours—the ultimate indignity—a slap in the face from a firm that has no interest in your concerns. It would be folly to try to estimate the number of customers who have been lost forever by business firms that take a cavalier attitude toward the promises they have made.

Because of this situation, a positive improvement in your customer satisfaction quotient is guaranteed if you will establish the sanctity of a promise made to a customer. Breaking that promise, except under the most unforeseen circumstances, should be treated as something akin to defaming one's parents.

Remember, though, that it isn't enough to establish this vow solely within the precincts of your own resolve. Every employee in your organization must view the matter with the same sense of urgency. Once it has been determined that a promise cannot be kept, your customer must be notified *immediately* and advised as to what alternative arrangements can be made.

TELEPHONE COMPLAINTS

Fielding customer gripes by telephone has one major advantage over the in-person variety—the customer can't reach over the desk and punch you in the nose. On all other counts, though, telephone complaints are more difficult to resolve.

Often, a telephone complaint is initiated while the customer is still highly agitated. Since no one enjoys talking to an angry person, there is always the risk that the conversation will get off to a bad start, especially if the customer appears to be taking out his frustrations on you personally. The lack of face-to-face contact makes the job even more difficult. A professional demeanor and a warm smile are the tools of a good customer relations professional, but they can't be seen over the telephone—at least not yet.

It is for these reasons that your customers must be greeted with a friendly manner and a pleasant voice by the first person who answers your telephones; by your secretary or anyone else who may be between you and your customers; and, finally, by you or your customer relations representative. It isn't going to help matters any if an already angry customer is greeted by an icy-voiced operator or a secretary bent on keeping the boss from finding out that there are dissatisfied customers out there.

I have long been bemused by corporations that spend huge sums of money trying to buy customer goodwill through expensive advertisements in the media while allowing rude and disinterested operators to assault every customer who tries to reach them by telephone in response to those same advertisements.

If you want to conduct an interesting experiment, try calling your office through the same number that your customers use. If your voice will be recognized, have someone else place the call while you listen.

If the nature or size of your service operation is such that initial complaints must be handled at a lower level, make certain that your representatives are well trained for the job. Customer relations is a very exacting job; don't expect your employees to know how to handle complaints on instinct alone.

Nor should you kid yourself about basic human nature. Not everyone has the sort of even temperament required to deal with irate customers, especially by way of the relatively impersonal telephone. An employee can be an invaluable asset in one capacity but a total disaster when it comes to dealing with customer problems. It's up to you to be perceptive enough to spot this kind of situation and to take steps to see to it that that sort of employee is not allowed to louse up your customer relations efforts.

Most Bell Telephone companies offer excellent training for personnel who must use the telephone. I suggest that you take advantage of this help offered by the world's leading authorities on the proper use of the telephone. Another good thing about it is the price. It's usually free.

When a complaint reaches your office, try to keep in mind that the customer has a problem that he feels is serious enough to warrant the attention of the "top brass." In this regard, you will want to remember that listening is the most powerful tool at your command when taking a telephone complaint. All the reasons for being a good listener during in-person contacts can be multiplied by 2 when you are using the telephone. It is especially annoying to be cut off in midsentence or to be told you are wrong by someone you can't even see.

Allow the customer to talk himself out completely while you take notes. And don't forget to make good use of those silent pauses.

Many telephone complaints will be of such a nature that they cannot be resolved to the customer's satisfaction during the initial conversation—either you or the customer may need to get additional information. In these cases, there is another psychological tool that can be used to your advantage.

After assuring the customer that you will do everything reasonable to resolve the matter, tell him that *you* will call *him* back. Many experts agree that the person initiating the call in a business situation has the psychological edge in the conversation; or is in charge, so to speak. Also, if you have done your initial work well, the customer will have had the opportunity to settle down, and should be easier to deal with.

One reminder: don't forget the ogre of broken promises. Once you've made a commitment to call the customer back, you are putting your reputation and that of your company right on the line. One certain way to alienate a customer—perhaps forever—is to cause her to spend some part of her limited supply of time waiting for a telephone call that either never comes or does not come when promised. If you find that you cannot arrive at the resolution of the problem by the promised time, call the customer anyway to let her know that you're still working on it.

I'm reminded of the time a neighbor of mine had such an experience. A local auto dealer had ordered a minor part needed for his brand new car. When the part didn't arrive at the promised time, the dealer telephoned on two different occasions to let him know that everything possible was being done to track down the part. It was a joy to observe the psychology of the situation. My neighbor was very impressed with the dealer's interest and, after the second call, almost began to feel obligated for the special attention he was getting. His annoyance at his own inconvenience was practically forgotten.

Once you have reached the point where a proposed solution to the problem must be offered, always try to speak in positive, rather than negative, terms. Try to avoid telling the customer what you cannot do. Instead, focus on what you *can* do.

HOW TO SAY "NO"

There is another piece of semantic legend in our business that I feel has done more harm to the customer than good. I'm referring to that old bromide, "The customer is always right."

The fact is, of course, that the customer is not always right. Customers are sometimes prone to exaggerate their problems and to seek totally unrealistic concessions. This characteristic is becoming more and more evident in our society as cynicism spreads its ugly influence. There is actually a book in print (*How I Turn Ordinary Complaints into Thousands of Dollars* by Ralph Charell, Stein and Day, Briarcliff Manor, N.Y., 1974.) that teaches as its main premise how to take advantage of the strong desire of today's large corporations to avoid customer dissatisfaction. The thesis of the book, I believe, is clearly indicated in the title, "How I Turn *Ordinary Complaints* into Thousands of Dollars" [italics added].

To pretend that unreasonable—or even dishonest—customers don't exist is to be unfair to the overwhelming majority who are neither of these things, who expect nothing more than the satisfaction they have paid for. That is why I feel it is a mistake to perpetuate such neat little aphorisms as "The customer is always right."

The *intent* behind the phrase is, of course, faultless. I subscribe to it wholeheartedly. But unless it is carefully explained, it is best phrased in other words. The intent is to make a company's employees understand that—*right or wrong*—the customer is to be satisfied. Even beginning-level employees can often see that a customer's position may be entirely wrong. To pretend that this cannot happen can create confusion on the part of the employee and perhaps cause him to believe that the company's policy is a sham.

In that context, many of today's progressive companies handle that problem by training lower-echelon employees to turn a customer's complaint or request over to their superior if, for any reason, they are unable to satisfy the customer's demands. In other words, they are allowed to say "yes" to a customer, but they are not permitted to say "no." This is a sensible approach to the task of teaching employees the importance of customer satisfaction.

Someone Has To Do It

Someone, though, must eventually say "no" to some customers. That is a fact of life, and in your company, that responsibility may well settle on your shoulders.

The real challenge in saying "no" to a customer is in being able to do so without losing her business to your firm. Obviously, the job of turning down a customer would be a cinch if there were no need for concern about the customer's reaction. To refuse a customer's request while retaining her goodwill, though, will call for the best of your professional skills.

When you are involved in a difficult customer situation, then, the important part of the problem is not in deciding whether the customer is right or wrong. With very few exceptions, the customer who persists until his complaint reaches you is certain in his own mind that he has a justifiable complaint. Even where the circumstances seem to contradict the customer's claims, it is important to avoid challenging him in a direct way. Your job is to bring the matter to a conclusion without alienating the customer, even when you have to say "no."

If you're like most people, there's one part of this responsibility that will prove to be very difficult. It takes determination to keep your own attitude toward a customer from being unduly influenced by that tiny percentage of people who will deliberately take advantage of your policy of customer satisfaction. I remember an excellent example of how this philosophy was practiced by an expert.

Some years ago, the man who was then the president of Rich's of Atlanta was being interviewed on a television talk show. Rich's, as you may know, is an elegant institution which, until recently, was one of the last of the great family-owned department stores in the country.

The president was asked if some people didn't take advantage of Rich's liberal policies on customer satisfaction, to which he replied:

> Of course. For example, I can't tell you how delightful it is to see Mrs. Smythe of the local social register picking out a lovely formal gown in Rich's on a Friday afternoon, when you happen to know that the governor's ball is all set for Saturday evening.
> It's even nicer when you tune in to the eleven o'clock news on Saturday in time to see a news clip of Mrs. Smythe dancing with the governor.
> But when you come in to work on Monday morning to see Mrs. Smythe returning your $600 gown because she "doesn't like the color," you have to swallow hard and remind yourself that most people don't behave in that fashion.

While the management of Rich's may have had occasion to "swallow hard," over the years, they haven't seen the necessity of altering their policy one little bit.

There is, of course, no way to completely avoid having someone take advantage of you if your policy of customer satisfaction has any teeth in it. The point to remember is that the percentage of people who deliberately set out to exploit your policies will be very small. And don't worry, rascals and thieves won't come pounding on your door as the word spreads.

The word will spread, of course, but for every person bent on cheating you, there will be ten or a hundred good customers who will be attracted to your firm precisely because of your reputation. Consider the cost of satisfying those few schemers as advertising expenses: you can be sure that they will brag to their friends about their exploits. Those dollars will be among the most effective advertising dollars you will ever spend.

Don't Antagonize

Every now and then, despite your most determined efforts, it will become necessary for you to refuse some particularly outrageous demand or unjustified complaint. When that happens, you will want to remember that there is a right and a wrong way to say "no."

Avoid a flat turndown without a proper explanation of why you are unable to satisfy the customer's demand and how hard you tried to do so. Let him know that you stretched your thinking to the limit in your attempt to find a way to say "yes." If some of the facts appear to be in contradiction to the customer's claims, avoid any direct challenge that might embarrass him. Embarrassment often causes a customer to become defensive and even more difficult to deal with. If possible, try to quote statistics or other facts that objectively support your position. Make liberal use of such phrases as "I can certainly understand why you felt the way you did" or "Here are a few things that you wouldn't have had any way to know about." These are good ways to avoid having the customer conclude that you regard him as an adversary. Finally, don't forget to let the customer know that you value his patronage and that you earnestly hope that he will continue to favor you with his business.

Despite the number of customers who may not show any outward sign of favorable response after being turned down in a professional manner, you will be surprised at how many will return to do business with you again.

THE CUSTOMER SATISFACTION AUDIT

While observance of the basic principles of good customer relations will improve the likelihood of optimum performance in your organization, there is only one way to be certain that your customers are being satisfied. Ask them.

Rules, regulations, and statistical analyses are fine, as far as they go. But what really matters is the customer's perceptions of your service. Satisfaction is a highly subjective concept that does not readily lend itself to quantitative analysis. What it does lend itself to is a sincere inquiry. Every service manager should conduct periodic surveys of her customers in order to determine whether internal programs and policies are working the way they're supposed to. The most common forms of customer satisfaction surveys are conducted by mail or telephone. In certain types of low-volume, highly specialized service operations, in-person surveys may be desirable.

In my view, the most practical form of satisfaction audit for most types of service organizations is the mail survey. It can be conducted on a permanent, spot-check basis at relatively little cost. If the survey form is well designed, it can be completed by the customer in a few minutes and will provide all the necessary information. Some suggested formats for mail surveys are contained in Chapter 15.

There are, of course, some disadvantages to this least expensive form of customer satisfaction analysis. The rate of customer response will sometimes be maddeningly small. Answers from more than 1 out of 5 customers surveyed would be a better-than-average result, with 1 out of 10 being a more likely objective. A postage-paid envelope and a brief questionnaire are absolutely essential if reasonable customer participation is to be expected.

Another characteristic of the mail survey is the high proportion of responses from customers with complaints to air. A happy customer, it seems, is less likely to go to the trouble of replying, while a customer with a gripe will seize the chance to be heard. For this reason, the mail survey is considered by some to be more of a public relations tool than an accurate yardstick for precise measurements of customer satisfaction. If the mail survey is kept in perspective, though, and conducted regularly on a uniform basis, it can be a useful tool for service managers.

The Telephone Method

Telephone surveys will generally provide a more balanced view of overall customer satisfaction since random calls will reach both satisfied and unsatisfied customers. Even customers who are not disposed to bother with questionnaires received in the mail can usually be persuaded to spend a minute or two on the telephone with a caller genuinely interested in listening to their opinions.

Another advantage of the telephone survey is the additional information that will often turn up. People who are reluctant to commit their criticisms to writing are often more willing to discuss them during a telephone call. The customer's tone of voice and phrasing will sometimes tell you more than you could have learned from any questionnaire.

The basic disadvantage of the telephone survey is the cost. If it is to be effective, the persons making the calls must be well trained, be able to interpret and record customers' comments accurately, and have a pleasant, professional telephone manner. Needless to say, people like that aren't usually found hanging around with nothing to do.

Many service organizations have successful survey programs that combine both telephone and mail techniques. The larger mail sampling combined with the personal touch of occasional telephone inquiries (often by the service manager himself) can be formed into an extremely effective measurement of the level of customer satisfaction. In addition, the combination has a powerful effect as a public relations tool.

The customer satisfaction audit is a form of listening. It will provide your customers with a forum for airing their feelings, and it will demonstrate that you are willing to listen. This is a powerful and effective tool that no service manager can afford to ignore. However, you should never allow yourself to forget that complaints uncovered during any form of customer audit must be handled and resolved promptly and thoroughly. To do anything less is to damage your credibility and destroy any value in the survey itself.

As a service manager, you will find that many of the people who work for you, especially technicians, are more interested in things than in people. It would be nice, of course, if the average mechanic or technician were as skilled in dealing with people as in dealing with the machinery he repairs. The fact is, however, that he is not, and that's where you come in.

Today's professional service manager recognizes that the end product of his organization—the reason it exists—is customer satisfaction. The main thrust of that objective must originate with the service manager through the setting of high standards and personal example.

YOUR PERSONAL DEVELOPMENT

One of the most effective methods of all for continuing your own program for personal development is contact with leaders in your profession. Just getting to know others who must deal with the same problems can provide encouragement and lead to a desire to excel. One of the best ways to develop contacts with other professionals is through participation in one or more of the associations that have been formed with that purpose in mind.

While there are a number of associations of service industry executives, there are two in particular that I recommend to you:

> The National Association of Service Managers
> 5940 W. Touhy Ave.
> Chicago, IL 60648
>
> The Society of Consumer Affairs Professionals
> 4900 Leesburg Pike, Suite 3H
> Alexandria, Va. 22302

Membership in either or both of these organizations will expose you to the latest service management techniques while giving you the opportunity to rub elbows with some of the most accomplished executives that our profession has to offer. Write for information.

There are many other similar organizations, some of which are oriented to a particular branch of the service industry. Even if you're not a joiner by nature, involvement with at least one trade association will work to your advantage.

Chapter 13
Managing a Healthy Business

Imagine for a moment that you have just been told that your only responsibility as a service manager is to satisfy customers. Remember now, your *only* responsibility is to give your customers whatever is needed to make them happy. No need to fret about expenses. No need to concern yourself with the problem of developing new sources of income for the business. No profit-and-loss statement (P&L) at the end of the month. A bottomless purse at your disposal. All you have to do is make your customers happy.

A service manager's Camelot.

Under those conditions, there would be no need for you to be reading this or any other book on the subject. What do you do about the lady with the 9-month-old car that's getting poor gas mileage? Easy. Just give her a brand new one.

Or what about the chap with the 4-year-old television set who thinks it should have lasted longer before it needed service? Repair it. At no charge, naturally.

Or what do you tell the sales manager who could close a deal for six copying machines if only she had a little something extra to throw in? No problem. Just tell her that your department will service them free for 5 years, or maybe 6.

It's a nice thought, isn't it? But, like a real-life Camelot, it just isn't destined to be. It is true, of course, that a service manager's job is satisfying customers. The trouble is that it must be done in the real world. And we all know what that means.

THE DISCIPLINE OF THE P&L

Depending on corporate philosophy and on certain accounting decisions, a service department may function as a profit center or as a cost center. In many ways, though, these phrases have only relative meaning; they are accounting terms that have more similarities than differences.

Whether your organization functions as a full profit center under the strict discipline of a P&L or as a cost center where the financial responsibility is to keep the net cost of operations at the lowest practical level, or whether you are the owner-manager of your own service company, you are managing a business. As with any business, the idea is to develop the highest possible income while spending the least practical amount of money, all the while satisfying customers.

In short, today's service manager must also be a good business person.

ACCOUNTING

Most service managers are neither financial experts nor accountants—nor do they have to be. However, the kind of success that every business manager hopes to attain demands at least a grasp of the fundamentals of business economics. Nothing fancy, you understand; just the basics. And they're not nearly so difficult as that grouchy old guy with the green eyeshade would have us believe.

There are two basic accounting tools that allow a business manager to see exactly how well, or poorly, his business is doing: the profit-and-loss statement (sometimes called an operating statement) and the balance sheet. Let's talk about the P&L first.

The profit-and-loss statement is exactly that. It tells the business manager whether she made a profit for a given period or whether she (gulp) lost money. Theoretically, a P&L can be put together as often or as seldom as management wants it. Your accountant could prepare a P&L for you every day or just once a year. Neither would be of much practical help. The preparation of a daily P&L would be an obvious waste of money, while a report only once a year would allow your business to go down the drain in between visits to your accountant.

Experience and custom have dictated the end of each calendar month as the logical time for summing up fiscal success or failure. Your business will almost certainly follow that pattern.

In its simplest form, the P&L consists of three sections. The first section lists all sources of income for the period, the second details all expenses incurred, and the third summarizes the results. In diagram form, it would look something like this:

$$\frac{\begin{array}{r}\text{dollars of income}\\ -\text{dollars of expense}\end{array}}{\text{dollars of profit or loss}}$$

The Information You Need

In actual practice, we need more information if the P&L is to do the job we ask of it. We need to see a breakdown of the various sources of income, and we want more detail about how our money is being spent. Bear in mind that there are an infinite number of variations that quite properly fill the requirements of an acceptable P&L. Some firms might require a finer breakdown or expenses, for example. Others might prefer to lump some of the individual categories into a miscellaneous entry in order to simplify the format. For this reason there is no precise uniformity in this essential operating tool. Rather, it is designed to suit the individual needs of the specific firm that it serves. Figure 13.1 shows a typical format for use by service organizations.

As you can see, income is broken down into the four segments that make up the total in a typical service organization. Expenses, on the other hand, are separated into fifteen different categories. This fine definition of expenses allows management to keep a close eye on exactly where the money is being spent.

Understanding Ratios

One of the most valuable aspects of the operating statement is the column labeled "ratio." This figure simply expresses the dollars spent as a percentage of total income. The result is a percentage, or ratio, that provides a handy comparison to previous performance or to industry standards.

For example, in our illustration the supplies expense ratio for XYZ is running 2.5 %. That may be good or bad depending on what that ratio has been in the past and on what the average is for comparable service operations. Let's say that the service manager at XYZ has been able to hold supply expenses to 2.1% until now. The ratio indicates that supply expenses are now rising at a faster rate than income.

CHAPTER 13

XYZ SERVICE COMPANY, INC.
OPERATING STATEMENT—
PERIOD ENDING SEPTEMBER 1981

	Net sales	Cost of sales	Gross profit	GM%
Parts	$ 44,500	$26,375	$18,125	40.7
Demand labor	58,600	26,282	32,318	55.2
Warranty labor	23,450	12,368	11,082	47.3
Service contracts	4,650	1,900	2,750	59.1
Totals	$131,200	$66,925	$64,275	49.0

Less: Operating expenses:			Ratio
Office salaries	$10,234		7.8
Owner/office salaries	15,000		11.4
Payroll taxes	4,660		3.6
Other taxes	800		0.6
Rent	2,400		1.8
Utilities	1,450		1.1
Telephone	1,200		0.9
Insurance	4,610		3.5
Travel and entertainment	445		0.3
Accounting and legal	690		0.5
Advertising	3,060		2.3
Supplies	3,325		2.5
Trucks and cars	4,199		3.2
Miscellaneous	1,150		0.9
Depreciation	2,360		1.8
Total operating expenses		55,583	42.4
Operating profit		$ 8,692	6.6

Add: Other income:			
Interest	$ 265		0.2
Bad debts recovered	400		0.3
Supplier rebates	575		0.4
Miscellaneous	666		0.5
Total other income		1,906	1.4

Less: Other expenses:			
Bad debts	$ 750		0.6
Interest paid	575		0.4
Miscellaneous	600		0.5
Total other expenses		−1,925	1.4
Profit for the period (before taxes)		$ 8,673	6.6
Less: Federal and state income taxes		2,081	1.6
Net profit for the period		$ 6,592	5.0

FIGURE 13.1. Typical operating statement.

Assuming that other expenses have remained at approximately their former ratios, it's time for a very close look at what's happening in the supply account.

However, if all or most of the expense ratios are rising, that's a red flag signaling serious trouble ahead. It means that overall expenses are rising at a faster pace than income. It doesn't take an economist to know what that will mean if it is allowed to continue. Under those conditions, it's up to the manager to determine whether the problem is due to a failure to develop sufficient income, poor control of expenses, or some combination of both.

This, of course, is just one example of how a P&L can provide vital information about current operating conditions. The alert manager will use it to help spot potential trouble areas before they become serious problems.

I've kept the sample P&L simple in order to make it easier to illustrate its basic structure. In actual practice, most P&Ls will contain additional information. Usually, figures for the month being reported as well as for the year to date will be included. This form of reporting provides another parameter against which the monthly figures can be compared.

Also, the bottom section of the statement may contain additional entries to provide for miscellaneous income items, such as savings account interest and rebates from suppliers; miscellaneous expenses, such as interest paid; and federal and local income taxes.

Balance Sheet

The P&L serves the specific purpose of documenting the financial performance of a company over a given period of time—normally a month or a year. The other half of the accounting one-two punch is called the balance sheet.

The balance sheet is a sort of physical exam. If the P&L tells you how well the runner made out in the race, the balance sheet tells you what kind of shape she was in after the race was over. In other words, the balance sheet provides a picture of the fiscal condition of a company at a fixed point in time, ususally the last day of the month and/or the last day of the year.

If you have trouble seeing the distinction, allow me one more analogy. Let's say that you made $1,000 in salary last month. After you paid all the bills, you had 50 bucks left to stash away in the bank. In a manner of speaking, you made $50 profit for the month. The bottom line of your personal P&L, if you had one, would show all of that information—but that's all it would show.

From that fact, we'd have no way to know whether that 50 bucks was all you owned in this world or whether you were a millionaire working just to keep from getting leg cramps. But if we could sneak a peek at your personal balance sheet, we'd have the complete picture of your financial condition at the end of the month. We'd know how many bank accounts you had; how much money you had in them; how much real estate you owned; how many krugerrands you had hidden in the attic; and how much was left over after you subtracted all your mortgages and other outstanding debts.

The balance sheet, then, is a sort of snapshot: a picture that freezes the action at a given point in time so that we can examine a company's entire financial skeleton. As you can see from Figure 13.2, the balance sheet centers around what is really a very simple formula:

Assets minus liabilities equals net worth

While balance sheets can be and often are designed to look very intimidating, they all boil down to "assets minus liabilities equals net worth." Here's what those terms mean:

Assets

Everything owned by the company for which a dollar value can be assigned is called an asset: not only such obvious things as cash and inventory but also furniture, office equipment, real estate—anything that has a dollar value. Certain items that will eventually wear out, such as furniture and office quipment, will be carried at a value that is reduced each month. Thus they are carried on the books at their "depreciated value." Depreciation provides a basis for assigning value to certain fixed assets, and for deducting the proper portion of the initial cost of those assets each year for income tax purposes.

Liabilities

We all have liabilities. So do businesses. There are such things as the mortgage on that building that we so cleverly listed at full market value as an asset; payments due on that inventory on our shelves; taxes due Uncle Sam that we haven't paid yet; and payments due on the money we borrowed to buy that new test equipment. Liabilities, then, include any financial obligations that must be paid.

Net Worth

After you subtract everything that you owe from everything that you own, you are left with your net worth.

ABC SERVICE COMPANY, INC.
BALANCE SHEET—DECEMBER 31, 1981

Current Assets:

Cash	$ 9,390	
Accounts receivable	17,340	
Inventory	21,550	
Total current assets		$48,280

Fixed assets:

Furniture and fixtures	$ 1,790	
Trucks and cars	33,500	
Equipment	15,000	
	$50,290	
Less: Accumulated depreciation	− 25,000	
Total fixed assets		24,790

Total assets $73,070

Liabilities:

Accounts payable	$12,550	
Employee taxes payable	2,890	
Sales taxes payable	650	
Miscellaneous taxes payable	90	
Federal and state income taxes	4,162	
Note payable, bank	7,500	
Total liabilities		$27,842

Net worth:

Capital stock	$ 1,000	
Retained earnings	31,044	
Profit for the period	13,184	
Total net worth		45,228

Total liabilities and net worth........................... $73,070

FIGURE 13.2. Typical balance sheet.

That, of course, is a blatantly simplistic explanation of what is really a much more complex subject. For example, both assets and liabilities are usually broken down further into two different categories: current and fixed.

Current Assets

These are assets that are in the form of cash or that will be converted into cash during normal operation of the business; for example, accounts receivable and inventories.

Fixed Assets

All property of a fixed, or permanent, nature used in the business but not intended for sale is considered to be fixed, or permanent, assets; examples include land, buildings, furniture and fixtures, and tools and machinery.

Liabilities that are due and payable within a year are usually considered current. Those that are payable over a period longer than a year—a mortgage, for example—are classified as fixed liabilities.

For firms that really want to get down to the nitty-gritty of fiscal analysis, these terms are broken down still further into additional subcategories.

The P&L and the balance sheet, then, are the two basic forms for reporting on the fiscal performance and health of a business. Working together, they constitute a sort of road map that tells a business manager not only where he has been but where he may be going as well.

Basic Ratios

Once you are familiar with the terms used on the P&L and balance sheet, you'll be ready to understand and benefit from the basic ratios used in accounting. Ratios are simply a means for expressing the mathematical relationships that exist between one set of figures and another.

Figure 13.3 lists ten of the most commonly used accounting ratios and gives a brief description of how they can be applied to your business.

In this intriguing world of numbers, there is an ever-increasing flow of ideas and new formulas for use in business management. For example, The University of Illinois School of Business developed this formula for a quick diagnosis of the health of a business:

$$\frac{1}{N} \times \frac{P - O}{O} \times 100$$

THE BASIC RATIOS	QUESTIONS THE RATIOS ADDRESS
1. Current ratio $$\frac{\text{Current assets}}{\text{Current liabilities}}$$	Is my company solvent? Do I have enough liquid assets to meet the debts falling due in the next week (month, year)?
2. Quick ratio $$\frac{\text{Cash, marketable securities, receivables}}{\text{Current liabilities}}$$	How well can I cover my debts falling due with my truly liquid assets? (Inventory and prepayments are current assets but are not very liquid.)
3. Debt ratio $$\frac{\text{Total liabilities}}{\text{Total assets}}$$	Is my company too highly leveraged? Is it financed with too much debt relative to its equity and retained earnings?
4. Inventory turnover $$\frac{\text{Cost of goods sold}}{\text{Average inventory}}$$	How many times has inventory "sold out" during the year? How well am I managing my inventory? Do I have enough stock on hand to meet sales demand?
5. Working capital turnover $$\frac{\text{Net sales}}{\text{(Current assets less current liabilities)}}$$	Is the working capital invested in my business generating enough revenue, or is it, perhaps, stretched too far?
6. Inventory to working capital $$\frac{\text{Year-end inventory}}{\text{Year-end capital}}$$	How much of my working capital is tied up in inventory?
7. Net profit $$\frac{\text{Net profit}}{\text{Net sales}}$$	How much does my company make on each dollar of sales after all expenses have been paid?
8. Receivables turnover $$\frac{\text{Net credit sales}}{\text{Average receivables}}$$	Are my credit terms too generous? How effective are my billing and collection procedures? Is too much money (working capital) tied up in receivables?
9. Return on investment $$\frac{\text{Before-tax net profit (after owner's salary)}}{\text{Net worth}}$$	Am I making a good return, or a poor return, on the funds invested in the business?

FIGURE 13.3. The basic accounting ratios.

In the formula, N equals the number of years that you have been in business, P is your present investment in dollars, and O is your original investment. Here's an example of how it works:

You have been in business for 10 years. Your original investment was $10,000. Your present investment is $20,000. Fill in these figures in the proper places and do the simple algebra. The answer is 10 which is a comparative figure.

Rework the formula each year using the appropriate figures for those years. If the comparative figure is greater than the figure derived the previous year, your business is doing alright. If it is lower, watch out! Your business is declining.

It goes without saying that this kind of brief discussion of accounting principles must be superficial at best. Accounting is a profession that requires years of intensive study in order to gain real proficiency. Nevertheless, as with medicine, a grounding in the basics is both valuable and relatively easy to attain. I recommend that you use this chapter as a stepping-off point to a broader understanding of how accounting can help you run a more profitable business. In this regard, you may want to get hold of a copy of *Accounting for Non-Accountants* (Hawthorne, New York, 1968) by John N. Myer. This dandy book sidesteps much of the clinical arcana of interest only to professional accountants and leaves a bare-bones explanation of the accounting process and its applications in the everyday world of business.

MANAGING FOR PROFIT

Accounting provides the road map, but you must still drive the car.

A good accounting system properly employed and understood can provide the information you need to help make sound business decisions. The leadership to make the decisions—and to follow through on them—is where you come in.

When you strip away all the fancy rhetoric, managing a business for profit boils down to two simple concepts: reduce expenses and increase income. While such an approach may appear to be hopelessly simplified, it can be a big help in getting and keeping a clear focus on your priorities.

An executive I once knew used to tell his subordinates, "Every now and then, on a regular basis, stop what you're doing and ask yourself this question: 'Is what I'm doing right now going to increase income or reduce expenses?'" If the answer is not immediately and unarguably 'yes,' drop the project at once and get back to the basics." Since this is a chapter on managing for profits, let's take a look at how that philosophy might work.

Developing Income

Above the bottom line, the P&L is divided neatly into two parts. At the top each of the principal sources of sales (income) is listed. Below that are shown the expenses. It's a point of interest, I believe, that income is always the first entry. As some unknown sage once said about the world of business, "Nothing happens until somebody sells something." That's true even in the service business.

Finding ways to increase the flow of income into your business is the most challenging and exciting part of being a service manager—and the one most often neglected. Regardless of the type of service business involved, the product you have to offer *is* a salable commodity, and selling it can be a rewarding part of your business life.

It's for that reason I suggest that you review Chapter 10 every now and then. Unless you are an exception as a service manager, the chances are that your natural talents are strongest in other areas of the business. Reminding yourself that service income lies out there waiting for you to discover it may well stimulate you into developing new and original ideas for improving the top half of that monthly P&L.

Is selling service contracts right for your service department? Can you develop new customers through direct mail programs? What about preventive maintenance? Does your service operation have walk-in customer traffic? If so, are your employees trained in the art of suggestion selling? What about the direct route? Can you approach businesses and institutions that may be potential customers for your firm?

Those are just a few income-producing ideas, but they and others you may come up with can provide a jumping-off point for sharpening your service-sales promotion skills.

Developing new ideas (and breathing new life into old ones) for increasing the flow of income into your business is a job that will continue as long as the business itself. Because customers come and go, and because expenses have a way of rising year after year, the need for fresh revenue will always be one of your most important responsibilities.

Collecting Your Fees

In the service business, developing income is one thing—getting it into the bank can be quite another.

No one, it seems, likes the idea of paying for intangibles. There's something vaguely disquieting about dishing out hard-earned money for a product that cannot be seen, heard, touched, or worn to church on Sunday. As bad as the record is for life's basic necessities, such as dental and medical care, it's far worse for the kind of services that we as professional service managers furnish to our customers. It is for this reason that every service manager should take specific actions to minimize the profit leaks that result when we fail to collect money that has been earned.

The most obvious form of earned but uncollected income is the bad debt—the customer who offers no argument about having accepted and used your product, but who simply refuses to pay for it. Shakespeare offered some startlingly succinct advice on avoiding this irksome problem when he wrote, "Neither a borrower nor a lender be." If you fail to collect for your services at the time they are performed, you have made a lender of yourself and a borrower of your customer. Shame.

On the other hand, work performed on a C.O.D. basis is unarguably a clear solution to the whole dilemma.

I suggest that you take heed of the Bard's advice and establish a policy that requires payment on completion of the work. The very nature of the work performed by service organizations seems to invite the kind of judgments that justify slow pay or even no pay by some customers. Because the amounts of money involved will usually be too small to justify legal action, and because disputed claims between servicer and customer can be impossible to resolve, offering to bill your customers is an invitation to the kind of headaches that you don't need.

Of course, work that is paid for promptly upon completion can be a problem, too, if it is paid for with a bad check. Fortunately, most checks that come back from the bank marked "insufficient funds" are due to carelessness and not larceny. Be sure to submit them a second time unless your bank has a specific policy that prohibits the practice. This allows your customer time to realize the mistake and make the necessary deposit to his account. Most banks will permit the depositing of checks to previously overdrawn accounts a second time.

Once the check fails to clear a second time, you're stuck with it. A diplomatic but firm telephone call is now in order. One service dealer I know has a firm policy of not accepting checks from customers who do not have telephones. His experience has caused him to believe that too often no telephone means no money.

Credit Cards

In the world of practical reality, a policy of no credit whatever will almost certainly mean the loss of some customers. In our society today, "pay as you go" is almost a foreign language to some people. For this reason, you may well decide that extending some form of credit is a lesser evil than losing a percentage of your potential market.

Unless you are part of a large company with a professional credit organization, bank cards are the only form of credit that you should offer. Collecting credit accounts is no job for an amateur, and the cost of carrying accounts receivable is an additional expense that most service dealers would do well to avoid.

Most of the well-known credit cards, such as MasterCard and Visa, are franchised through local banks which are then authorized to issue the cards. The issuer assumes the job of billing and collecting as well as all responsibilities for uncollected accounts.

For this service, the participating merchant pays a percentage of the amounts billed to the credit card. The rates charged by the credit card issuers for this service vary with the type and size of the participating company. At the time of this writing, the rates for service organizations are averaging about 6%. That means you would receive only $47 for every $50 billed to your customers. That 6%, of course, can make a big difference on the bottom line for some service organizations. It's an added cost of doing business that should not be regarded lightly. It must be carefully weighed against the alternatives of a flat no-credit policy or an attempt to set up your own credit and billing systems with the attendant risks of uncollected accounts.

I would not presume to attempt to influence such a personal thing as your philosophy with regard to credit and whether or not you want to give it a place in your business. If you feel that extending credit is necessary, though, I strongly suggest that you avoid the problems inherent in trying to set up your own system, unless your company is large enough to support a professional credit organization.

While the fees charged by the credit card companies will be a significant addition to your cost of doing business, they will almost certainly be less than the amounts you would spend in clerical payroll and losses from uncollected accounts.

THE TECHNICIAN'S ROLE

It's sad but true that customers aren't the only ones who think that today's service charges are too high. The fact is that many of the technicians who are expected to collect for their work have the feeling that they are being used as pawns in a scheme to rip off their customers.

I have had many technicians confide in me that they were uncomfortable asking their customers to pay the rates that they were expected to collect. Some have even told me that they often feel guilty when it's time to present the bill to a customer. That sort of attitude can usually be traced to manangement's failure to demonstrate that the company's service rates are reasonable and based directly on the cost of doing business. The inevitable result, if the misunderstanding is allowed to continue, will be an attempt by some technicians to "hedge" on the quoted service rates, especially on home service calls. That is, they alter the description on the repair order of the work done so that a lower charge to the customer is indicated. That simple procedure solves two problems quite nicely for the technician who must deal with customers at their homes or businesses. It tempers her guilt feelings, and makes it less likely that she'll have to defend her charge to a hostile customer. After all, she reasons, the company doesn't need the money as badly as the customer does.

Or does it?

Let's say that your monthly P&L tells you that your uncanny management skills are producing a respectable net profit of about 10%. Now let's say that one of your technicians is about to tote up the bill for a snaggletoothed customer with a decidedly unfriendly demeanor. The correct charge comes to $48, but friendly Mr. Technician takes one look at that towering hulk and decides that $48 may be too much after all. A few scribblings on his service order and, *voilà*, the total comes out to an easier-to-swallow $39. The technician is happy, the customer has stumbled on one of today's rare bargains, and you don't even know that you've become a philanthropist. Your potential profit of $4.80 (10% of $48) has disappeared, and you've actually *lost* $4 or $5 on the call. It doesn't take a great deal of imagination to figure out the eventual result for any company that permits such a scenario to be repeated often enough.

The distressing fact is that adopting a professional and an accurate method for setting your service rates is not enough, in itself, to ensure that you will receive them. If your technicians do not have confidence in your rate structure, or if they have not been well schooled in the need for charging the proper amount on every job, the chances are that your service department is failing to collect money that it has earned.

It Can Happen Here

One of the most pernicious aspects of this particular problem is the difficulty that so many service managers seem to have in bringing themselves to believe that such a thing could happen in *their* service departments. From my experience, that attitude is an almost certain guarantee that it is—or will be.

There are several steps that you can take to minimize the likelihood of this nasty profit leak in your service organization. None are difficult to administer, and all are consistent with the sort of sound management principles discussed in this book.

The basic foundation for your program—and I can't stress this too strongly—is a pricing structure that really is based on your cost of doing business and is fairly calculated. A sloppy attitude toward the job of establishing your service rates cannot be hidden from your technicians, and will surely cause them to look with contempt on the rate structure you are asking them to implement.

Get the Technician on Your Side

Once you're satisfied that your prices are right, sit down with your technicians and other key employees to give them a broad overview of the hows and whys of setting service rates. The idea in this is not to bore them with a lot of statistical analyses (nor to divulge any confidential company data) but rather to acquaint them with a few of the hard facts—to discuss some of the hidden costs involved in completing a service call. As I'm sure you know, there is an unfortunate but persistent tendency for some technicians (and customers) to conclude that hourly labor rates should be set at the technician's wage rate "plus a little for profit."

In the world of uncompromising reality, an hourly charge of from 2½ to 4 times the technician's average hourly wage is necessary for most types of service organizations to generate a satisfactory profit. Too often, technicians themselves have no clear idea of the supporting costs required to keep them at work.

Another problem of this type is the insistence of some customers to try to equate the price of the parts used in a repair job to the price charged for labor. I couldn't count the times over the years that I have found myself trying to explain to a customer that there is no relationship between the value of the parts used and the time required to make the repair.

In television, or any form of electronics work, to use one example, the diagnosis of the problem is often the most time-consuming and thus the most costly part of the repair. Yet there is still the customer who suspiciously demands, "Why are you charging me $30 to replace a $2 part?" If your business is one in which this problem occurs, the training of your technicians should include help on how to speak to this issue when the need arises.

Once your technicians have a better understanding of what is meant by overhead, they will be in a better position to deal with customers on the delicate subject of labor rates. In turn, you will be in a better position to ask for their help and support in collecting the full amount that has been earned on every repair job. One service manager I know has had excellent results in this area by appealing directly to the pride of his technicians. "You are professionals," he reminds them. "You want to be treated as professionals and paid as professionals. Don't demean your profession by suggesting that your personal skills aren't worth the going rate."

Properly handled, that kind of approach will go a long way toward eliminating this problem from your service organization. Coupled with the following final step, it can lead to measurable improvements in your income and profit picture.

Just as a good service manager carefully screens work orders *before* they are scheduled, she screens them at least as carefully *after* they are completed. Comparing time spent on the job with descriptions of the work performed will often alert the trained eye to discrepancies that can mean lost service income. Depending on the size of your service organization and the persistence of the problem, the screening of completed jobs may have to be done at a 100% rate, or an occasional spot check may be all you need to plug the leak. In any case, the job can never be considered complete. Because human nature tends to work against us in this case, bulldog tenacity is your best insurance against this unkind assault on your profit-and-loss statement.

What About Expenses?

With no risk whatever of being accused of profundity, I can safely observe that no amount of income flowing into a business is enough if an equal or greater amount is flowing right back out again in the form of expenses. Or . . . the other half of the job of managing for a profit calls for keeping operating expenses at the lowest possible level, consistent with the overall objectives of the company. Or . . . spend a little less than you take in.

Once all of the items of income on your P&L are brought down to a total, the list of expenses begins. On some P&Ls, these are grouped into categories. Fixed and semifixed expenses are those that cannot be significantly affected by day-to-day management control.

The others—controllable expenses—are the little devils that pop up everywhere and seem to be able to multiply like rabbits. These are outgoing dollars that must be brought under your sternest scrutiny. One bit of inspiration in this regard is the sure knowledge that every dollar of unnecessary expense eliminated from your P&L is translated into an additional dollar of profit on the bottom line.

An Expense Control Checklist

In Chapter 11, we talked about some of the basic expenses that are an important part of the cost structure of most service organizations. Here are a few others that will respond to professional management control techniques.

Employee benefits. An attractive benefit package is necessary these days in order to attract and hold top-caliber employees. Most benefit programs will include some form of paid-absence schedule for illness and other personal reasons. While this benefit is an essential ingredient in any benefit program, it is also one of the most abused.

Most companies with large numbers of employees have learned the hard way that absences for illnesses are not always legitimate. If absences are not monitored carefully, your costs for illness payments can easily develop into a major source of unnecessary expense. The antidote: a carefully defined policy of allowable illness payments; a no-exceptions rule requiring a doctor's certificate for absences over 3 days; and follow-through interviews and investigations of employees who consistently abuse their illness benefits.

Be advised, though, that a fair and absolutely consistent policy in enforcing your rules is a necessity. Any action that could be interpreted as favoritism or uneven enforcement on your part will be a certain guarantee of morale problems.

Employee defalcations. Most of us prefer to think of our working associates as being honest. However, a naive disregard for the ever-present risk of employee theft is one mistake that you should not make. Unpleasant though it may be to contemplate, the fact is that employee theft is a major problem in business today. Perhaps your business is an exception to this rule. If so, your interest will be in keeping it that way.

One security expert told me that there is no way for a company to protect itself completely from an employee who is a careful and dedicated thief. Unless he overdoes it, the apprehension of such a criminal often comes down to nothing more than a lucky accident. I'm sure that he's right, especially in our business. Fortunately, though, such thieves are relatively scarce. Of more concern to you as a business manager is the fact that part of our population consists of basically honest folks who can be inclined toward helping themselves if temptation is continually thrust in their faces.

You, of course, would not be so indiscreet as to place your employees in such a position.

Or would you?

The fact is that most businesses are riddled with systems and procedures that literally invite employee dishonesty. The list of potential problem areas is much too long to adequately cover here, but there are some general guidelines that can help you benefit from the experiences of others.

First, it doesn't take a profound thinker to figure out that service technicians can find themselves in need of repair parts from time to time to conduct business other than yours. It is for this reason that your inventory control procedures must be designed with security in mind. As a service manager, your biggest exposure to employee defalcation is in your parts department.

Second, you must contend with the risk of the employee who diverts some of the moneys he collects from customers into her own pocket. There are a number of checks and balances that can be built into your operating procedures to make it more difficult for such a practice to go undetected. One of the most effective of these is the customer satisfaction audit letter. A sample of an effective letter for this purpose is included in Chapter 15.

Third, don't forget your accountant or company comptroller. By training, and often by instinct, a good accountant is well equipped to evaluate your susceptibility to employee theft. I don't think I have ever met a successful accountant who wasn't suspicious by nature—just the quality you're looking for in your efforts to provide security for your company's assets.

Daily Open to Spend. Many of the expenses appearing in the bottom half of your P&L are those that are paid out in dribs and drabs, daily or weekly. One of the best tools for helping to control this type of expense is the daily open to spend (DOS) which is illustrated in figure 13.4. The DOS is nothing more than a form designed for daily entries. At the beginning of the month, the amount that has been budgeted for these expenses is entered on the form. Each day, the amounts paid out are entered and subtracted from the previous open-to-spend amount. Thus, as the month progresses, a quick glance at the form will tell you how much of your original budget remains to be spent.

MANAGING A HEALTHY BUSINESS 187

Month	May 1982						
Account	Supplies			Amount Budgeted	$400.00		

Approved by		Requisition or P.O. Number	Purchased From	Cost	Open to Spend	Date Rec'd
Date	Initial					
5/2	J.K.	07936	Silver Electronics (solder)	12.50	387.50	5/3
5/7	J.K.	07951	Ajax Printers (work orders)	110.00	277.50	
5/12	R.M.	07977	Silver Electronics (tuner cleaner)	6.40	271.10	5/14
5/14	J.K.	07990	Keystone Electric (coax cable)	61.05	210.05	5/17

FIGURE 13.4. Daily open-to-spend form.

One variation of this method calls for dividing the original budgeted amount by the number of workdays in the month. Then the open-to-spend amount is reduced each day by the daily allocation. The result is a report that tells you exactly how much over or under your expenditures are running at any point during the month. This approach is good for the types of expenses that usually are spread more or less evenly throughout the month.

Necessarily, much of this chapter has been devoted to the hard analysis of fiscal realities. In order to manage a business for optimum profits, it is necessary to be aware of and to understand the basic arithmetic of income and expense. I don't know of any way to avoid that obvious requirement.

However, as you apply yourself to the task of learning as much as you can about balance sheets, current ratios, and cash flow, you may want to remember something else of importance. Jervis B. Webb, who is chairman of one of the largest family-owned enterprises in the United States, put it quite effectively, "Never forget: Managing a business is managing people. Don't let all the numbers and ratios confuse that point!"

Chapter 14
Legal Considerations

When it comes to matters of the law, there is no substitute for a good attorney, despite what Mr. Shakespeare had to say on the subject:

> The first thing we do, let's
> kill all the lawyers.
> *King Henry VI, Part II*

Perhaps when the Bard wrote that provocative line in 1591, things were different. Today (though I do know a few businesspersons who might find the idea intriguing), the gaggle of laws that affect the operations of all businesses have made such a harsh program highly impractical. The web of legal intricacies in today's society and our demonstrated propensity for suing each other have combined to provide lots of security for lawyers. It would, in fact, be difficult to imagine any turning of the modern wheels of commerce without an assist from our legal friends.

As an individual, the odds are that you will find yourself in need of the services of an attorney on at least several occasions during your lifetime. As a business executive, the likelihood becomes a certainty.

Never mind that most of our lawmakers are themselves lawyers, and that the very laws that make it so difficult for ordinary folk to conduct their business affairs were conceived by those same lawyers upon whom we must depend to interpret them. The fact is that the cycle is inexorably in motion: more laws propounded by lawyers. More lawyers needed to guide us through the resulting maze. More laws propounded by lawyers. *Ad infinitum.*

To show you just how much I believe in our ultimate destiny vis-á-vis lawyers, I am about to follow the stern advice of my own counselor by advising you of the following: I am not a lawyer, nor have I received any training that would qualify me to render legal advice. Be aware, then, that the ruminations that follow are the thoughts of a fellow layman (unless, of course, you happen to be a lawyer yourself; in which case, I hope that you are not a vindictive sort).

The purpose of this chapter is simply to highlight a few of the broad areas in which the legal process has reached out and touched our profession, and to alert you to some of the consequences. Remember, when it comes to specific legal problems, there is no substitute for an attorney with the appropriate experience.

Now that I have properly disposed of that obligation, I'll offer some thoughts on a subject that once was very simple indeed, but which, over the years, has evolved into a complex legal concept.

WARRANTIES AND GUARANTEES

Ever since the first craftsmen set out to provide goods and services for use by others, the concept of guaranteed performance was inherently understood. The mill operator who bought a new grinding wheel from the local stonemason had a right to expect that it would hold up under the demands normally placed on grinding wheels. The blacksmith commissioned to shoe a horse was expected to stand behind both his workmanship and the shoes fashioned from his hearth.

Of course, in those early days, there was little in the way of formality behind promises of quality and performance. The guarantee, if it was specified at all, was sealed with a handshake. In many cases, it was simply implied—an unspoken but clearly understood agreement.

When products or services failed to live up to expectations, there was little in the way of structured help in resolving the dispute. With litigation still an unrecognized concept, the principals found their own ways to settle things.

Gradually, as life became more complicated, a personal relationship between the buyer and seller was no longer an adequate means for handling this responsibility. Along with the industrial revolution came the impersonal mass production of goods, nationwide marketing, and the involvement of third parties such as distributors and retailers.

With the ultimate consumer making his purchase from a retailer who had no connection whatever with the manufacturer, whose factory may have been located thousands of miles away, the need for a specific and binding form of protection for the buyer became evident. Thus warranties and guarantees, as we know them, gradually came into use. Today's legal standards provide for a clear distinction between these two terms. A warranty provides assurance to the buyer that the product is as described, meets all specifications, and is free of defects in materials or workmanship. Generally, the warranty will specify some period of time for which it applies. A guarantee, on the other hand, provides the buyer with the assurance that the product will perform in a manner that is consistent with the provisions of the warranty. Generally, the guarantee will provide for repair or replacement, also for a specified period of time.

If you have difficulty discerning the subtle differences between warranty and guarantee, relax. So do I. Furthermore, I suspect that if you were to question the next thousand people passing the intersection of 42d and Broadway, you'd be lucky to find two who could define the difference.

What to do? Easy. Just (forgive me, counselor) do as almost everyone else does—use the terms interchangeably. Better yet, choose one term and use it exclusively. You won't be alone if you do. Many big corporations and some government agencies which deal intimately with the subject have formally elected to make one term suffice.

As for me, I prefer to use the increasigly popular "warranty" to cover all aspects of the warranty/guarantee issue.

What Consumers Think

Regardless of what you choose to call it, though, it is an important subject in our profession. A major survey of consumer opinion conducted in 1976–1977 by a research organization associated with Harvard University found that a lot of consumers were unhappy with product quality, warranty coverage, and product servicing.

- 61% said they believed the quality of most products and services had declined during the last decade.
- 78% thought products have a shorter life than they used to.
- 48% saw a growing gap between product claims and actual product performance.

- More than half found warranties difficult to understand.
- 64% found it more difficult than it used to be to get things repaired.

A perfect foundation for consumer legislation.

THE MAGNUSON-MOSS WARRANTY ACT

If there is one piece of legislation that serves to illustrate the point at which we have arrived in the third-party influence of the buyer/seller relationship, it is the so-called Magnuson-Moss Warranty Act. Signed into law in June 1975, the act applies to consumer products and services sold with a written warranty. While it does not require that a seller furnish a warranty, it mandates specific requirements for the wording of any warranty that is provided. Authority to enforce the act has been vested in the Federal Trade Commission.

I'd like to recommend that you obtain a copy of the act and familiarize yourself with it since it contains information important to every service manager. However, I'll have to admit that the likelihood of a busy service manager plowing through that exquisite example of bureaucratese seems remote indeed.

To give you an idea of how convoluted the text of Magnuson-Moss is, I'll tell you that the *Federal Register* published "Interpretations of the Magnuson-Moss Warranty Act" on August 16, 1976. Because there still were countless people who could not understand the interpretations, further explanations of the interpretations were published on July 13, 1977. I suspect that we haven't yet seen the end of the "explanations."

With that background as a caution, I'll attempt to sketch in briefly the act's principal points affecting the service industry. Bear in mind, though, that the legislation itself and the subsequent interpretations are far lengthier than this entire chapter.

The Magnuson-Moss Warranty Act does not require the seller of consumer products or services to provide a written warranty. However, it does provide specific requirements for those businesses that elect to provide their customers with that benefit.

Full or Limited Warranty

The act provides for two separate classifications of warranties: the full warranty and the limited warranty. In order to qualify as a full warranty, the document must meet a number of specifications and requirements.

- It contains a statement of duration, such as "full 90-day warranty," "full 1-year warranty," or "full 40,000-mile warranty."
- Service must be provided within a "reasonable" period of time. Since legal minds have been wrestling with the definition of "reasonable time" for decades, this one should prove to be interesting. (Keep in mind, though, that some state and local laws mandate more definitive time requirements.)
- No charge can be made for any repairs or replacements of products during the period of a full warranty.
- The customer cannot be required to do anything "unreasonable" in order to obtain service. Such things as mailing a registration card in order to qualify for warranty protection or shipping the merchandise to a repair station at customer expense have been defined as unreasonable under the act.
- A product must be replaced at no charge or a refund of the full purchase price must be given if it cannot be repaired after a reasonable number of attempts. (Unfortunately, "reasonable number of attempts" has yet to be clearly defined.)

Warranties that do not meet all the above requirements do not qualify as full warranties, and must be designated as limited. Both full and limited warranties must carry the word "warranty" in the heading, although use of the word "guarantee" is permitted elsewhere in the text.

The act also provides that both full and limited warranties must pass with the product from the original owners to any subsequent owners during the terms of the warranty. In other words, a written warranty can no longer restrict coverage to the original owner. Nor may any written warranty contain any statement disclaiming the warrantor's liability under the concept of implied warranties. (More on implied warranties later.)

While much of the basic thrust of the act is aimed at the manufacturer and retailer of consumer goods, replacement parts and components used in repairs are covered. Warranties on services are not covered. Therefore, any warranty that applies solely to the workmanship involved in a repair is not covered by the act. However, if you supply your customers with a written warranty that covers both the parts provided to effect a repair and the workmanship, the warranty must comply with all provisions of the act.

If you do provide such a warranty (and I surely hope that you do), you should have it reviewed by an attorney familiar with consumer law. Remember, as verbose as all this may sound as set forth here, it is but the sketchiest description of a long and complex law.

Implied Warranties

The Magnuson-Moss Warranty Act sets forth certain parameters for *written* warranties. As I mentioned earlier, a seller of products or services is not required by law to furnish the buyer with a written warranty of any sort. The act simply says that if you do decide to furnish a warranty in writing, that document must conform to the law.

Obviously, then, one easy way to avoid all this fuss and responsibility over warranties is to decide not to provide any warranty at all. Right?

Wrong.

Over the years, the courts of our judicial systems have repeatedly established that the buyer of a product or service is entitled to assume that the purchase will fulfill reasonable (there's that word again) expectations—whether or not the seller has chosen to guarantee performance by way of a written warranty. To say that another way, the seller of a product or service has provided a warranty whether she is aware of it or not. Let's consider this admittedly oversimplified example:

The XYZ Tire Manufacturing Company advertises and sells what it describes as its best radial tire. However, one of its retail outlets decides not to provide any sort of written warranty to its customers.

Buyer Jones buys a set and, to his dismay, finds that they are completely worn out after only 4000 miles. Is Jones out of luck? Not necessarily.

If he decided to take XYZ and the retailer to court, odds are that he would collect some form of reimbursement. Given the current state of the art, it is widely known that even the least expensive brand of radial tire can be counted on for a minimum of 30,000 to 35,000 miles. Unless XYZ could establish that Jones subjected the tires to some form of improper use, the laws of implied warranty would probably hold the defendants liable. In accordance with the laws of implied warranty, buyer Jones had a right to expect his tires to perform their jobs safely for a reasonable period of time (miles), considering current state of the art and industry standards.

In this fictional account, XYZ might well find a third party (the courts) deciding what a reasonable warranty should have provided. It is this situation that contributes to the motivation for most businesses to provide specific written warranties for the products and services that they sell. After all, better to decide on a reasonable understanding of warranty terms with your customers *before* they buy than to have a third party called in to resolve the matter after the fact.

However, bear in mind that providing a specific, limited warranty cannot be counted on to relieve the seller of any responsibilities that might come under the heading of implied warranty. The product you sell must be fit for the obvious purpose for which it is intended, even if you choose to avoid the subject in the written warranty you provide.

Warranties are governed by both federal and state laws and regulations. While only written warranties are covered by Federal Warranty Law, all types of warranties are covered by state laws. Under the Federal Warranty Law, written warranties *must* carry this statement:

> This warranty gives you specific legal rights, and you may also have other rights which vary from state to state.

PRODUCT LIABILITY

There probably is no area of civil law in America that has undergone as much wrenching change as have the laws regarding product liability.

Since the earliest days of our system of jurisprudence, persons who suffered personal or financial damage as the result of their use of a product were allowed to seek legal redress. However—and this is the crux of the matter—it was the responsibility of the injured party to prove that the product was, in some way, defective or inadequate. Further, negligence or poor judgment on the part of the user of the product was considered to be a mitigating circumstance that almost always nullified any claim that the user may have brought against the seller of the product.

One of the landmark tort cases that may have started the current trend was the 1916 case of *MacPherson* v. *Buick Motor Company*. MacPherson sued when one of the wheels of his buick collapsed. He won the case. What made *MacPherson* v. *Buick* so important was that it was the first time that the buyer of a product was successful in bypassing the seller and collecting from the manufacturer. Prior to that time, the buyer of a product could collect damages only from the seller, and only if it could be proved that the seller was responsible for or knew about the defect. The manufacturer was, in effect, insulated from legal action.

Not so today.

In recent years, there has been a remarkable tendency in our courts to award damages arising from the use of a product without regard to who may or may not have been at fault. As incredible as it may seem to some of us, the manner in which the product was used no longer seems to be a matter of relevance.

One widely discussed case involved a man who decided that a power lawn mower he was using would make a good hedge trimmer. The results were predictable. The mower slipped from his grasp and severely injured him. The manufacturer was held liable and the man was awarded a large judgment.

How could this be? The mower wasn't defective. The manufacturer had produced a product that satisfied current industry standards for quality and safety; yet despite the obvious and gross misuse of the product, the manufacturer was held liable.

Why? According to the judgment of the court, the manufacturer should have foreseen the possibility that someone might consider putting his product to such a misuse and, therefore, should have placed a warning against doing so in the printed instructions.

An offbeat example? Not at all. The court records of every state contain cases similar in principle. There is, for example, the Oklahoma man who was awarded a $600,000 judgment from a glue manufacturer. The instructions on the glue can warned of the flammability of the product and called for opening windows when using it indoors. As it turned out, there were no windows in the man's workroom for him to open. Conclusion of the court: he should be awarded damages for his burns.

Or consider the Maryland teenager who poured cologne on a lit candle in order to give it a scent. She also collected damages. The manufacturer of the cologne had failed to warn her about the fire that resulted.

Absurd? In the view of some, yes. Absurd or not, however, such happenings are part of the litigious society in which we are living. At least in the previous examples the manufacturers were known and identified. Consider another case.

In 1976, a California resident suffering from cancer filed a lawsuit claiming that a drug her mother had taken 26 years earlier to prevent miscarriage was responsible for her malady. The trouble was that there was no way, after so many years, to prove who had actually manufactured the drug taken by the woman; it had been produced by perhaps a dozen different companies.

The plaintiff solved that problem by naming the five largest producers of the drug on the grounds that anyone of them *might* have been the one that made the drug taken by her mother; therefore, *all* of them should be held liable for the cancer that *may* have been caused by the drug.

A ridiculous case, you say. Certain to be thrown out of court by an irate judge. Think again.

The woman won her case, a decision that was upheld by the California Supreme Court in 1980. The decision rocked the legal world. While there were some who viewed the matter as a "great victory for the consumer," and others who described it as a "legal disaster," just about everyone agreed that the case marked a radical change in product liability law.

One lawyer interpreted the decision as relieving the burden of proving liability from the plaintiff. "It shifts the burden to the manufacturer." he said, "who now must prove that he *didn't* do it" [italics added].

While mine may be the simplistic interpretation of a layman, it seems to me that the decision suggests that the plaintiff in a civil suit no longer need worry about proving the liability of the defendant. Instead, the defendant must somehow prove his innocence. Imagine, if you will, that same doctrine carried over into criminal law. Shades of our forefathers!

In any event, the case represents a completely new legal concept that will eventually have incalculable consequences in our business and social communities.

Whether you agree with my abhorrence of the "'let's sue the bastards" mentality so prevalent today, or whether you, too, feel that such cases represent "victories" for the consumer, there is one consequence that you will have to face as a business executive—insurance.

Insurance

You don't have to be a manufacturer in order to find yourself on the wrong end of a product liability lawsuit. By an extension of the same flawed logic illustrated in the cases just discussed, liability may extend to any business even remotely involved with the product. In many cases, defendants now include everyone from the manufacturer to the distributors, retailers, and even the service organization. Bear in mind that the servicer may not even be accused of negligence in the suit; having been involved with the product in any capacity, it seems, is enough to pose a potential liability.

Authorized in-warranty or franchised service organizations can be especially vulnerable to product liability lawsuits. It is for this reason that trade organizations, such as the National Appliance Service Association, are attempting to convince manufacturers to amend their agreements to provide indemnification for service organizations providing in-warranty service. Up to this point, predictably, the manufacturers have been slow to respond.

Though the service organization cited in a product liability suit (or any type of lawsuit) may eventually be held blameless, the necessary legal defense can incur catastrophic costs. The only sure defense against this sort of financial calamity is a well-designed insurance package.

Of course, if you are an employee of a large company, you can leave it to others to concern themselves with corporate insurance needs. As an owner/manager of a small service organization, though, you ought to know more about insurance needs than your insurance agent. . . . Well, almost.

The unfortunate truth is that the world of insurance is nearly as full of clinical arcana as a medical textbook. As a busy manager, you're not going to have the time to become an expert in insurance. What you can do, though, is acquaint yourself with enough of the basics to enable you to do a good job in picking your insurance agent or broker.

Once you've done that, you'll need to rely on her to advise you on specific coverages.

Take Your Pick

Speaking of coverages, here's just a sampling of the dizzying array of insurance types available today:

Accounts receivable insurance

Automobile insurance

Blanket contractual coverage

Broad-form property damage insurance

Business interruption insurance

Comprehensive general liability insurance

Disability insurance

Fire and flood insurance

Leasehold insurance

Medical-dental insurance

Owner's, landlord's, and tenant's insurance

Payroll insurance

Plate glass insurance

Product liability insurance

Sole-proprietorship life insurance

Surety bond for employees
Umbrella liability coverage
Vandalism and malicious-mischief insurance
Workers' compensation coverage

No, you certainly won't need all these coverages—no single company can afford to take out protection against every conceivable potential loss. That's where a reliable broker or agent comes in. Their training and experience qualify them to analyze your business and to recommend an insurance package suited to your specific needs.

Why not just forget the whole thing and operate without insurance? Perish the thought!

It would be foolish to the extreme to operate any form of service business in our society without at least the basic minimum coverage (and, of course, coverages such as unemployment or workers' compensation are mandated by law). In our litigious environment, a single damage claim can wipe out a business and its owners overnight if they are not covered by the proper kinds of insurance.

Despite the pain that premiums may seem to inflict, the concept of insurance is vitally important; it carries social as well as economic implications. The history of the insurance industry is both long and significant.

The first-known marine insurance was developed in Genoa, Italy in 1348. The owners of the fragile barks then sailing the Mediterranean were suffering high losses. In desperation, a group of owners decided to band together to share the risks. With contributions to a central fund, or "insurance pool", they were able to spread the financial risks evenly among all the participants.

The first fire insurance was to come much later. A year after the great London fire of 1666 destroyed 80% of the city's buildings, the first fire insurance group was organized.

From those simple origins, the insurance industry has grown to become one of the largest and most economically significant on earth.

You and Your Insurance Company

Insurance, then, can be seen as a means for buying protection against the possibility of heavy financial loss from an unexpected event. At the same time, it is a joint social action designed to distribute losses equally among a large group of people who pay in advance.

Of course, the crass arm of commercialism has reached deeply into the relationship between the insured (you) and the carrier (the insurance company)—a fact you would do well to keep in mind. Since you must rely heavily on the advice of your broker or agent once you have selected him, you should remember that he is, above all, a salesperson. Even the most knowledgeable and sincere among them must depend on you and other clients to pay the rent. Make it a point to buy your insurance from someone you know or have checked out thoroughly.

While we're on the subject, keep in mind that insurance companies exist to make a profit—a task for which they have proved to be eminently suited. One of the tools that has contributed greatly to this end is a generous supply of fine print.

Legally, an insurance contract is *uberrima fides*, that is, requiring the utmost good faith on the part of both parties. In plain English: if you fib on your application, you'll find out that you don't have insurance just when you need it. Even a little white lie could result in having your policy declared void.

Also, you must have what is known as "insurable interest" in the covered property. That is, you must be able to establish that you would suffer a direct financial loss if the property were damaged or destroyed. For example, you cannot take out fire insurance on your neighbor's home (unless you happen to own all or part of it) and expect to be paid if the place burns down. To allow you to do so would be nothing more than gambling, and insurance companies aren't allowed to gamble. (Not to mention the temptation to which you would be subjected under such an arrangement.)

Your insurance company may not show much concern about your insurable interest at the time that you take out your policy, but you can be certain that it will demonstrate a great deal of interest in the subject when and if you present a claim. A few policies, in fact, may require that you prove your sole and unconditional ownership of the property before benefits of the policy can be paid.

Will your insurance company try to cheat you? Probably not. Insurance companies are very closely regulated in every one of our fifty states. Every insurance carrier needs a license, and very few of them are likely to risk the loss of that precious piece of paper by indulging in outright mischief. "Fine printing," though, is something else. You can rest assured that insurance policies are meticulously written to afford every legal advantage for the insurance carrier. A good agent or broker notwithstanding, there's nothing like reading the fine print carefully.

But operate without insurance? Never!

Equal Opportunity

In 1964, the Congress of the United States set out to eliminate discrimination in the marketplace; it enacted the Civil Rights Act of 1964. Title VII of that act declares it to be unlawful for an employer "to fail or refuse to hire or to discharge any individual, or otherwise to discriminate against any individual with respect to his compensation, terms, conditions, or privileges of employment, because of such individual's race, color, religion, sex, or national origin."

If your job as service manager involves you in the hiring and firing process in your company, you will want to take careful heed of those provisions as well as similar laws at local and state levels. Technically, Title VII applies only to firms employing fifteen or more persons. In the practical world, though, discrimination against employees in any size firm will expose management to potential legal problems. If you are part of a large corporation, you will almost surely be well-schooled in your responsibilities under Title VII as well as Title 41 of the Code of Federal Regulations, which deals with the subject of affirmative action requirements.

These laws are enforced by an agency of the federal government called the Equal Employment Opportunity Commission, otherwise known as EEOC. This is a group with which you will probably want to avoid any involvement unless it is absolutely necessary.

While there is no substitute for guidance from a professional trained in civil rights legislation, a knowledge of the fundamentals will help you to comply with both the letter and the spirit of the laws concerning the hiring and firing of employees.

Remembering that the basic purpose of civil rights legislation is to prevent discrimination on the basis of race, color, sex, national origin, or age, you should make certain that any preemployment application forms you use do not require that the applicant furnish such information. Also, as an interviewer, you should avoid questioning the applicant on these subjects. Of course, information of this nature necessary for your records may be obtained and recorded *after* an applicant has been hired.

More important, perhaps, are the specifics of your handling of the release of an employee or the rejection of an applicant. Either of these responsibilities can expose you or your company to the risk of legal liability if the person involved is given any reason to believe that your action was the result of discrimination.

The use of business and personal references is a valuable aid in the selection of employees. However, when you elect not to hire an applicant because of an unsatisfactory reference, you should not mention the poor reference as your reason for not hiring, nor should you ever disclose any information supplied to you by a former employer or personal reference. When turning down an applicant, the conventional advice is to simply inform the applicant that someone else has been selected for the position.

Proceed with Caution

Incidentally, since all perspective employers may not be as circumspect in these matters as you are, you should exercise great discretion when answering a reference request involving one of your former employees. When your files contain negative information, you would do well to do no more than confirm that the person in question is indeed a former employee and supply the actual dates when employment began and ended.

If a prospective employer should persist in attempting to obtain additional information, you may want to provide details orally. In such a case, you should exercise restraint and take the necessary steps to verify the identity of the person to whom you are speaking.

Under no circumstances should you provide negative information in writing. To do so would be to make yourself extremely vulnerable to legal action. This precaution is advisable no matter how serious the offense of the former employee or how much proof you may feel that you have of the conduct that led to his dismissal.

On the other side of this coin is the need for you to screen your own job applicants very carefully. You should not restrict your own reference checking out of fear of lawsuits. The only certain protection against being sued would be to avoid any sort of personnel selection whatever—and that could be disastrous.

While there are no current laws that forbid careful investigation of an applicant's background, it would be wise to obtain the applicant's permission in writing before you contact previous employers and other references. This permission can be incorporated right into your application for employment form. If you use outside investigative agencies to provide background reports, it is imperative that the applicant be informed of your intent.

CONSUMER REPORTS

Background and character reports prepared by outside agencies often provide more detailed information on a prospective employee than might be obtained through more conventional reference checks. The use of such reports, however, is regulated by a law known as the Fair Credit Reporting Act, which became effective on April 25, 1971. The obvious purpose of this legislation is to protect the individual's right to privacy and to prevent unfair use of information contained in the files of reporting agencies.

Under the act, reports from outside agencies are called consumer reports, and are divided into two types:

1. Reports based on information already in the files of reporting agencies or available from public records
2. Reports based on investigation and containing subjective information on character, personal reputation, lifestyle, etc.

Obviously, the second type of report provides information in much more depth than the first. However, its use imposes greater disclosure obligations.

One of the most effective ways of minimizing the likelihood of future personnel problems is a careful screening of all job applicants. This must be carried out, though, with a watchful eye toward today's legal constraints.

The checking of references is an important part of a good screening process. However, you should review your methods with your personnel department or legal advisor to make certain that you are operating on a sound legal footing. Legal requirements in this field are constantly changing, and laws vary considerably from one state to another.

Service Legislation

As service managers, we have to pay heed to the same laws that govern the behavior of mortals everywhere—but alas, we also are blessed with a special selection of our own.

The earliest legislation aimed directly at the service industry was probably one of those ubiquitous licensing laws. There probably isn't a single branch of the industry that has escaped the gimlet eye of local licensing authorities somewhere.

Despite their checkered history, licensing laws continue to pop up at local levels in just about every state. Time and again, experience has shown that licensing service firms and individuals does little, if anything, to protect the consumer against incompetent or dishonest workmanship. Instead, the creation of local licensing boards seems to lead to bureaucratic bungling, petty graft, and the drawing up of impractical or unworkable legislation intended to "protect" the consumer against neighborhood businesses trying to serve him.

All this is not intended to suggest that incompetence and dishonesty does not exist within the precincts of our profession—quite the contrary. Ours, as any other business or profession, has at least its fair share of both. It's just that licensing laws have clearly proved themselves to be an aggravation of the problem and not a solution. In recognition of this, many communities have abandoned licensing laws and dismantled local licensing boards.

A case in point is the recent action taken by the Vermont state legislature. After many years of ineffective operation, the Radio/TV Technician's Licensing Board was abolished. According to the former chairman of the licensing board, it never issued a single regulation concerning TV shop operations. The board also lacked investigative authority, though it could request assistance from the state attorney general's office.

The picture that emerged from the legislative study that preceded the repeal of the Vermont licensing law was not an unusual one: an ill-conceived law enforced by a five member licensing panel without sufficient authority to do anything but approve or deny licenses. The result was a predictable failure to accomplish any of the objectives behind most licensing laws.

The Vermont experience is by no means unusual. The same scenario, with minor modifications, has been played out many times in other localities and almost surely will be again.

In her syndicated column, financial writer Sylvia Porter has observed that consumerists are dropping their support of licensing laws because the laws do not appear to be doing their intended jobs. One reason for this apparent reversal of popular opinion is that licensing laws do little or nothing in the way of weeding out the ne'er-do-wells in the service industry. Frequently, this can be traced to insufficient supervision and enforcement by local licensing boards created for the purpose.

Critics of licensing laws charge, among other things, that the laws frequently degenerate into nothing more than revenue-raising vehicles for local treasuries; have resulted in higher service prices; have failed to set workable qualifications for entering the trade; and have often fostered petty graft and fraud. Still, new licensing laws continue to pop up with determined regularity.

Because licensing laws remain in a constant state of flux, you should check with your legal advisor or state and local licensing authorities to see whether any current laws affect your business. Remember the old maxim, "Ignorance of the law is no excuse." It's up to you to determine your own status as far as licensing requirements are concerned.

There are other types of service legislation not concerned with licensing as such. One example is the new set of regulations recently put into effect by the Bureau of Electronic and Appliance Repair in the state of California. The lengthy list of regulations includes one that requires that appliance repairs be made "in a good and workmanlike manner." It will be interesting to note whether these new rules result in an improvement in the quality of workmanship in the California service industry.

Not everyone is opposed to licensing laws and other forms of legislation involving the service industry. There are, in fact, some strong supporters of licensing laws within the industry itself. However, as experience resulting from existing laws accumulates, the ranks of supporters grow thinner and thinner.

As I put the finishing touches on this chapter, I am struck by an interesting question. Have you ever noticed how many of our nation's laws affecting business are identified by the names of the legislators who first sponsored them? We have been blessed with the likes of the Taft-Hartley Law, the McCarran-Walters Act, the Smoot-Hawley Act, the Volstead Act, the Robinson-Patman Act, the Sherman Antitrust Act, and or course, our old favorite, the Magnuson-Moss Warranty Act.

The intriguing possibility occurs to me that if it weren't for this opportunity to enshrine one's name for posterity long after the last election has been lost, we might be able to stem the flood of such legislation. In the meantime, the tide flows on.

Chapter 15
Letters to Help You Manage

As harsh as it may sound, the unvarnished truth is that most service managers are unable to write a clear and effective business letter.

Please. Before you start tearing this book to shreds while shouting obscene references to my heritage, allow me to complete the thought: neither can most doctors, chemists, bus drivers, nor brain surgeons. It's odd but true that one of the most important means of communication in our complex society is outrageously abused by such a large number of people who really ought to know better.

I have been intrigued for many years by the high percentage of our population of sophisticated business executives who have never made the effort to learn how to compose a lucid business letter. I was puzzled at first. I had always assumed that education and experience were all that were needed to mold an effective communicator. Not so.

The truth of the matter is that most people—well-educated or not—are relatively ineffective when it comes to communicating through the use of the written word. Interestingly, not even an encyclopedic knowledge of such things as grammar, syntax, and the conjugation of verbs can provide assurance of letter-writing proficiency. There are some people in fact, who believe that "college professor" knowledge of the language may sometimes be a handicap when it comes to writing letters that must be clearly understood by the recipients.

The self-contained paradox in such a thought is, of course, quite obvious. Perhaps it would be more accurate just to say that a sharply honed knowledge of the technicalities of the English language is no *guarantee* of the ability to transfer one's thoughts to paper with accuracy and precision. Back in Chapter 3 I gave you some examples of hopelessly convoluted letters written by people whose knowledge of the language is much better than average. In contrast, I know a number of people with only the most modest of formal educations who are quite able to turn out beautifully concise and clear letters with little apparent effort.

Perhaps it can be said, then, that successfully communicating your thoughts by means of the written word is a special skill quite apart from a knowledge of the technical subtleties of the language.

This point, I believe, is well illustrated by the large body of accomplished professional and businessmen who are terrible letter writers. Many business executives whose powers of persuasion in face-to-face discussions are awesome, are pussy cats when faced with the need to translate their ideas into written form. Several professional men of my acquaintance will privately admit to their inability to compose a simple declarative sentence without considerable agonizing. Without a goodly portion of "whereas," "wherefore," and "pursuant to," some lawyers would be unable to communicate with the rest of us at all.

GOOD ADVICE FROM MALCOLM FORBES

Lest you come to think that all of this is but a shameful exaggeration on my part, consider the words of Malcolm Forbes, editor-in-chief of venerable *Forbe's Magazine*: "Over 10,000 business letters come across my desk every year. They seem to fall into three categories: stultifying if not stupid, mundane (most of them), and first-rate (rare)."

I can't imagine a more imposing set of credentials for evaluating business letters than those belonging to Mr. Forbes. With the permission of the copyright owner, here are some specific suggestions offered by Mr. Forbes in an essay written for International Paper Company:

KNOW WHAT YOU WANT

If you don't, write it down—in one sentence. 'I want to get an interview within the next two weeks.' That simple. List the major points you want to get across—it'll keep you on course.

If you're *answering* a letter, check the points that need answering and keep the letter in front of you while you write. This way you won't forget anything—*that* would cause another round of letters.

And for goodness' sake, answer promptly if you're going to answer at all. Don't sit on a letter—*that* invites the person on the other end to sit on whatever you want from *him*.

PLUNGE RIGHT IN

Call Him by Name.—not "Dear Sir, Madam, or Ms." "Dear Mr. Chrisanthopoulos"—and be sure to spell it right. That'll get him (thus you) off to a good start. (Usually you can get his name just by phoning his company—or from a business directory in your nearest library.)

Tell What Your Letter Is About in the First Paragraph. One or two sentences. Don't keep your reader guessing or he might file your letter away—even before he finishes it.

In the round file.

If you're answering a letter, refer to the date it was written. So the reader won't waste time hunting for it.

People who read business letters are as human as thee and me. Reading a letter shouldn't be a chore—*reward* the reader for the time he gives you.

WRITE SO HE'LL ENJOY IT

Write the Entire Letter from His Point of View.—what's in it for *him*? Beat him to the draw—surprise him by answering the questions and objections he might have.

Be Positive.—he'll be more receptive to what you have to say.

Be Nice. Contrary to the cliché, genuinely nice guys most often finish first or very near it. I admit it's not easy when you've got a gripe. To be agreeable while disagreeing—that's an art.

Be Natural—Write the Way You Talk. Imagine him sitting in front of you—what would you *say* to him?

Business jargon too often is cold, stiff, unnatural.

Suppose I came up to you and said, "I acknowledge receipt of your letter and beg to thank you." You'd think, "Huh? You're putting me on."

The acid test—read your letter *out loud* when you're done. You might get a shock—but you'll know for sure if it sounds natural.

Don't Be Cute or Flippant. The reader won't take you seriously. This doesn't mean you've got to be dull. You prefer your letter to knock 'em dead rather than bore 'em to death.

Three points to remember:

Have a Sense of Humor. That's refreshing *anywhere*—a nice surprise in a business letter.

Be Specific. If I tell you there's a new fuel that could save gasoline, you might not believe me. But suppose I tell you this:

'Gasohol'—10% alcohol, 90% gasoline—works as well as straight gasoline. Since you can make alcohol from grain or corn stalks, wood or waste, coal—even garbage, it's worth some real follow-through.

Now you've got something to sink your teeth into.

Lean Heavier on Nouns and Verbs, Lighter on Adjectives. Use the Active Voice Instead of the Passive. Your writing will have more guts.

Which of these is stronger?

Active voice: "I kicked out my money manager." Or, passive voice: "My money manager was kicked out by me."

GIVE IT THE BEST YOU'VE GOT

When you don't want something enough to make *the* effort, making *an* effort is a waste.

Make Your Letter Look Appetizing—or you'll strike out before you even get to bat. Type it—on good quality 8½ x 11 stationery. Keep it neat. And use paragraphing that makes it easier to read.

Keep Your Letter Short—to one page, if possible. Keep your paragraphs short. After all, who's going to benefit if your letter is quick and easy to read?

You.

For emphasis, *underline* important words. And sometimes indent sentences as well as paragraphs.

Like this. See how well it works? (But save it for something special.)

Make It Perfect. No typos, no misspellings, no factual errors. If you're sloppy and let mistakes slip by, the person reading your letter will think you don't know better or don't care. Do you?

Be Crystal Clear. You won't get what you're after if your reader doesn't get the message.

Don't Put on Airs. Pretense invariably impresses only the pretender.

Don't Exaggerate. Even once. Your reader will suspect everything else you write.

Edit Ruthlessly. Somebody said that words are like inflated money—the more you use, the less each one is worth. Go through your entire letter as many times as it takes. Annihilate all unnecessary words, sentences—even paragraphs.

SUM IT UP AND GET OUT The last paragraph should tell the reader exactly what you want *him* to do—or what *you're* going to do. Short and sweet. "May I have an appointment? Next Monday, the 16th, I'll call your secretary to see when it'll be convenient for you."

Close with something simple like, "Sincerely." And for heaven's sake sign legibly. The biggest ego trip I know is a completely illegible signature.

There are, as you undoubtedly know, many other disciples of clarity and precision in the written word. One of my favorites is Rudolph Flesch. In the event that you are fortunate enough to have developed an interest in improving your writing skills, I suggest that you beg, borrow, or steal a copy of anything written by Professor Flesch. In particular, *The Art of Readable Writing* (Collier, New York, 1962) should be considered a mandatory addition to your personal library. As is the case with most of Flesch's books, it is available in inexpensive paperback.

Finally, I want to recommend one more book to you: *The Elements of Style* (Macmillan, New York, 1972). This tiny paperback (about ¼-inch thick) is regarded by many as a genuine masterpiece of instruction in effective use of the language. Originally written by Dr. Strunk in 1935, it is viewed as indispensable by many of today's English instructors. Adhering to his own preachments about brevity, Dr. Strunk kept the book short enough that it can easily be read from cover to cover in a single evening. But don't let that fool you. If you buy a copy, I daresay that you will find yourself browsing through its fascinating pages many times through the years. Here's a sample:

> Vigorous writing is concise. A sentence should have no unnecessary words, a paragraph no unnecessary sentences, for the same reason that a drawing should have no unnecessary lines and a machine no unnecessary parts.

Top that for sheer poetry.

Enough theory. Let's get down to some specific suggestions and examples.

WRITING TO YOUR BOSS

Unless you are the owner of your own service business, you have a boss. If you do have a boss, you almost certainly will be required to communicate with him in writing—perhaps frequently. Doing it well will be to your advantage.

Use the Inverted Pyramid

There is perhaps no other circumstance where brevity and precision will be more important than in a letter addressed to your boss. For that reason, the "inverted pyramid" is something you should know about.

Developed in newspaper journalism, the inverted pyramid is the name given to that style of writing that crams the most important information into the opening lines of a news article. As the reader gets further into the piece, background information of lesser importance is developed.

Here is an example of a news article written in the inverted pyramid style. Note how the most important fact in the story is contained in the opening sentence, with details of lesser importance coming as the reader continues into the body of the piece.

> Pittsburgh, Pa.—John Wasko was convicted yesterday of first-degree murder in the death of an Allegheny County woman he had admitted shooting during a crime spree that claimed four lives.
>
> The jury deliberated about two hours before returning the verdict against Wasko, of Pittsburgh, one of two men accused in the string of killings committed last year.
>
> The verdict carries a mandatory life sentence.
>
> In a tape-recorded confession played for the jury Friday, Wasko said he shot Mary Lou Olden, 26, also of Pittsburgh, early on January 1, at the urging of his companion, Michael Coniglia.
>
> The two men were hitchhiking when Miss Olden gave then a ride.
>
> The victim died of gunshot wounds to the head and chest.

If this were a fiction story instead of a news article, the facts may well have been presented in precisely the reverse order of that in which they actually appear.

The purpose of the inverted pyramid, of course, is to capture the interest of the large number of us who are "scanners." We want our information quickly with a minimum of unnecessary verbiage. The inverted pyramid gives us the important facts "up front." Readers who are interested in supporting information can get it by continuing to read. Facts of least importance will be found only by those who elect to read the entire piece.

Without ever having heard of the inverted pyramid, many busy executives demand that memos and letters addressed to them be in that format. One executive I know advises his subordinates, "'Put your summary up front. After I read that, I'll know whether I want to continue further." Other executives, while they may not have given as much conscious thought to the subject, instinctively appreciate business letters that come to the point quickly. Chances are that your boss is among them.

Some Examples

Let's say that the boss received a complaint from a customer who was able to get her washing machine repaired by a competitor for much less than the estimate given by your service department. He asked you to look into the complaint and to report back to him in writing. Your reply might go something like this:

> Dear Mr. _____
>
> Regarding the complaint you got from Mrs. Wilcox.
>
> I'm afraid we goofed on this one. The technician did diagnose the problem correctly, but he neglected to explain that operation could be restored without making the complete repair.
>
> The gear case is badly worn and noisy, but was not replaced by the company that did the repair. It undoubtedly will fail in the near future.
>
> I called Mrs. Wilcox and gave her a complete explanation of all this. She appreciated our interest and assured me that she will come to us for her future service needs.
>
> Signed _____

If we examine this letter in terms of effective communication, we find that we can give it a reasonably good report. The boss probably noticed it too. The subject and the reason for the letter are spelled out in the short opening sentence. This is followed by a brief description of the problem and, finally, by the good news that you have resolved the complaint and there is no further action needed by the boss. All in less than 100 words.

While not all problems can be handled with such dispatch, the written communications concerning them almost always can be. Any executive receiving a letter such as the one above could hardly help but be pleased.

Let's consider another example. This time, your boss has expressed concern over the drop in gross profit in your parts department recently. She's asked for an analysis of the problem and your thoughts about it.

> Dear Ms. _____
>
> About our gross profit on parts. Here's what it looks like so far this year:
>
> | January | 48.2% |
> | February | 47.9% |
> | March | 47.7% |
> | April | 47.8% |
> | May | 47.8% |
> | June | 47.9% |
>
> Please note that a reversal of the decline began in April. I believe that the upward trend will continue steadily until we get back to our usual 48.5%.
>
> The trouble, I found, was due to our switching to a new supplier for rebuilt timers. The failure rate on these units has proved to be alarmingly high, causing a rise in our returns and allowances account. Reimbursement from the supplier has been slow.

We've gone back to our old source now. The resulting lowering of our allowances plus reimbursements from the discontinued source will allow us to regain our old gross profit within another 60 days.
If anything should happen to change this projection, I'll let you know.
Signed _____

Again, you've written a brief but responsive letter. It won't take the boss long to read it, and she'll understand exactly what you're saying.

LETTERS TO CUSTOMERS

Perhaps the greatest demands on a service manager's letter-writing skills come in the form of the need to reply to customer's letters of inquiry or complaint. Many a customer has been won or forever lost on the basis of a single letter—or a single sentence within a letter.

I remember a letter I once wrote to a well-known typewriter manufacturer. The reply I received from their customer relations (?) director was a classic of ineptitude and unresponsiveness.

In my letter, I courteously explained that I was a long-time user as well as a booster of the firm's products. My problem was with their typewriter-ribbon cartridges. After the third one jammed and became useless about halfway through its length, I wrote to call their attention to the problem and to the fact that I did not receive full use of the three cartridges in question.

The reply subtley berated me for not proving my "claim" by mailing back the defective cartridges. The implication that I was in some way trying to cheat the company was unarguably clear. Although their letter was accompanied by several replacement cartridges, its tone left me so furious that the attempt to reimburse my loss was completely meaningless to me.

Had the writer of the letter been more keenly tuned in to the demands of his profession, he would have clearly seen that the same three cartridges (or no cartridges at all) accompanied by a courteous "thank you" for calling attention to the problem would have created a dedicated customer and a valuable walking advertisement for the company. A positive rather than a negative result for the same effort and cost.

You, of course, will never be guilty of such an obvious assault against the best interests of your company.

In an attempt to help business letter writers avoid such gaffes, the U. S. Postal Service has developed what they call ten "magic" phrases. Their use should minimize the likelihood that any of your letters will alienate, rather than ingratiate, customers.

1. I apologize.
2. Thank you for letting us know about this.
3. I would feel the same way if I were in your position.
4. We appreciate your interest.
5. We are pleased to. . . .
6. We are sorry to hear of the problem you have experienced with. . . .
7. We hope you find this useful (or helpful).
8. We share your concern.
9. I want you to know.
10. If I can be of further help, please let me know.

A liberal sprinkling of these phrases (or similar ones) in your letters will surely increase your "customer satisfaction quotient."

Let's consider a few examples of letters that satisfy the requirements we've been discussing.

LETTERS THAT SAY "NO"

Regardless of your dedication to customer satisfaction, you will occasionally find yourself in a position of having to say "no." That's never an easy job for a concerned professional, but if it's done carefully, you may save a customer that might otherwise be lost to your company.

Any hint of curtness in a turndown letter is certain to produce a resentful customer who can be depended upon to broadcast ill feelings to others. The first order of business when saying "no," then, is to say it with courtesy and understanding. Some other hints:

1. Start out by thanking the customer for writing.
2. Indicate that you understand how the customer feels.
3. Explain courteously *why* you are not able to allow the customer's request.
4. Express your sincere regret for your inability to say "yes" in this case.

Here's how one major appliance manufacturer handles the problem:

    Dear Customer _____
        Thank you for taking the time to tell us about your recent experience with your ABC washer.

Yes, we certainly do expect our products to last longer than 2 years. As a matter of fact, our records show an average life of more than 13 years for our clothes washers.

However, occasional failures of mechanical parts can be expected in any machine that does the kind of hard work done by a modern automatic washer. Replacement of the worn parts, as was true in your case, will usually restore the machine to normal functions. Such failures do not mean that the life of the machine has been adversely affected.

Experience and careful record keeping over the years have shown us that failures caused by defects in manufacture almost always happen during the first few months of product life. For that reason, our company, as well as most others, have established a 1-year warranty on parts and labor.

In order to be absolutely fair to all ABC customers, it is necessary that we apply the warranty uniformly to all. I do hope that you can appreciate the necessity of this. To extend the warranty for some owners and not for others would be unfair.

While we are unable to honor your request for a refund of the repair charges, we do regret any inconvenience that the incident may have caused you.

Please be assured, Mrs. _____, that we sincerely appreciate your patronage, and all of us here at ABC look forward to the pleasure of serving your future needs.

Sincerely _____

Requests for Technical Help

For some service organizations, written requests for technical help for do-it-yourselfers is a perplexing problem. While customer satisfaction is the fundamental responsibility of every service organization, requests for written technical advice can pose certain legal risks. Given today's litigious environment, a do-it-yourselfer who causes damage or injury while attempting to follow your well-intentioned advice may well be transformed at the twist of a screwdriver from a valued customer to a hungry plaintiff.

Of course, depending on the merchandise you service, such risks may or may not be a significant factor in your organization. In any case, if you do find it advisable to turn down requests for technical advice, you should make every effort to do so in a manner that will avoid alienation of your customer. Here's an example of how one firm does it:

Dear _____

Thank you for your letter requesting our help in diagnosing and repairing your ABC microwave oven.

We were very pleased to hear, Mr. _____, of the satisfactory service you have been receiving from our product. I am sorry to tell you, though, that we are unable to honor your request for technical assistance.

Microwave ovens pose very serious dangers when repairs are attempted by anyone other than a qualified technician. Encouraging our customers to expose themselves to such risks simply would not be in the best interests of them or us. I do hope that you understand.

Enclosed with this letter is a copy of the parts list and owner's manual originally packaged with your model. This information details the limits of repairs and adjustments that can be safely made by the user. Should your ABC oven require service of a technical nature, you should contact our nearest authorized service dealer.

Again, let me thank you for your use of ABC products. We do hope that we may look forward to your continued patronage.

Sincerely _____

Of course, the recipient of such a letter may well go ahead with his attempt to make repairs. The company's position, though, will not have been compromised by your letter.

Saying "no" to a customer does not have to be a difficult job. For someone not concerned with keeping valuable customers, the job is not at all difficult. For a professional service manager, though, each case will be a new and difficult challenge.

LETTERS FROM SATISFIED CUSTOMERS

"And what is so rare as a day in June?" Well, for one thing, try complimentary letters from customers. It's human nature, I suppose. When we're happy with a product or service, we can always tell someone tomorrow. When we're angry, though, we want to tell the world—right now!

For that reason, the customer who takes the time to write a complimentary letter should be treated as a very special person. He deserves a prompt reply—one that fully expresses your appreciation and thanks for his patronage. Here's an example from a national service organization.

Dear _____

Thank you so much for your recent letter.

As you may know, satisfied customers seldom take the time and trouble to write about their experiences. For that reason, we here at ABC are especially appreciative when we receive a letter such as yours.

Customer satisfaction is very important to us, and it gives us a real boost to get a good report from a happy customer.

I know that our technician, Mr. _____, will be especially pleased to see your nice comments about his work. Your letter will be made part of his personnel file.

Once again, thank you for your letter and for the opportunity to be of service.

Sincerely _____

CONSUMER AGENCIES

It is a fact of life today that third parties are frequently invited into disputes between a customer and the company that has provided a product or service. As consumerism becomes more deeply rooted in our marketplace, the customer who takes a complaint to a government agency, a state or local congressional representative, the Better Business Bureau, the local newspaper "Action Line" column, or any form of consumer activist group will become even more common.

Even-handedness and uniformity in resolving complaints that reach you through an outside agency are especially important. Settlements or concessions beyond your normal guidelines may appear to offer an opportunity to gain favor; in time, though, they will backfire. Generosity that appears to be an appeasement to the agency, rather than a genuine attempt to win back the customer, will only serve to make the agency (and the customer) suspicious of your motives—and will eventually result in even more complaints directed to the agency rather than to you.

You are not alone if you should happen to feel a twinge of resentment when you receive a letter of complaint from a third party, not even a customer of your firm, asking for a direct reply. However, in the event that you feel the urge to ignore such a letter or to dash off a nasty "none of your business" reply, I urge you to resist the temptation. Although the experience can be galling, you shouldn't permit yourself to minimize the significance of the fact that one of your customers has felt the need to seek help from a third party. Furthermore, negative publicity—or worse, depending on the agency—may well result from any intransigence on your part, justified or not.

On the other hand, a professional response to a consumer agency will help to establish your credibility and make it easier to deal with the agency in the future. Here is a reply to a consumer agency concerning service rates:

> Dear _____
>   Thank you for the opportunity to explain our system for establishing repair charges.
>   We're sorry that our customer, Mrs. _____, felt it necessary to contact you. Here at ABC, customer satisfaction is an important part of our business philosophy. Naturally, we were distressed to learn in this manner of her problem.
>   In order to provide uniformity in this important part of our business, we make use of a nationally available flat-rate pricing manual. This system, used by thousands of service companies nationwide, establishes a fixed time value for every repair job. The publisher analyzes many thousands of actual repairs to arrive at an average time for completion; thus, the customer is assured of paying

for no more than the average time required for any specific repair. Our own hourly rate is then applied against these time factors to arrive at the exact labor charge. Our current hourly rate is $30.

Of course, some individual jobs require less, and some more, time than the average. This cannot be avoided. The advantage to our customer, though, is in knowing *in advance* exactly what the repair charge will be. An inexperienced technician or any unusual circumstances that would require extra time on the job become our responsibility and not the customer's.

I hope this provides you with the information you need in order to reply to Mrs. _____. If I can be of any further help, please let me know.

Sincerely _____

This is another reply to a question about repair charges:

Dear _____

Thank you for your letter of January 24. I was disappointed to learn that our customer, Mrs. _____, felt it necessary to take her complaint to a third party. Nevertheless, I appreciate the opportunity to respond.

Let me begin by saying that I agree comletely that $74 is a lot of money to pay for the repair of an air conditioner.

Unfortunately, we here at ABC are caught up in the same inflationary pressures that are a worry to everyone today. The prices that we must pay for the labor and other elements that go into professional repair service are constantly rising. The result is that service rates must go up in price just like everything else.

The technician's wage rate is only one of the factors that contribute to our hourly rate of $32 for home service. Such things as truck and travel costs, tools and test equipment, insurance, technical training, rent, and salaries of backup personnel are just some of the other expenses that must be paid.

Please be assured that our service rates are the lowest possible, consistent with today's economy and with our guarantee of quality service. In our experience, bargain-basement service is no bargain at all in the long run.

If and when economic conditions should permit, you can be certain that ABC will be among the first to lower our charges to reflect those changes.

Sincerely _____

You may or may not choose to send your customer a carbon copy of a letter to an agency. Some service executives advise against the practice, suggesting the possibility that this may set off another round of letters from the customer. This has not been my experience. I prefer to let the customer see a straightforward reply because there is less likelihood that the customer or the agency will infer that there is anything to hide.

SALES PROMOTION LETTERS

Selling anything, especially intangibles, by means of the written word is a devilishly difficult task not recommended for amateurs (see Chapter 10). In addition to the sort of writing skills discussed in this chapter, sales letters demand psychological insights and motivational techniques too subtle for most of us to master. Here's a letter said to have brought good response for an automobile agency:

> Dear Mr. _____
> It takes the two of us together to see that your Cadillac gets the recommended maintenance it requires.
> Your part is to bring your Cadillac in for recommended maintenance services when it needs them. Our part is to keep you informed about your Cadillac's maintenance schedule and provide the quality service your Cadillac needs. We want you to get the most from your car, and we're doing our best to see that you do.
> That's why we're sending you the enclosed folder. It briefly describes why it's important to you to have recommended maintenance services performed on a timely, regular basis.
> ABC Cadillac Co. shares your responsibility of seeing to it that your Cadillac is properly maintained. We do our best to remind you when maintenance services are due. We have the people, tools, equipment, and GM-approved replacement parts to help keep your Cadillac running the way it was built to run.
> Stop in and see us whenever you need service or have a question about your car. We'll do our part to keep you completely satisfied with your Cadillac.
> Sincerely _____

That excellent letter was probably commissioned by General Motors from among the most talented writers in the business.

Here's a letter used by Tom Thomas, president of Certified Electronics in Pueblo, Colorado, to find out whether his customers are as satisfied as he wants them to be with his TV repair service:

> Dear _____
> It will always be our pleasure to serve you!
> Thank you so much for your patronage. We genuinely appreciate you as our customer, and you have our assurance that we shall make every effort to maintain the type of relationship so necessary for your continued confidence and goodwill.
> Our sole intention is to maintain our position as the most professional television service facility in Pueblo. We, therefore, frequently ask our customers to give us their comments as to the type of job we are doing.
> We would like you to take just a moment and help us by completing the information below and returning it to us in the postage-free envelope. We value your opinion, and for taking the time to help us, we will send you a free gift, a copy of the *Guinness Sports Record Book*. The book is excellent and offers pictures and facts about all the world of sports.
> If you care to respond to the questions and to receive the free *Sports Record Book*, simply fill in and mail the letter (we must have it with your name on it so we'll know who to send the book to!). Either way, we again wish to thank you for your patronage and sincerely hope that you remain our customer.
> Sincerely _____

At the bottom of the letter, there is a series of questions involving the quality of the service rendered. A postage-paid reply envelope is also included. Mr. Thomas may not have called upon the best advertising talent available on Madison Avenue to compose his letter, but I believe that we can safely assume that it gives his customers a nice, warm feeling to receive one.

Letter writing, as I mentioned earlier, is not everyone's long suit. And it probably would be possible for a reasonably successful service manager to avoid the task almost entirely—if he were determined to do so. It makes more sense, though, to recognize that effective written communications are an extremely valuable tool for helping to bridge the gap between people who, for one reason or another, are unable to meet face to face.

Customers, bosses, subordinates. At some point, relations among all of these people will be affected—either positively or negatively—by way of the written word. With a little effort, you can raise yourself a notch above those who have denied themselves this important means for improving effectiveness on the job.

Necessarily, this chapter is limited to a sprinkling of sample letters. If you feel that you would like to explore the subject further, I recommend the *Customer Service Manual* by Benjamin French (Prentice-Hall, Englewood Cliffs, N.J., 1976). It has what may be the largest collection of model letters, paragraphs, and forms directly applicable to service management ever put together in a single volume.

Ideally, every business contact that you make would be in person. Since that obviously cannot be the case, why not take the necessary steps to ensure that your letters help you to do an even better job of professional service management.

ADDITIONAL READINGS

True professionals recognize the responsibility for keeping up with the latest innovations, techniques, and just plain news relevant to their work. Books and magazines pertinent to the field are valuable tools, assisting the professionals in attaining their goals. In the service business, we are fortunate to be able to choose from a list that represents just about every specialized activity in the industry. While the following list is by no means complete, it does include a selection of the most respected journals in the field:

Automotive Equipment

BRAKE & FRONT END SERVICE
   11 S. Forge St.
   Akron, Ohio 44304
CANADIAN AUTOMOTIVE TRADE MAGAZINE
   MacLean-Hunter Ltd.,
   481 University Ave.
   Toronto, Ontario MSW 1A7
   Canada
THE CHEK-CHART SERVICE BULLETIN
   Box 6227,
   San Jose, CA 95159

MOTOR MAGAZINE
>Hearst Corporation
>224 W. 57th St.
>New York, N.Y. 10019

MOTOR SERVICE
>Hunter Publishing Co.
>53 W. Jackson Blvd.
>Chicago, IL 60604

SERVICE STATION AND GARAGE MANAGEMENT
>109 Vanderhoof Ave., Suite 101
>Toronto, Ontario M4G 2J2
>Canada

Aviation

INTERNATIONAL AVIATION MECHANICS JOURNAL
>211 S. 4th St.
>Basin, WY 82410

Electrical Equipment

ELECTRICAL APPARATUS
>Barks Publications, Inc.
>400 N. Michigan Ave.
>Chicago, IL 60611

Electronics

SERVICE SHOP (Official organ of the
National Electronic Service Dealers Association)
>2708 W. Berry St.
>Fort Worth, Texas, 76109

TWO-WAY RADIO DEALER
>Titsch Publishing Co.
>Box 5400-TA
>Denver, CO 80217

Appliances

APPLIANCE SERVICE NEWS
>P.O. Box 789
>Lombard, IL 60148

Heavy Duty Equipment

HEAVY DUTY EQUIPMENT MAINTENANCE
>7300 N. Cicero Ave.
>Lincolnwood, IL 60646

ADDITIONAL READINGS

Security Alarms

A.I.D. (ALARM INSTALLER AND DEALER)
Fortuna Publishing Co., Inc.
Box 9200
Calabasas, CA 91302

Heating, Air Conditioning

AIR CONDITIONING, HEATING AND REFRIGERATION NEWS
Box 2600
Troy, MI 48084
CONTRACTOR MAGAZINE
Berkshire Common
Pittsfield, MA 01201
HEATING, PLUMBING, AIR CONDITIONING
1450 Don Mills Rd.
Don Mills, Ontario M3B 2X7
Canada

General Merchandise

CHAIN STORE AGE, GENERAL MERCHANDISE EDITION
425 Park Ave.
New York, N.Y. 10022

By one definition, management is the art of getting things done through other people. Whether the subject can be legitimately summed up so neatly is open to question. However, there is little room for doubt about the need for today's manager to demonstrate a high degree of interpersonal skills. The following are a few of my favorite books on this subject:

Effective Management

Fred J. Carvell, *Human Relations in Business*, Macmillan Book Company, New York, 1980.
Peter F. Drucker, *The Effective Executive*, Harper & Row, 1967.
Ray A. Killian, *Managers Must Lead*, Amacom, 1979.
Lawrence L. Steinmetz, *Human Relations: People and Work*, Harper & Row, 1979.

Index

Accomplishment, need for sense of, 27
Accounting, 170–171
    assets, 174
    balance sheet, 173–176
    basic ratios, 176–178
    current assets, 176
    fixed assets, 176
    liabilities, 174
    net worth, 174–176
    ratios, 171–173
Accounting for Non-Accountants (Meyer), 178
Acme Visible Records, 95–96
Advancement, need for employee, 25
Advertising:
    by direct mail, 140–142
    by Yellow Pages, 137–140
Affirmative action, 200–201
Andreason, Alan, 9
Art of Readable Writing, The (Flesch), 209
Assets, 174
    current, 176
    fixed, 176

Balance sheet, 173–176
Bench stocks, 83–84
Bernatavicius, Al, 130

Best, Arthur, 9
Better Light Better Sight Bureau, 81
Bleuel, William H., 125
Broken promises, 160–161
Bryan, William Jennings, 37
Burns, James McGregor, 17
Business community, service industry and, 7–8
Business letters, 205–206
    to the boss, 209–212
    to consumer agencies, 216–217
    to customers, 212–215
    Malcolm Forbes' advice on, 206–209
    requests for technical help, 214–215
    responding to letters from satisfied customers, 215
    for sales promotion, 217–219
    (*See also* Communication skills)

California Bureau of Electronic and Appliance Repair, 204
California Supreme Court, 196
Carnegie, Andrew, 16
Carry-in service, 86-87
Chilton's Professional Labor Guide and Parts Manual, 116
Citizens band (CB) radio, 69–70

223

Civil Rights Act (1964), Title VII, 200
Civil Tongue, A (Newman), 34
C.O.D. billing, 180
Communication skills, 29-30
   good listening, 30
   good vocabulary, 30–32
   improving, 35–37
   meeting manners, 41–42
   misinterpretation, problems of, 32–35
   speech, making a, 38–39
   the spoken word, 37–38
   the written word, 39–41
   (*See also* Business letters)
Complaints, customer, 158–161
   satisfaction audit, 166–168
   by telephone, 161–163
   unreasonable, handling, 163–166, 213–214
Consumer:
   contemporary, 4
   warranties and guarantees for (*see* Warranties)
   (*See also* Customers)
Consumer agencies, letters to, 216–217
Consumer reports, 201–202
Contracts, service (*see* Service contracts)
Cook, Alistair, 36
Cost of goods, 103
   (*See also* Expenses, controlling)
Credit cards, 181
Current assets, 176
Customer satisfaction audit, 166–168
Customer Service Manual (French), 219
Customers:
   broken promises to, 160–161
   business letters to, 212–215
   demands for service from, 9–10
   expectations of, 11–12
   importance of, 156–158
   letters from satisfied, 215
   listening to, 158–160
   saying "no" to, 163–166, 213–214
   service manager and, 155–168
   telephone complaints from, 161–163
   (*See also* Consumer; Legal considerations; Selling services; Service contracts)

Daily open to spend (DOS), 186–187
Dewey, John, 31
Dignity of employee, 18–20, 25–26
Direct mail:
   advertising by, 140–142
   in service contracts, 129–131
Discipline, need for employee, 21–24
Dispatching (*see* Routing and dispatching)
DOS (daily open to spend), 186–187
Drop-off, road calls and, 76
Durant, William Crapo, 2

E. F. Johnson Company, 71
Economy TV, 84
80/20 rule for inventories, 92
Elements of Style, The (Strunk), 209
Employees:
   accessibility to management, 26–27
   accomplishment, need for sense of, 27
   advancement, need for, 25
   benefits for, 185
   defalcations by, 185–186
   discipline for, 21–24
   equal employment opportunity for, 200–201
   fundamental physical needs of, 25–28
   grievances of, 24–25
   personal dignity of, 18–20, 25–26
   personal recognition of, 20–21, 26
   recreation and leisure time for, 25
   security for, 26
   working conditions of, 26
   (*See also* Legal considerations; Technicians)
Energy, controlling expenses on, 154
Energy Products and Services Association (E.P.S.A.), 11
Equal employment opportunity, 200–201
Equal Employment Opportunity Commission (EEOC), 200
Estimates, charging for, 118–119
   (*See also* Service rates)
Expense control checklist, 185–187
Expenses, controlling:
   on energy, 154
   and a healthy business, 184–187

Expenses, controlling (*Cont.*):
  on paper and printing, 150–151
  on payrolls, 146–148
  on supplies, 148–151
  on technical payroll, 146–147
  on telephones, 151–154

Factory concept for service industry, 44–45, 79–82
  (*See also* Shop layout and work flow)
Fair Credit Reporting Act (1971), 202
Federal Trade Commission, 191
Federal Warranty Law, 191–194
Fees, collecting, 179–180
Feigelman, Nathan, 139
Financial incentives, productivity and, 61–62
Fixed assets, 176
Flat-rate system, 114–118
Flesch, Rudolph, 209
Forbes, Malcolm, 206–209
Ford, Henry, 16
French, Benjamin, 219
Full warranties, 191–193

General Electric, 69, 71
General Motors Corporation, 2
Glass, Dick, 120
GNP (gross national product), service industry as percentage of, 2–3
Grayson, Charles Jackson, Jr., 44, 51, 55
Grid routing, 77
Gross profit, 103
Guarantees, 189–191

Hagstrom Co., 77
Hawthorne Research, 48
Healthy business, 169–170
  accounting, 170–178
  managing for profit, 178–181
  profit and loss statement, 170–178
  role of technician in, 181–187
Hearne Bros., 77
Hearst, William Randolph, 31
Hoge, Cecil C., Jr., 130

Hourly rate system, 108–110
  determining costs in, 110–112
Housekeeping:
  productivity and, 61
  shop layout and, 87–88
Human relations, laws of, 17–25

Implied warranties, 193–194
Income, developing, 179
Insurance, 196–199
Inventories:
  components of, 94–95
  deletions in, 97–98
  determining size of, 93–94
  80/20 rule for, 92
  level of service and, 90–92
  minimum quantity (MQ), 98–100
  order quantity (OQ), 98–100
  out-of-stocks, 98–100
  profit from parts department, 102–104
  purpose of, 89–90
  record-keeping, 95–97
  stocking service vehicles, 100–102
  turnovers and, 94

Job security, 26

Laws of human relations, 17–25
Lawyers (*see* Legal considerations)
Leadership (Burns), 17
Legal considerations, 188-189
  consumer reports, 201–202
  equal employment opportunity, 200–201
  insurance, 196–199
  Magnum-Moss Warranty Act, 191–194
  product liability, 194–197
  service legislation, 202–204
  warranties and guarantees, 189–191
Legislation:
  consumer protection, 201–202
  product liability, 194–196
  service, 202–204
  warranties, 191–194
Letters, business (*see* Business letters)

Liabilities, 174
Licensing laws, 202–204
Lighting, 81
Limited warranties, 191–193
Listening, art of, 30, 158–160

MacPherson v. *Buick Motor Company*, 194
Magnum-Moss Warranty Act (1975), 191–194
Maintenance, preventive (PM), 142–143
Manager (*see* Service manager)
Manners, meeting, 41–42
 (*See also* Communication skills)
Markup, 102–103
Masten, Thorton P., 126
Meeting manners, 41–42
 (*See also* Communication skills)
Meyer, John M., 178
Minimum quantity (MQ), 98–100
Money and Motivation (Whyte), 48
Motivation, productivity and, 46–49
Motor Parts and Time Guide, 116
Motorola, 71

National Appliance Service Association, 196
National Association of Retail Dealers of America (NARDA), 50, 95
National Association of Service Managers, The, 168
NEBS, 143
Net profit, 103–104
Net worth, 174–176
Newman, Edwin, 34

O'Connor, Johnson, 31
Order quantity (OQ), 98–100
Oregon Professional Electronics Association (OPEA), 138
Out-of-stocks, 98–100

Paper, controlling expenses on, 150–151
Paperwork, productivity and, 53–55
Parkinson, C. Northcote, 64

Patton, Joseph D., Jr., 125
Payroll, 147–148
 technical, 146–147
"People skills," importance of, 14–17
Personal dignity, need for, 18–20, 25–26
Personal recognition, need for, 20–21, 26
Persuasion, art of, 15–17
Preventive maintenance (PM), 142–143
Principles and Practices (Bleuel and Patton), 125
Printing, controlling expenses on, 150–151
Product liability, 194–196
 insurance for, 196–197
Product Service Management (Masten), 126
Productive-time ratio for service rates, 112
 travel time in, 112–114
Productivity, 43–44
 financial incentives and, 61–62
 housekeeping and, 61
 improvement of, 53–62
 measurement of, 49–53
 motivation and, 46–49
 paperwork and, 53–55
 profits and, 45–46
 the service factory concept, 44–45
 service manager and, 53–62
 stage setting in, 55–57
 technicians and, 57, 59–61
 time-wasters, avoiding, 57–58
 (*See also* Routing and dispatching)
Profit:
 managing for, 178–181
 net, 103–104
 from parts department, 102–104
 productivity and, 45–46
Profit and loss (P&L) statement, 170–178
 daily open to spend (DOS), 186–187
Promises, broken, 160–161

Raker, Harry, 138
Rates (*see* Service rates)
Ratios, 171–173
 basic, 176–178
RCA, 69, 71
RCA Service Company, 132
Recognition of employees, 20–21, 26

Index

Record-keeping:
  of repair parts inventories, 95–97
  for shop, 85–86
Recreation time for employees, 25
Repair parts:
  accessibility to, 82–84
  inventories of (*see* Inventories)
  location of department, 84
  profits from, 102–104
Road calls, 63–64
  alternative dispatching systems, 67–74
  daily gathering of technicians, 75–77
  drop-off, 76
  the old system of daily operations, 64–65
  one-call-at-a-time dispatching, 67–68
  planning routes carefully, 66–67
  suggested changes in, 65–67
  two-day routing, 76–77
  two-way radio, 69–74
Road technicians, 57
  time limits on diagnosis by, 59
  training of, 59–60
  (*See also* Road calls)
Roebuck, Alvah C., 2
Routing and dispatching:
  alternative systems, 67–74
  daily gathering of technicians, 75–77
  drop-off, 76
  full route system, 63–67
  grid routing, 77
  one-call-at-a-time, 67–68
  road calls, 63–77
  shop technicians, 77–78
  two-day routing, 76–77
  two-way radio, 69–74

Sales promotion letters, 217–219
Schrank, Robert, 43–44, 55
Schwab, Charles, 16
Sears, Richard W., 2
Security, job, 26
Selling services, 135–136
  deception in, 139–140
  by direct mail, 140–142
  first step in, 136–137
  new business from old customers, 142–143

Selling services (*Cont.*):
  new customers, bringing in, 137–140
  professional image, 143–145
  by Yellow Pages, 137–140
  (*See also* Service contracts)
Service, level of, and repair parts inventories, 90–92
Service contracts:
  advantages and disadvantages of, 122–123
  direct mail programs, 129–131
  fulfillment costs, 123–124
  genesis of, 121–122
  selling, 125–128
  selling renewals, 128–131
  wording, 131–134
  (*See also* Selling services)
Service factory concept, 44–45, 79–82
  (*See also* Shop layout and work flow)
Service industry:
  business community and, 7–8
  contemporary consumer and, 4
  corporate development of, 5–6
  customer demands and, 9–10
  customer expectations and, 11–12
  early growth in, 2–3
  effects of changing technology on, 4–5
  healthy business in (*see* Healthy business)
  legal considerations (*see* Legal considerations)
  origins of, 1–2
  as a "people business," 13–28
  as percentage of GNP, 2–3
  productivity in (*see* Productivity)
  selling services (*see* Selling services)
  television, influence of, 6–7
  today, 3–4
  (*See also* Service manager)
Service legislation, 202–204
Service manager:
  accessibility to, 26–27
  associations for, 168
  business letters (*see* Business letters)
  communication skills for (*see* Communication skills)
  customer and, 155–168
  customer complaints (*see* Complaints, customer)

228   Index

Service manager (Cont.):
  handling fundamental physical needs of employees, 25–28
  healthy business and (see Healthy business)
  laws of human relations with employees, 17–25
  life as, 10–11
  "people skills" for, 14–17
  personal development of, 168
  productivity and, 53–62
  role defined, 155–156
Service rates:
  care in setting, 105–107
  charging for estimates, 118–119
  flat-rate systems, 114–118
  hourly rate system, 108—112
  inflation and, 119
  moderate or premium, 119–120
  other systems for determining, 118
  policy rules for setting, 107–108
  productive-time ratio, 112–114
  service as an intangible, 106–107
Service Shop Management Guide (Glass), 120
Service vehicles:
  controlling expenses on energy, 154
  repair parts inventories in, 100–102
  (See also Routing and dispatching)
Shop layout and work flow:
  bench stocks, 83–84
  carry-in service, 86–87
  factory concept, 44–45, 79–82
  housekeeping, 87–88
  lighting, 81
  repair parts, accessibility to, 82–84
  repair parts department, location of, 84
  shop records, 85-86
  storage areas, 84–85
  work areas, 81–82
Shop records, 85–86
Shop technicians, 77–78
Society of Consumer Affairs Professionals, The, 168
Speech, making a, 38–39
  (See also Communication skills)
Sperry Tech Labor Pricing Guide, 116
Spoken-word skills, 37–38
  making a speech, 38–39

Spoken-word skills (Cont.):
  (See also Communication skills)
Stockkeeping unit (SKU), 95, 96, 98–99
Storage areas, 84–85
Strunk, William, Jr., 209
Supplies, controlling expenses on, 148–151

Technical payroll, 146–147
Technicians:
  productivity and, 57, 59–61
  road (see Road technicians)
  role of, in healthy business, 181–187
  shop, 77–78
  time limits on diagnosis, 59
  training of, 59–60
  two-man job, 60–61
  (See also Employees)
Technology, effects of changing, 4–5
Telephone:
  customer complaints by, 161–163
  customer satisfaction audit by, 167–168
  expenses on, controlling, 151–154
  Yellow Pages advertising, 137–140
Television industry, 5–7
Ten Thousand Working Days (Schrank), 43, 55
Time-wasters, productivity and, 57–58
Travel time, service rates and, 112–114
Trucks (see Service vehicles)
Turnovers, repair parts inventories and, 94
TV Digest Magazine, 7
Two-way radios, road calls and, 69–74

VISIrecord Systems, 95
Vocabulary, 30–32
  (See also Business letters; Communication skills)

Wanamaker, John, 157
Warranties, 189–191
  full or limited, 191–193
  implied, 193–194
  Magnum-Moss Warranty Act, 191–194
WATS (wide area telephone service), 152

Webb, Jervis B., 187
Western Electric Company, 48
Whyte, William F., 48
Work areas, 81–82
Work flow (*see* Shop layout and work flow)
Workers (*see* Employees; Technicians)

Working conditions, 26
Written-word skills, 39–41
   (*See also* Business letters; Communication skills)

Yellow Pages advertising, 137–140